LOOKING OUT FOR #1
is Robert J. Ringer's unorthodox and sometimes startling approach to handling the people and things that make up your everyday world. The author dispenses with myths and intellectual discussions and gets down to realistic, workable ideas that lead to a rewarding life filled with more pleasure and fewer complications.

By the time you have finished, you'll clearly understand how to get from where you are now to where you want to be—with friends, lovers, finances, and all other areas of your personal world. There has never been a single source of usable, real-life wisdom to equal *LOOKING OUT FOR #1*.

LOOKING OUT
FOR #1

by Robert J. Ringer

Illustrations by Jack Medoff

FAWCETT CREST • NEW YORK

A Fawcett Crest Book
Published by Ballantine Books

Copyright © 1977 by Robert J. Ringer

All rights reserved under International and Pan-American Copyright Conventions. Published in the United States by Ballantine Books, a division of Random House, Inc., New York, and simultaneously in Canada by Random House of Canada Limited, Toronto.

ISBN 0-449-21010-3

This edition published by arrangement with Los Angeles Book Corporation

Selection of the Literary Guild

Manufactured in the United States of America

First Fawcett Crest Edition: June 1978
First Ballantine Books Edition: May 1983

OPM 41 40 39 38 37 36 35 34 33 32

Contents

Dedicated to the hope that somewhere in our universe there exists a civilization whose inhabitants possess sole dominion over their own lives, where every individual has the ability to recognize and the courage to acknowledge reality, and where governments as we know them do not exist.

Introduction

Anyone who is familiar with my philosophy would be disappointed if I didn't say that my sole reason for writing this book was to make as much money as possible.

Perhaps without realizing it, you have, by purchasing this book, entered into a value-for-value relationship with me. I'm exchanging my ideas—ideas which I believe can make your life more pleasurable—for your money. This value-for-value approach enables you to dispense with the notion that I'm doing you some kind of favor by sharing these ideas; I'm not. That's your safety valve in this transaction—the security of knowing that I'm interested in making money by selling you more books in the years ahead and that I recognize that I'm likely to retain you as a customer only if this book is worth its price to you.

There are no ulterior motives involved. I'm not out to convert you to a cause, to enlist your aid in destroying an "evil," or to gain your support for or against anything. If you understand that the means to my end is to provide you with a valuable product, then you're already in the proper frame of mind for the realities which lie ahead.

A CLEAN SLATE

Before moving forward, it will be extremely helpful to you to attempt to clear your mind of all preconceived ideas, whether they concern friendship, love, business or any other aspect of life. I realize this is easier said than done, but do try to make the effort; it will be worth your while.

Also clear your mind of any preconceived image you may have of me. Don't picture me as "conservative," because I'm not. Don't think of me as "liberal," because I'm not that either. I am an individual and, as such, I have many facets to my personality. I acknowledge you as a unique human being, different from all others, and for your own selfish purposes you will be far better off if you grant me the same concession. What I have to say will seem much more consistent to you if you don't attempt to label me.

Since my emphasis is solely on the individual, there is no male/female distinction in my philosophy. Therefore, wherever a specific gender is used, you may assume that the opposite gender is automatically interchangeable (except, of course, where a particular male or female pronoun is employed for obvious reasons).

FASTEN YOUR SEAT BELT.

Clear your mind, then. Forget foundationless traditions, forget the "moral" standards others may have tried to cram down your throat, forget the beliefs people may have tried to intimidate you into accepting as "right." Allow your intellect to take control as you read, and, most important, think of yourself—Number One—as a unique individual.

It is not my intention to give you legal advice, to act as a marriage counselor, or to prompt you to take radical action based on the assumption that what I have to say should be construed as some sort of guarantee. Should you fail, I have no desire to bear any guilt; by the same token, I don't expect to share in your "profits" should you succeed—whether your success be in love, finance, or any other area discussed in these pages. You and you alone will be responsible for your success or failure.

However, because we have entered into the only kind of transaction (value for value) which I believe to be rational, I can honestly say that I wish you all the success in the world in clearing the hurdles which may now stand between you and a better life.

—*The Tortoise*

Looking Out For
Number One

WHAT IS IT?

Looking out for Number One is the conscious, rational effort to spend as much time as possible doing those things which bring you the greatest amount of pleasure and less time on those which cause pain. Everyone automatically makes the effort to be happy, so the key word is "rational."

To act rationally, and thus to experience pleasure and avoid pain on a consistent basis, you have to be aware of what you're doing and why you're doing it. If you are not aware, you're not living life; you're merely passing through. Because people always do that which they *think* will bring them the greatest pleasure, selfishness is not the issue. Therefore, when people engage in what appear to be altruistic acts, they are not being selfless, as they might like to believe (and might like to have you believe).

What they are doing is acting with a lack of awareness. Either they are not completely aware of what they're doing, or they are not aware of why they're doing it, or both. In any case, they are acting selfishly—but not rationally.

If you wish consciously and consistently to make wise pleasure/pain decisions, you must lift yourself to a high level of awareness. This means elevating your cerebral machinery to the point where you act more often, and eventually most often, out of choice—*your* choice. If you're not basing your actions on rational choice, you're out of control, and anything out of control is dangerous to both itself and its surroundings.

While the high point on the Awareness Meter is taking action based only on your own rational choices, the absolute pits is taking action based on what others choose for you. If you've been in the habit of doing the latter, the good news is that you have only one way to go from here: up.

WHAT'S THE PAYOFF?

Why is it important to act out of choice? What's in it for you? You already know: more pleasure and less pain—a better life for Number One.

In everyday terms, it means feeling refreshed instead of tired. It means making enough money to be able comfortably to afford the material things you want out of life instead of being bitter about not having them. It means enjoying love relationships instead of longing for them. It means experiencing warm friendships instead of concentrating your thoughts on people for whom you harbor negative feelings. It means feeling healthy instead of lousy. It means having a relatively clear mind instead of one that is cluttered and confused. It means more free time instead of never enough time.

Looking out for Number One is important because it leads to a simple, uncomplicated life in which you spend

11

more time doing those things which give you the greatest amount of pleasure. It's the discovery of where it's all at—the realization that life is worth living and that it can and should be a joy rather than a dread. The natural offspring of this realization are feelings of self-control and self-esteem, which in turn perpetuate still more joy in your life.

Feelin' Good

What is joy? Rather than go around in a circle of technical definitions, I think you and I inherently understand what it means. When you experience pleasure or an absence of pain, you know one thing: you're *feelin' good*.

When you boil it all down, I think that's what everyone's main objective in life really is—to feel good. Happiness isn't a mysterious condition that needs to be dissected carefully by wordologists or psychologists. It's your state of mind when you're experiencing something pleasurable; it's when you feel good.

We sometimes lose sight of the fact that our primary objective is really to be as happy as possible and that all our other objectives, great and small, are only a means to that end. To the degree we achieve our subobjectives, and to the extent these subobjectives are rational, we feel good.

There is no such thing as simply being happy or unhappy; it's a matter of degree. You can be happier today than yesterday, twice as happy yesterday as you were a month ago, and hope to be much happier in the future than you've ever been before. The degree of your happiness at any given moment will depend upon the rationality of your objectives and the success you have in obtaining them. The more rational they are, the easier they are to obtain.

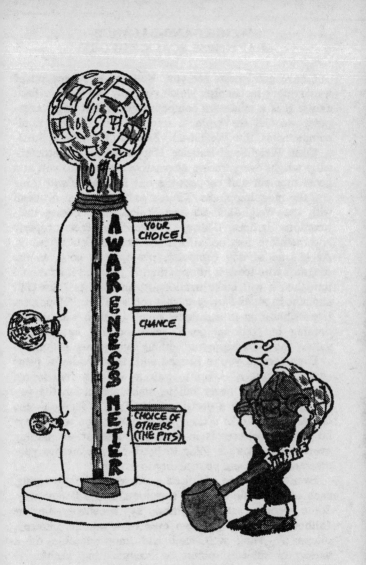

WEIGHT-AND-BALANCE
HAPPINESS SCALE THEORY

I have good news for you. You are in possession of a marvelous mechanism which you may not have realized exists. It is a miniature computer within that larger computer we call the brain. I refer to this amazing mini-computer as the Weight-and-Balance Happiness Scale.

Your Weight-and-Balance Happiness Scale automatically weighs every known alternative available to you at a given moment and chooses the one it *believes* will bring you the most happiness. There's only one slight problem with the Weight-and-Balance Scale: it sometimes malfunctions. It doesn't always ascertain the facts properly and therefore does not always produce the right decisions. As is true of any computer, it's only as good as the operator who feeds it information. If you feed it irrational thoughts, it will make irrational decisions. As John Galt explains in *Atlas Shrugged*, that spells defeat: "Happiness is possible only to a rational man, the man who desires nothing but rational goals, seeks nothing but rational values and finds his joy in nothing but rational actions." [1]

Even though you're blessed with this wonderful piece of equipment, it is up to you to keep it functioning properly. It will never fail to make a decision for you (even not making a decision is, in fact, a decision—the decision not to take action), and that decision will always be what it believes is in your best interest. Its batting average, however, is going to be directly related to your awareness level and your ability to reason.

Even if everyone exercised good reason before acting, each of us would seek his happiness in a different way. Some people seek happiness by becoming martyrs (although I doubt this can ever be a rational choice), others by being well read and knowledgeable on a variety of subjects, others by accumulating wealth. As Louise Ropes Loomis said in paraphrasing Aristotle, "The end for which we all more or less strive is happiness. Our differences in behavior are due to our different notions of what happiness is." [2]

The trouble begins when *others* try to tell you what makes you happy. "If someone says that giving is the key to happiness," asks Harry Browne, "isn't he saying that's the key to *his* happiness?" [3] He cautions that you delude yourself if you assume that such a person's opinions are binding upon you.

How do you know when your Weight-and-Balance Happiness Scale is functioning properly? The pleasure/pain compartments of your brain will always give you an easy-to-read printout. Mentally, you either feel good or you don't.

If you're feelin' good, don't ask questions; your Scale is doing right by you. But if you're troubled, you've got some hurdles to clear, and clearing hurdles translates into work (mostly mental).

It's that old inescapable cosmic reality again: no such thing as something for nothing. The greater the happiness you wish to achieve, the greater the price you must pay to achieve it. It's up to you to decide how great a price you're willing to pay, and it's to your advantage to decide on that price *before* you take action.

What other alternatives do you really have? You didn't choose to be born, but the reality is that you're here. So aside from paying the price necessary for a better life, you have only two other options.

One is simply to do away with yourself, which, although many make that decision each year, hardly seems like a rational alternative. A second choice is inaction—accepting things as they are and living with the confusion, frustration, conflict, and other negatives that may be making life more a burden than a celebration.

Most people take the latter course—inaction—because it seems easiest. But I believe such people cheat themselves by thinking short-term. They're exchanging a relatively small number of periodic sharp pains for a lifetime of dull, chronic pain. This helps explain much of the bitterness you see all around you. A continuously dreary life is, figuratively speaking, a living death. Why worry about life after death if you're not even living this one?

It seems to me that the wisest choice, long-term, is to pay the price necessary to develop your ability to think rationally. This may mean making radical changes in your lifestyle, in your work, or even where you live. But changes should be made only after careful reasoning convinces you that they're warranted. Much of what it takes to make you happy may be right under your nose.

VOLCANIC ASH THEORY

My memory reaches back to some poignant scenes from an old movie, *Fanny*. In this film, Fanny is desperately in love with young Marius, and he with her. Fanny wants to marry him, but Marius, in his words, is "so divided—so torn!"

Marius relates to Fanny a story an old seaman had told him when he was just a boy. The mariner had vividly described "the isles beneath the winds where black trees grow," saying that "when you cut them they are gold inside—and smell of camphor and pepper."

"That's when it happened," Marius continued, his eyes glimmering with excitement, "this deep, painful wish I have. It makes me dizzy, as though I were falling forward always . . . toward the sea." So Marius, despite his deep love for Fanny, goes off to sea in search of the wonders the old mariner had described.

More than a year later, when he returns home for a brief visit, he calls on Fanny, who has by then married another man. In a touching scene, Fanny asks Marius if he saw "the isles beneath the winds."

Marius replies that he did.

"What were they like?" Fanny inquires.

"Have you ever seen photographs of the craters of the

16

moon? That's what they were like—volcanic ash. Oh, Fanny, I left with such high hopes!"

Happiness is where you find it. It's very possible that it may not be where you are today. But then again it could be staring you right in the face. Whether it is or is not presently close by, don't be carried away by illusions and make dramatic moves based on emotion. Those isles of happiness may turn out to be nothing more than volcanic ash.

Most important, remember that happiness is not what someone else deems it to be. Happiness is that which makes *you* feel good.

Is winning necessary to happiness?

I'm often asked if one has to "win" to be happy. The answer is yes, on two counts. First, since your main objective is happiness, it is important that you "win"— that you achieve that objective. Second, since happiness is really the result of accomplishing a series of subobjectives, the realization of as many of them as possible is imperative.

The frustration comes from choosing the wrong objectives or from having too many of them. The problem of wrong objectives stems from irrational thinking; the problem of too many objectives results from societal pressure regarding the generally accepted concept of winning. When people say "he's a winner," they usually mean to imply that the person wins at just about everything he tries. "He's competitive" conjures up an image of a tense person who never takes time to relax, who tends to go all out whether he's negotiating a business deal or playing a weekend game of golf.

While winning is the act of gaining your objectives— being victorious—it doesn't mean you have to be a pig about it. You can't have all the candy in the store, if for no other reason than because none of us has the unlimited time, energy and talent necessary to grab all the goodies.

So don't kill yourself trying. Leave some for the rest of us, because we're going to get our share whether you like it or not. We're going to get it because we have greater talent in some areas and may be able to devote more time and energy to those specific areas than you. Time, particularly, is a fixed commodity which limits what you can accomplish in a lifetime.

Winning merely for the sake of winning elevates it to an end in itself and thereby relegates the main objective—happiness—to a position of lesser importance. That's the predicament of the man who knows no other life but work. He gets so caught up in making money that he forgets to take time out to enjoy it.

It's wise to decide which objectives are most important to your happiness and to set priorities accordingly. Don't place an equal value on becoming a championship tennis player, a renowned socialite, a financial empire-builder, a gourmet cook, a notorious lover, and a topflight chess master. I've known people who have tried to accomplish even more than that, and if they were happy, then happiness means being out of breath, being tense, and having high blood pressure.

Not all your objectives must revolve around having winning "scores." Your objective in playing tennis on a Saturday afternoon may be to relax and enjoy the company of another person. If at the end of the day you've relaxed and had fun, then you've won. You've achieved your objective whether you won or lost at tennis. In this case, the actual score had nothing to do with "winning."

That isn't to say you should not have tried to win the tennis match; it's a matter of perspective. It's no mortal sin if you don't feel a life-and-death urge to beat your opponent when your main objective is to relax and have fun. It's a fine line, and you must be the one to decide where it is drawn. You alone can determine which things in your life are most important to you. And those that aren't? Well, if you should come out with winning scores in any of the less important "games," consider them bonuses. But the highest "score" does not have to be your paramount objective in every activity you undertake.

The so-called competitive attitude, as we have come to view it, can lead to several bad consequences. It can drain energy that is needed to accomplish more important objectives. It can make you look foolish for trying to compete fiercely in an activity into which you are not willing or able to put the necessary time and effort, or for which you do not have the natural ability. It can totally frustrate you, which can adversely affect your attitude when facing more important challenges. And it can make enemies of people who might be valuable acquaintances if you were dealing with them on a casual and relaxed basis.

Everyone wants to win at the game of happiness, but don't go overboard and feel you have to be intensely competitive at everything in order to achieve this main objective. You may only succeed in driving yourself mad.

IS IT RIGHT?

Is looking out for Number One "right"? As a preface, I find it necessary to describe an old nemesis of mine—a creature who's been running around loose on Planet Earth over the millennia, steadily increasing in number. He is the Absolute Moralist. His mission in life is to whip you and me into line. Like Satan, he disguises himself in various human forms. He may appear as a politician on one occasion, next as a minister, and still later as your mother-in-law.

Whatever his disguise, he is relentless. He'll stalk you to your grave if you let him. If he senses that you're one of his prey—that you do not base your actions on rational self-choice—he'll punish you unmercifully. He will make guilt your bedfellow until you're convinced you're a bad guy.

The Absolute Moralist is the creature—looking deceptively like any ordinary human being—who spends his life deciding what is right for *you*. If he gives to charity, he'll try to shame you into "understanding" that it's your moral duty to give to charity too (usually the charity of his choice). If he believes in Christ, he's certain that it's his moral duty to help you "see the light." (In the most extreme cases, he may even feel morally obliged to kill you in order to "save" you from your disbelief.) If he doesn't smoke or drink, it takes little effort for him "logically" to conclude that smoking and drinking are wrong for you. In essence, all he wants is to run your life. There is only one thing which can frustrate him into leaving you alone, and that is your firm decision never to allow him to impose his beliefs on you.

In deciding whether it's right to look out for Number One, I suggest that the first thing you do is eliminate from consideration all unsolicited moral opinions of others. Morality—the quality of character—is a very personal and private matter. No other living person has the right to decide what is moral (right or wrong) for you. I further suggest that you make a prompt and thorough effort to eliminate from your life all individuals who claim—by words or actions, directly or by inference—to possess such a right. You should concern yourself only with whether looking out for Number One is moral from your own rational, aware viewpoint.

Looking out for Number One means spending more time doing those things which give you pleasure. It does not, however, give you carte blanche to do whatever you please. It is not hedonistic in concept, because the looking-out-for-Number-One philosophy does not end with the hedonistic assertion that man's primary moral duty lies in the pursuit of pleasure.

Looking out for Number One adds a rational, civilized tag: man's primary moral duty lies in the pursuit of pleasure *so long as he does not forcibly interfere with the rights of others*. If you picked up this book in the hope that it might explain how to get ahead in life by trampling on the rights of your fellow man, I'm afraid you've made a bad choice. I suggest instead that you read *Life and Death of Adolf Hitler, The Communist Manifesto,* or the U.S. Internal Revenue Code.

There is a rational reason why forcible interference with others has no place in the philosophy of looking out for Number One. It's simply not in your best interest. In the long run it will bring you more pain than pleasure— the exact opposite of what you wish to accomplish. It's possible that you may, on occasion, experience short-term pleasure by violating the rights of others, but I assure you that the long-term losses (i.e., pain) from such actions will more than offset any short-term enjoyment.

Why? Because the syndrome of bad-cause/bad-effect is a cosmic reality. I'm not referring here to any kind of mysticism. Rather, I see this as one of the many universal laws of Nature which always seems to enforce itself. I cannot explain this phenomenon any more than I can explain where space ends or time began, but I have perceived its workings, clearly and without fail, over many years.

With absolute morality and hedonism out of the way, I perhaps can best answer the question *Is it right?* by asking you one: Can you see any rational reason why you *shouldn't* try to make your life more pleasurable and less painful, so long as you do not forcibly interfere with the rights of others?

You have but one life to live. Is there anything unreasonable about watching over that life carefully and doing everything within your power to make it a pleasant and fulfilling one? Is it wrong to be aware of what you're doing and why you're doing it? Is it evil to act out of free choice rather than out of the choice of others or out of blind chance?

Remember, selfishness is not the issue. So-called self-sacrifice is just an irrationally selfish act (doing what you think will make you feel good) committed under the influence of a low awareness level. The truth is that it won't make you feel good—certainly not in the long run, after bitterness over what you've "sacrificed" has had a chance to fester within you. At its extreme, this bitterness eventually can develop into a serious case of absolute moralitis. A person's irrational decision to be self-sacrificial can lead to a bitterness so great that it can be soothed only by his preaching to others the virtue of committing the same error.

You may mean well, but don't try so hard to sacrifice for others. It's unfair to them and a disaster for you. The sad irony is that if you persist in swimming in the danger-ous and uncivilized waters of self-sacrifice, those for whom you "sacrifice" often will be worse off for your efforts. If instead you spend your time looking out for Number One, those people for whom you care most will benefit by your actions. It's only when you try to pervert the laws of Nature and make the other person's happiness your first responsibility, relegating yourself to the Number Two position, that you run into trouble. It has never worked, and it will not work for you. It's a law of Nature. The idea that self-sacrifice is virtuous is a law of *man*. If you're going to expend your energies fighting laws, fight man-made laws; they are worth resisting. The laws of Nature will not budge an inch no matter how great your efforts.

That looking out for Number One brings happiness to others, in addition to Number One, is one of the beautiful realities of life. At best, it benefits you and one or more other persons. At worst, it benefits only you and interferes with no one else. Even in the latter case, it actually is a benefit to others because the happy individual is one more person on this earth who does not represent a po-tential burden to the rest of the population.

That, in my opinion, is enough to make it right. If you practice the principles of looking out for Number One, you'll find it easier to develop rewarding relationships with other human beings, both friends and lovers. It will enhance your ability to be a warm and sensitive person and to enjoy all that life has to offer.

IS IT EASY?

If you're over twenty-one, you already know that nothing worthwhile is easy. This involves another cosmic reality that millions either refuse to believe or cannot understand. It's called price paying.

That every pleasurable thing in life has a price attached to it is a hard enough reality in itself. What makes the game of life infinitely more difficult, however, is its vicissitude.

CHANGING CIRCUMSTANCES THEORY

The one absolutely predictable thing in life is that circumstances will always change. You can positively count on it. What is not known is *when* they will change.

You can make detailed plans to lead a happier life, but if you die, those plans go out the window when the ultimate changing circumstance—death—occurs. What you normally cannot know, in advance, is when it will occur.

Do everything you can to experience the joys of life, but be flexible in your planning. It's dangerous to base your actions on the assumption that everything is going to continue as it is. Nothing could be further from the truth, and, because circumstances do change suddenly, you often are caught by surprise.

I once knew a woman who freaked out every time there was the slightest unexpected change in her life, which meant that she was upset every day. If there was a power failure in her house, it was a major catastrophe. When her duties at work shifted, she developed a migraine headache. The day her favorite restaurant went out of business, it was no longer any fun to go out to dinner. She lives in a near-constant state of tension because she cannot adapt to the unceasing change of circumstance that surrounds everyone's life.

One day you're on top of the world financially; the next day you're faced with the possibility of being put out of business because of a new product on the market. Today you look forward to getting to the office; tomorrow you have a new supervisor whose personality conflicts with yours. For years you've been accustomed to whipping in and out of the gas station in minutes; suddenly there's an oil boycott, and getting your tank filled becomes an hour-long ordeal.

Lovers and relatives die; close friends move away; buildings are torn down and replaced by new ones. Changing tastes catch a performer by surprise and make him a has-been; an athlete discovers that he doesn't fit in with the new coach's plans. Nothing lasts forever, and the individual who is not attuned to that reality often finds himself in a quandary and can't figure out why. I believe that the insecurity of a rapidly changing world is one of the chief causes of depression. The person who cannot adapt to the reality of change is constantly off guard and therefore unprepared to make the rational decisions necessary to look out for himself.

You may be familiar with Murphy's Law:

> *Nothing is as easy as it looks.*
> *Everything takes longer than you expect.*
> *And if anything can go wrong—it will*
> *At the worst possible moment!*

A wise observation on the part of Murphy. One of the reasons his law holds true is the reality that nothing seems to stay in one place long enough to pin it down. Trying to make a situation work out can sometimes give a guy the feeling that life is a greased watermelon; he can never quite seem to pick it up. He often comes close, but it always manages to slip out of his grasp at the last moment.

Believe it or not, though, some things do work out.

And the better you understand the realities of the Changing Circumstances Theory and Murphy's Law, the easier it becomes to succeed. Your best insurance in this regard is a theory I explained in *Winning Through Intimidation:*

THEORY OF SUSTENANCE OF A POSITIVE ATTITUDE THROUGH THE ASSUMPTION OF A NEGATIVE RESULT

The old adage that "you can't win 'em all" is misleading. A more realistic perspective would be to say that you can't *lose* 'em all. Because lose you will—and often—à la Murphy's Law. Constant change and other factors beyond your control assure you of that. And unless your perspective is correct, losing not only becomes a drag, but it also can shatter your self-image and fill you with frustration.

A big turning point for me was the day I began viewing short-term losses as battles rather than wars. I have long since lost interest in winning every "battle"; I'm now concerned only with winning the "war." Since I know, in advance, that most things don't work out (due to factors beyond my control), they register in my mind only as unsuccessful battles along the path toward the larger objective of winning the war. If you take this realistic attitude, the positive result is that you won't be mentally devastated when things go wrong. This allows you to retain the "positive" attitude which might be lost if every setback came as a surprise to you.

I realize I'm going to lose ten, twenty, or perhaps fifty battles before I succeed, but the crucial point is that I try to be prepared to win each time out. The fact that I acknowledge the obvious reality that life has an annoying habit of not cooperating with one's plans is all the more reason why I can't afford not to be ready when everything does happen to fall into place. Even though I assume the worst, I do more than just hope for the best. I prepare for it.

While you're enduring all of life's bumps and bruises in a daily stream of lost battles, there is a freebie in each situation. It comes in the form of an educational experience. All you need to do is extract the lesson learned and use it to be better prepared the next time around. The negative result itself is history. Forget it. The knowledge gained, however, can prove to be far more valuable than a victorious battle.

> In South Africa, they dig for diamonds. Tons of earth are moved to find a little pebble not as large as a little fingernail. The miners are looking for the diamonds, not the dirt. They are willing to lift all the dirt in order to find the jewels. In daily life, people forget this principle and become pessimists because there is more dirt than diamonds. When trouble comes, don't be frightened by the negatives. Look for the positives and dig them out. They are so valuable it doesn't matter if you have to handle tons of dirt.[4]

It sounds paradoxical, but in reality the "Sustenance" Theory prepares you for long-term success by preparing you mentally for short-term failure. It helps you move the dirt between you and *your* diamonds.

This mental preparation is another form of price paying. You must face the inescapable reality that absolutely everything in life has a price: love, friendship, material gain, a relaxed mind, the freedom to come and go as you please—anything which adds pleasure to your existence. All things worth obtaining must be paid for. If you delude yourself into thinking otherwise, you only open the door to endless frustration.

I consciously attempt to analyze, at the outset, the price of anything I desire. Whether the necessary payment will be in money, time, energy, discomfort, or any other form, I try not to kid myself. And once I've made up my mind that something is worth the price, I like to pay it and get it over with. Don't develop the habit of prolonging the payment. The sooner you get it out of the way, the sooner you can enjoy the rewards of a clear mind and a happier life.

What it basically amounts to is the long-term solution versus short-term patching. Dispense with the rationalization that you will temporarily resolve a problem, to get past a rough spot in your path, with the intention of working out a permanent solution later. Later never seems to come, and the result is that the problem only festers and grows. The sooner you understand the wisdom in taking the time, expending the mental effort and summoning the courage to work out long-term, permanent solutions (i.e., total and final payment), the more pleasurable your life will become.

Don't try to buy happiness on the installment plan. If you drag your payments out, you will never quite reach the point where you can enjoy life with a clear mind. Remember, looking out for Number One carries a heavy price: *conscious, rational effort*. Begin paying the price today so you can start enjoying the pleasurable benefits as soon as possible.

If you fail to take the proper action, I can assure you of one thing: no one else is going to perform the job of looking out for you as well as you yourself.

In a matter of pages, the ball will be in your court. I wish I could be the bearer of good tidings and tell you that you have unlimited time to stare at the ball and decide what you're going to do with it. Alas, my friend, it isn't so. Like all games, this one, too, will end. And the clock is running as you read this sentence.

How much time? No one knows for sure, but I like to use age sixty-five as a nice round figure and look at anything beyond that as a bonus. That means if you're thirty-five years old and you theoretically could freeze time long enough to do some calculating, you have precisely 10,950 days left in your game; or 262,800 hours; or 15,768,000 minutes; or 946,080,000 seconds. Choose the time unit that makes you most comfortable, but do acknowledge the reality that the clock is running.

The Perspective Hurdle

". . . the first step is what counts. First beginnings are hardest to make and as small and inconspicuous as they are potent in influence, but once they are made, it is easy to add the rest."—ARISTOTLE [1]

While I might take issue with Aristotle on the latter part of his statement—that it's easy to add the rest—experience leads me to concur with him that the first step is usually the hardest. The Perspective Hurdle is *your* first step, the first hurdle which must be cleared in the pursuit of a more pleasurable life. You cannot deal effectively with the other roadblocks in your path unless you first are able to place them in proper perspective.

If you allow any problem to be magnified beyond its merits, you will lack the proper mental focus to cope with it rationally. At the extreme, a person who does not have a reasonable perspective on his problems might tend to react to a spilled cup of coffee and nuclear war with about the same degree of emotional stress. What such a person lacks is an understanding of relativity.

```
WELCOME TO BURGER KING

# 1
    1 FFM WHOP   $     3.99@
         1 DINE
    2 SALES          124445
   SUBTOTAL      $     3.99
TAX              $     0.32
TOTAL            $     4.31
YOUR ORDER NUMBER IS     45




AMT TENDERED     $     4.31
CHANGE           $     0.00

TIME 12:44PM DATE  1/17/04
```

THEORY OF RELATIVITY

This theory states that few people take the trouble to consider facts in a relative light, and that until one does so, one cannot intelligently settle on a proper course of action. In other words, that you and I have problems is not startling. We already realize that. What's crucial is the extent of those problems. Problems relative to what?

You have a hangnail? That's painful, true, but painful relative to what? You're unemployed? Relative to a hangnail, that's worse. Relative to a guy who lives in an underdeveloped country and whose yearly income is $250, it's not all that serious. You're ill? That can be grim, but the severity of even that situation must be measured against the literally infinite number of plights in which some four billion people find themselves daily.

Human dilemmas like loneliness, financial failure and government interference seem at times to overwhelm us. They prod some to drink, others to take narcotics; they can produce ulcers, migraine headaches and high blood pressure. At best, difficulties can cause constant worry; at worst, they can precipitate serious mental and emotional disorders.

But wait. What if none of it matters? What if you're allowing yourself to be irritated, when, with just a slight reorientation in your perspective, you could be taking the first step toward making pleasure the dominant experience of your existence?

ALL DRESSED UP BUT NO PLACE TO GO?

In my early twenties, while I was stumbling around the streets of New York hoping to promote a deal—any kind of deal—I had the good fortune to be introduced to a wealthy old Wall Streeter. (A Wall Streeter, as used here, is an investor who spends each day watching the ticker tape and maneuvering money in and out of stocks at hopefully opportune moments.)

Harold Hart epitomized the typical Lower-East-Side-to-Park-Avenue success story. Having begun his struggle as a poor youngster, Mr. Hart had eventually amassed a considerable stack of chips, purportedly in the area of $50 million. At the time I first met him, he was already in his early seventies.

He had it all: a chauffeured limousine to take him to and from "work," a splendid wardrobe complete with silk top hat, and a breathtaking apartment decorated in Early Rich.

I had the opportunity to visit this gentleman at his Park Avenue palace on several occasions and came to know him quite well. The purpose of our meetings (at least my purpose) was to try to induce him to invest in some perfectly sound venture, such as a sulfur mine in Tibet or a gold-panning expedition in New Zealand.

I don't remember the nature of the proposed venture, but it's safe to assume it was one of those typical LSD Deals I often hypnotized myself into working on. (If you're new to the term *LSD Deal*, it's the kind of endeavor on which most promoters waste their time—a deal that could only be created by a person under the influence of LSD and which has absolutely no chance of ever coming to pass.) While I failed, of course, to get the investment money I was naive enough to seek, I obtained far more than I had bargained for in the way of food for thought.

The biggie came one evening when I went to visit Mr. Hart on one of my LSD-Deal missions. When I arrived, I found him resting tranquilly in his favorite chair, garbed in silk robe and pajamas, with servants waiting on him hand and foot. I sat there awhile, watching as he stared blankly into space. Finally he muttered, "You know, Nature has played a great hoax on man. You work your ass off all your life, go through an endless number of struggles, play all the petty little games, and—if you're lucky—you finally make it to the top.

"Well, I made it long ago, and you know what? It's

"How about a nice little sulfur mine in Tibet this evening?"

all bullshit. It doesn't mean a damn thing. I tell you, Nature's made a fool of man, and the biggest fool of all is me. Here I sit, in poor health, exhausted from years of playing the game, well aware that time is running out, and I keep asking myself, 'Now what, Genius? What's your next brilliant move going to be?' All that time I spent worrying, maneuvering . . . it was meaningless. Life is nothing but a big hoax. We think we're so damn important, but the truth is we're nothing."

A few months after that pleasant little dissertation in his apartment, Harold Hart died. That was many years ago, but today his words, and the tone in which he spoke them, still ring in my ears.

Has Nature made a fool of man? Is it all a hoax? After considerable experience, and after years of thinking, reading and philosophizing with knowledgeable people in fields ranging from science to religion, the one thing of which I'm certain is that I still am not in a position to give a confident answer. Nor has anyone else convinced me that he has the answer, though many have tried. But of one thing I am confident: even if man does have a definite purpose in our vast universe—if our actions here on earth *are* important—it doesn't necessarily follow that every problem we face is significant when placed against the perspective of an endlessly complex world and an even more incomprehensible universe.

You might argue that all this is fine in theory, but that you cannot relate to the Big Picture—to things that are not a part of your day-to-day life. In response, I would have to say that if you *don't* bring your problems into realistic focus as they relate to the Big Picture, you're making the mistake of sidestepping the first hurdle instead of clearing it. The truth is that it's not that people *can't* relate to the Big Picture, it's that they're so caught up in their problems that they won't allow themselves to take the time to do it.

What exactly is the Big Picture? Perhaps if a person were well-enough informed he could begin to summarize it in 10,000 pages. But since that would hardly be practical (or necessary for our purposes), we'll settle instead for a quick hopscotch across the universe, around our planet, and through life in general in an effort to get at least a small glimpse of this Big Picture.

THE UNIVERSE

Let's take a look at this gob of infinity we call the universe. Damn, but it sure is a huge place. Whole books have been written on individual facets of it, but it's sufficient here merely to reflect on a couple of random items.

As an individual, the thing which most impresses me about the size of the universe is how insignificant I am by comparison. In fact, there is no comparison. Pitted against the infinite universe, the earth is hardly the equivalent of a grain of sand on a beach. On a comparative basis, then, I wouldn't rate even the status of an atom within that one grain of sand.

If that's my stature in the universe, where does that leave my problems on the scale of eminence? Sure, they're important to *me*, but placed in perspective against the Big Picture, they're hardly worth a yawn. This incomprehensible disparity helps me keep the roadblocks in my life cut down to more realistic size, making them much easier to deal with.

Is anybody out there?

A possibility that has always fascinated me is that of life on other planets. I'm not speaking of microbes, but of intelligent life, most likely in some kind of humanoid form. Some scientific guesstimates on the probability of extraterrestrial life range as high as fifty million civilizations in our galaxy alone—I repeat, *in our galaxy alone*. It's a fascinating thought. But I'm not hard to impress; if there's just one other planet in the whole universe inhabited by an intelligent civilization, it would excite me.

Whatever happened to the Super Bowl?

But let's not think so small. I was reflecting only on our own little galaxy. Recently, scientists confirmed the existence of a new galaxy estimated to be five to ten times larger than ours and to contain trillions of stars. (Estimates on the number of stars in our Milky Way galaxy, by comparison, range from 100 to 250 billion). We are further told that the light we now see from this galaxy, through high-powered telescopes, has been traveling through space at the rate of six trillion miles a year for eight billion years. If all this hasn't sufficiently boggled your mind, consider that this galaxy is purported to be traveling away from our planet at the rate of 2.7 trillion miles per year and is one million times fainter than any object visible to the naked eye.

Whew!

In the meantime, we have nervous breakdowns because we can't get the horizontal hold adjusted on our color TV sets five minutes before Super Bowl kickoff. It could be worse. We could be living on a planet in that newly discovered galaxy, in which case we would be moving away from the Super Bowl at the rate of nearly three trillion miles a year.

Man, talk about a hoax! What if our whole universe is nothing more than a Ping-Pong ball falling off a table in a giant's world? And what if you and I happen to be living at a time when the ball is about to hit the floor?

I don't know about you, but the picture out there in space is a little too big for me. The infinite boundaries and the mysteries concealed within them do more than just help our perspective; they overwhelm us. Let's literally come down to Earth—to our little speck of dust—and look at a handful of realities which are a little more comprehensible.

THE EARTH

First of all, if you think the average lifetime is relatively short, you're going to think it's a lot shorter when you consider this next item. According to Carl Sagan, famed exobiologist, "If the eons that comprise the lifetime of Earth were compressed into the span of a single year . . . recorded history would occupy the last 30 seconds of the last day of such a year." [2] This means, for example, that the combined length of time it took to fight the two World Wars—which I would have to classify, by Earthly standards, as pretty serious problems—would occupy only a millifraction of a second in the lifetime of Earth.

From that perspective, when someone is a half-hour late picking you up, does it really deserve the status of a major irritation? If you tried to squeeze such an event into Sagan's time frame, there wouldn't be an element small enough to record it.

The Horrors of Living in Scarsdale

While our everyday problems are certainly real, they're hardly catastrophic when put in proper perspective. Consider the fact that in the late thirties and early forties, a madman named Adolf Hitler, through brilliant political maneuvering and virtual mass hypnosis, was successful in morbidly slaughtering some six million members of the Jewish faith.

In Scarsdale, more than thirty years later, a descendant of one of those victims believes he is burdened by enormous difficulties. Someone at the office is vying for his position, his doctor has just informed him that he must give up smoking or face grave consequences, and his mistress is threatening to cut him off if he doesn't leave his wife. Were this man suddenly to find himself in Auschwitz in 1942, he would, by contrast, be incapable of identifying such future hypothetical circumstances as problems.

Now, if you're in Hiroshima and it's 1945, I'd say you've got a big problem. But if you've recently been chiseled in a business deal, I'm sure that by calming down and reviewing the situation rationally, you'll find a way to survive.

Is middle age depressing you? Some people aren't bothered by such downers. In parts of the world where the average life expectancy is thirty-seven years, men and women are spared the distressing experience of a fortieth birthday party.

Are grocery bills getting you down? Perhaps 10,000 people die every day of starvation, while millions more suffer from malnutrition.

Sick of the high cost of rent? Maybe you'd rather be a pavement dweller in Calcutta. These lucky stiffs are born, live and die on the pavement. The only thing they have to worry about is finding a rag to spread under their heads at night.

While these kinds of horrors continue along at their normal, accepted pace, we throw tantrums over being relegated to a poorly located table in a fancy restaurant, are frustrated because we can't seem to lose weight, and bitch endlessly about monthly bills. Problems? Relative to what?

Since it is both unnatural and impossible to concentrate continuously on the pain and suffering of others, it's understandable that we get upset when we pull a ligament playing handball or worry frantically about the work load piling up at the office when we're laid up with the flu. But if our view is always restricted to our own small environments, the most minor difficulty can seem a major hassle and consume unwarranted amounts of time and energy.

Get you and your so-called problems into proper focus. When cut down to their true relative size, you'll find them much easier to handle. Is your present greatest concern really all that important when placed against the backdrop of the Big Picture?

An experience related thousands of years ago by a fellow named Chuang-tzu probably did as much for my perspective as did the words of Harold Hart. This Taoist expressed the following thought back in the days when people weren't flooded by tension over such concerns as who would win the World Series. He had time to reflect.

> Once upon a time, I . . . dreamt I was a butterfly, fluttering hither and thither, to all intents and purposes a butterfly. I was conscious only of following my fancies as a butterfly, and was unconscious of my individuality as a man. Suddenly I awoke, and there I lay, myself again. Now I do not know whether I was then a man dreaming that I was a butterfly, or whether I am now a butterfly dreaming that I am a man.[3]

Hell, you're worrying yourself sick over unpaid bills, a lover who refuses to see things your way, a garage mechanic who sticks you with a bill that's a hundred dollars over his original estimate, and for all you know you're nothing but a damn butterfly having a bad dream.

Far out? Maybe. But don't make the mistake of hiding from it all simply by protesting that it's not realistic to relate your problems to the Big Picture—that you, as an individual, can relate only to your own day-to-day problems. If you expect to be effective in looking out for Number One—if you wish to remove the hurdles which presently prevent you from spending a majority of your time engaging in pleasurable activities —you'll have to be willing to expand your scope of vision beyond your own little world. Your vision—not your efforts. The latter *should* be focused on your own problems.

Most people carry more baggage than necessary on their journey through life. And, like the airlines, Nature charges us for excess baggage. If you're like most people and can't afford the price, you'd be wise to lighten your load—rid yourself of as many so-called problems as possible. Slow down; relax; think. Reflect on your problems; don't pressure-cook them. Take them one hurdle at a time.

After rational analysis, you may find that some of your problems aren't problems at all. And of those which remain, the question that still must be answered is: problems relative to what?

The Reality Hurdle

Proper assessment of reality can be as crucial to life as oxygen. To try to make it through this world without a reasonable understanding of reality is like stumbling around in a dark room laden with land mines.

Being aware of what you're doing and why you're doing it—the prerequisite for looking out for Number One—is, in effect, being conscious of realities. This understanding of realities gives you the ammunition to make rational choices for yourself rather than allowing your behavior to be controlled by mere chance or the choice of others.

In simple terms, in order to clear the Reality Hurdle, you must become a realist. A realist is a person who believes in basing his life on facts and who dislikes anything that seems imaginary, impractical, theoretical, or utopian.

The biggest problem people have with reality is that they tend to confuse it with their likes and dislikes. One's personal feelings regarding a given reality are not relevant to the reality itself; scorning others for pointing out realities does not in any way change those realities; and to deceive oneself about reality is worst of all— literally fatal in some cases. In the words of Bishop Butler, "Things and actions are what they are, and the consequences of them will be what they will be; why then should we desire to be deceived?"

The Bishop hit the nail dead center. You've heard it before in simple Tortoise language, as the

THEORY OF REALITY

Reality isn't the way you wish things to be, nor the way they appear to be, but the way they actually are. Either you acknowledge reality and use it to your benefit or it will automatically work against you.

That's the nice thing about reality—you *do* have the choice of employing it on your behalf, rather than sitting around like a dum-dum and allowing it to beat you over the head. Since not everything in life is within your control, it's nice to know that the acknowledgement of reality and the opportunity to use it to your benefit are.

The danger in confusing your preferences with realities is explained in the

"IS'S" VERSUS "OUGHT TO'S" THEORY

The degree of complications in an individual's life corresponds to his insistence on dwelling on the way he thinks the world *ought to* be rather than the way it actually *is*.

I, for one, feel that the world *ought to* have no governments or nations—that it should consist of billions of free individuals who have the right to do whatever pleases them so long as they do not forcibly interfere with the rights of others.

I believe that technology *ought to* advance at an even

40

more rapid pace than in the past, but without a price tag of air and water pollution.

I think there *ought to* be no such thing as prejudice—racial, religious, sexual, or otherwise.

It also seems there *ought to* be no necessity to work for a living. Why shouldn't people have everything they want in life without having to toil so hard?

Hey, this is starting to get exciting! How about a gorgeous, intelligent, sensitive, understanding woman for every man, and a handsome, intelligent, sensitive, understanding man for every woman? That *ought to* be a reality, wouldn't you agree?

And while we're at it, there also *ought to* be a Tooth Fairy, there *ought to* be no need to waste a third of your life sleeping, and, speaking of life, there *ought to* be no such thing as death. Who in the hell needs to die?

Wow! I got so worked up concentrating on all the things that *ought to* be that I almost succeeded in hypnotizing myself. And that's exactly what an "ought-to" life is—a life of self-hypnosis, a life based on fantasy rather than fact.

It's very easy to fall into the trap of allowing your desires and emotions to play tricks on you, creating illusions intended to pass for reality. While a person spends his time dwelling on "ought to's" and makes plans accordingly, the world continues right on its merry way dealing in "is's."

What will *always* be irrelevant to reality are your wishes. When you allow your desires to become confused with the facts, you're heading for trouble. Simply stated by Ayn Rand, ". . . facts cannot be altered by a wish, but they *can* destroy the wisher." [1] Avoid the pitfall of confusing the way you think things ought to be with the way they really are. Never be so afraid of the truth that you refuse to acknowledge it. How are you to deal effectively with facts if you deny their existence?

Is living in an unreal world of "ought to's" really all

that bad? I can best answer that by asking another question: Is it really so hazardous to jump off a ten-story building if one has a strong conviction that men ought to be able to fly?

This example, however farfetched, is used to make clearly visible the dangers that lie in the path of the man who lives a life of "ought to's." Such a man may succeed in acting out of choice, but it will not be rational choice. You cannot consciously make rational choices unless you're aware, and if you do not have the ability to recognize and the courage to acknowledge reality, you're not aware.

REALITY VERSUS PERCEPTION OF REALITY

I've often heard it argued that reality is not an absolute, that it is different things to different people. The premise here is that each of us perceives situations differently and, therefore, that reality changes from person to person.

Those who make this argument are partially right in their words, but completely wrong in their conclusion. Each person does perceive reality differently, but reality could care less. It doesn't change to fit the perception; reality is fact. What reality is not in all cases is a *known*. And that's where perception of reality comes in. Reality is the given; perception of reality is the variable.

One of the obstacles to an accurate perception of reality is what I call the Paradigm Restriction. We all are confined not only to the planet on which we live, but metaphorically speaking we reside within our own little worlds. It's tough to comprehend ideas and circumstances we aren't accustomed to hearing and seeing within the invisible perimeters that surround our lives. Yet common sense tells us that all we have learned and understand certainly does not comprise all the knowledge that exists on earth, let alone throughout the universe. The antidote for the Paradigm Restriction is an open mind. This means the rejection of custom and tradition as a basis of fact and, in its place, the acceptance of logic and reason.

Clearing the Reality Hurdle, then, means two things: correctly perceiving reality and having the courage to acknowledge it to yourself. This is where those two unforgettable characters, the Mr. Magoo and the Ostrich, encounter all their problems.

A Mr. Magoo is someone who does not have the ability to perceive the facts correctly. He is totally out of touch with reality. He really thinks, no matter how many times he fails, that pie-in-the-sky business deals can be closed. He actually believes that politicians are better equipped than he is to determine what's right for him. He truly has faith that other people will act in his best interest rather than in their own.

Alas, though, Nature does not accept ignorance as an excuse. As David Seabury observed, "Nature brooks no disobedience of her laws. She hurts us just as much when we are loving and ignorant as when we are hateful and stupid. We suffer from mistakes in any case. Not once has any man been excused by her for good motives." [2]

Unless somewhere in the mysterious depths of a Magoo's brain there lies a yet undeveloped reality-perception seed, his fate is cast. If he does possess such a dormant seed, there's always the faint hope that he can overcome the odds and learn to perceive reality correctly. But if the seed has been undernourished and generally neglected in the past, it will take hard work to develop it to a mature, useful state. If not even the seed exists, then about all you can do for a Magoo is offer him your sympathy.

An Ostrich is an entirely different phenomenon. He's the individual who has the ability to perceive reality correctly, but who refuses to do so, preferring instead to live in the fantasyland of "ought to's."

Sounds incredible, doesn't it? Yet the Ostrich family

numbers in the hundreds of millions. The truth is that the Ostrich is more pathetic than the Magoo, because the individual who knows the facts, but refuses to acknowledge them for what they are, is really the greatest of all fools.

Don't confuse the Ostrich with the Liar—a really dangerous species. The Liar correctly perceives a given reality but, for his own reasons, purposely hides the true facts. The Liar knows not from "ought to's." That's not his game. With him it's not a matter of a lack of courage, but, rather, of premeditated deceit.

So, except for the Liar, when a person speaks of reality, remember that what he is really referring to is his perception of reality. Everything that has ever been written, taught or believed is based not on reality, but on someone's perception of it. Everything in this book, for example, is based on *my* perception of reality. That's really what I'm selling—my perception of realities and my ideas on how to deal with them.

You're free to accept or reject any or all of my interpretations of reality. Where we differ, one of us will suffer negative consequences to the degree to which he is incorrect in his perception. To the degree either of us is correct in his perception of a given reality, his results will be increasingly positive. But the one thing that will be completely unaffected by our views is reality itself.

THE HUMAN NATURE GROUP

This entire book is a discussion of realities, but I've chosen to group three realities here for special attention. They are so fundamental in nature that they must be emphasized early to help lay a strong foundation for the realities discussed in future chapters. These realities are set apart by the fact that they are present to the same degree in all people; that's why I categorize them as the Human Nature Group. They are as basic to Homo sapiens as are five fingers to each of his hands.

Human-Nature Reality No. 1: Self-Interest

Like millions before me, I grew up cringing at the term *self-interest*. No four-letter word could compare in negative stature. Four-letter words were the ones you uttered secretly behind your parents' backs. Self-interest was a term you didn't utter at all. You learned to hiss and boo roundly anyone who proclaimed it a virtue.

Okay, without any pangs of self-consciousness, let's get it out in the open once and for all: *All* people act in their own self-interest *all* the time. There, that wasn't so hard, was it? Then why was it so hush-hush in the first place? What is it about self-interest that makes it such a menace to certain individuals?

The people who most dread widespread knowledge of the reality of self-interest are those who would like you to continue acting in *their* best interests. *Rational* selfishness is not a problem (i.e., selfishness that doesn't involve forcible interference in the lives of others). The problem is the *irrational* selfishness of those who don't want you to act in your best interest—who want selfishly to interfere in your life by encouraging you to do what *they* think is right. The individual who chastises you for being selfish is usually being irrationally selfish himself. That fact alone would not present a problem to civilization. The trouble begins when he becomes overzealous in encouraging you to do those things which give him happiness.

How can this person—an Absolute Moralist—coerce you into thinking of his needs first if you logically arrive at the conclusion that there is nothing immoral about acting in your own self-interest—that it's perfectly normal? The answer is that he can't. He believes that once you break the reasoning barrier and realize that to be selfish is not only natural, but virtuous, you can no longer serve his purpose.

That's where the fallacy in his reasoning lies. The fact is that you could serve his purpose much better if he were willing to deal with you on a value-for-value basis. But that's the catch. He is not willing to offer you equal value for that which he seeks from you. He is not rational enough to understand that by appealing to your needs he could stimulate you to contribute value to his life voluntarily.

One dictionary defines selfishness, in part, as "caring only or chiefly for oneself; regarding one's own interest or advantage chiefly or solely." Like most dictionary definitions, this one tends to distort the issue. Whether you *solely* regard or *chiefly* regard your own interest are two different things. Again, selfishness is not the issue. You will always act selfishly, no matter how vehemently you resist or protest to the contrary, because such action is automatic. You have no choice in the matter.

What you can choose is whether you will be *rationally* selfish or *irrationally* selfish. And it's how you handle this ever-recurring choice that will determine whether your life will be filled primarily with pleasure or pain. If you're rationally selfish, then you *chiefly* regard your own interests, but not *solely*. Simple reasoning tells you that you must regard the interests of others (though not all others) in order to obtain your objectives. Fellow human beings represent potential values to you in business or personal relationships, and the rational individual understands that to harvest those values he must be willing to fill certain needs of others. In this way, the most rationally selfish individual is also the most "giving" person, since he best understands the soundness of value-for-value relationships.

When an "unselfish" person does something for you, you're not particularly impressed, because he "gives" to everyone, regardless of his admiration or respect for them. In fact, I fear such gifts, because I'm in the dark as to what the eventual payment—with compounded interest over a long period of time—might be. I'm not anxious to accumulate a lot of unspoken accounts payable. When, at some future date, the so-called unselfish person taps me on the shoulder and lets me know, in his own subtle way, that the due date has arrived, I may not be prepared for the shock.

Don't fool Number One. Understand that the gifts from the professed unselfish almost always have hidden price tags—usually bigger ones than you would have been willing to pay had the price been made visible from the outset. And unknown prices have a way of coming due when you can least afford them.

On the other hand, when you receive a "gift" from a truly selfish person, it is evidence of the value he places on you.

You can see now why looking out for Number One requires a conscious, rational effort. Subconsciously, you always think you're looking out for Number One, continually making decisions to take action (or not to take action), and it is precisely because it is you who makes these decisions that you are acting selfishly.

CASE IN POINT: It's Saturday, and all week you've been looking forward to playing tennis with a friend. But your wife has other plans for you—like watching the kids so she can spend time on some special interests. You reluctantly agree to baby-sit, though you really wanted to play tennis. Certainly, then, you didn't choose the thing you wanted most, right?

Wrong. You did choose what you wanted most. You always do. You did what you believed, at that time and under those circumstances, was in your best interest. In this instance, you made the decision (it may or may not have been a rational one) that the displeasure you would avoid (a potential conflict with your wife) was more important to you than the enjoyment you might derive from playing tennis.

It was your choice. It belongs to you. No one put a gun to your head. The only question is whether you made a rational choice, and that's something only you can determine.

CASE IN POINT: What if someone did put a gun to your head? Yes, you would still act selfishly, and if you

47

were rational you would probably cooperate with the person holding the gun.

If, for example, you refused to cooperate because you believed it would be cowardly on your part, you would then be engaging in an irrationally selfish act. Though there could be circumstances under which it would not be in your best interest to cooperate, even at gun point, "bravery" would not be a rational reason. If you resisted for the irrational desire to be "brave," you still would have been choosing what you thought was best for you. Can you imagine someone thinking that death would be in his best interest?

CASE IN POINT: You don't have to imagine it. Just look at the statistics on suicide. All over the world, people daily make the decision that death would be more pleasurable than life. And under certain circumstances, it is possible for such a decision to be an appropriate and rational one. In most instances, however, it is not.

But in any case, the person who takes his own life is simply choosing to do what he selfishly believes is best for him.

CASE IN POINT: What about the individual who risks his life to save another person? Is he, too, being selfish? I have a feeling that by now you know the answer. If you blindly and recklessly risk your life for a total stranger, you've made the decision—spur of the moment as it may be—that you will feel better risking your life, knowing you tried to rescue the stranger, than having to live with the thought that another human being died whom you might have been able to save. Since each emergency will vary according to the risks involved, your ability to make rational decisions quickly is put to a stern test when literal life-and-death situations arise. Therefore, you should lay out some guidelines in advance of such emergency situations, so you'll have a general idea of what you plan to do before they occur. And when you're laying out those guidelines, figure this thought into your formula: How do you know that the person for whom you risk your life is not an Adolf Hitler? Or an Attila the Hun? Or, worse yet, the head of some U.S. regulatory agency?

Therein lies the basic irrationality in risking your life for a stranger: you have no way of knowing for whom you risk it.

Does this mean you should be hostile, wary, or indifferent to strangers? To be hostile to someone you don't know is, of course, absurd. I think it's prudent to be wary of strangers for the same reason you're wary of crossing the street. Both pose potential dangers to you, but not to the extent that you should allow yourself to become paranoid. Your fear of strangers, until they've given you reason to think otherwise, should be no greater than your fear of crossing an intersection.

Indifference is another matter. It seems rational to me that I should be indifferent to the extent that I don't spend my life roaming the streets looking for people who need help. Since everyone needs help, where would I begin? But I'm not indifferent to strangers to the extent that I do respect their rights to live their lives as they please (so long as they do not interfere with mine) and attempt to be humane, friendly and even helpful, within the normal course of living and without sacrificing my own objectives.

With people you know, there is an entirely different value judgment to be made. You still act selfishly, but at least you're not in the dark. You can make a rational decision, for example, to risk your life for the woman you love if the pleasure you gain from her existence is great enough to warrant such action. If a person is prepared to die to keep from losing a cherished relationship, then perhaps selfishness isn't so horrible after all.

CASE IN POINT: Finally, there's the "Mahatma Gandhi argument." I think of the "Gandhi argument" as the last resort of the Magoos and Ostriches because they've brought it up so often in an effort to prove that it is possible to be unselfish.

All right, let's give it one last try. Can I honestly say that I believe Gandhi was acting selfishly when he "sacrificed" himself for the freedom of the Indian people? No, I can't say that I believe it. It would be more proper to say that I know it for a fact. I certainly was not a personal crony of Gandhi's, but I didn't have to be. I need only know that he was a human being and that the courses of action of all men, throughout history, have been chosen from the alternatives available to them at the time. Whatever Gandhi did, out of rational or irrational choice, he did because he chose to do it. If he acted in the hope of making millions of his countrymen happy, then that was the method he chose to seek his own happiness. It's only the means people choose to achieve their happiness which differ.

Mahatma Gandhi was not the first martyr, nor will he be the last. Chances are there's one in your family or among your friends. Martyrs are selfish people—the same as you and me—but with insatiable egos. The ego has a big appetite, and adulation is the foodstuff which makes it grow.

Yes, you "sacrifice" for your children for selfish reasons (which may or may not make them and you happy). Yes, you "sacrifice" for your husband for selfish reasons (which may or may not make him and you happy). Yes, you "sacrifice" for your parents for selfish reasons (which may or may not make them and you happy).

None of these examples, of course, really involves sacrifice at all. What is involved, at its highest level, is rational selfishness—acting on the belief that the good you hope to receive in return will be worth the time, effort and/or money you expend in doing something for the other person.

The summation is that there's no such thing as altruism in the so-called unselfish sense. There is only rational or irrational selfishness. Be on guard when warped idealists try to play word games with you. If by *altruism* a person literally means sacrificing for others, then what he's really

talking about is nothing more than irrational selfishness—
mistakenly doing what he thinks will make him feel best
by surrendering a higher value to a lower one. Be especially wary of those who actually believe they're altruistic, for they are the most vain and dangerous of all people.

THE PACKAGING OF SELF-INTEREST

Within the perimeters of selfishness, human beings can
be divided into three main groups.

THREE TYPE THEORY

This theory was first introduced in *Winning Through
Intimidation,* where it described the three types of people
in the business world. All three, though their methods
differed, were concerned with getting your "chips." The
refinement and expansion of this theory since then has
prompted me to move it out of the narrow world of
business and into the business of life. The basic theory
has not changed, but evolved. The identity of each type
has taken on a broader base.

A Type Number One is an individual who understands
and openly acknowledges that he always acts in his own
self-interest. A Type Number Two is a person who understands that he always acts in his own self-interest, but
tries to make you believe otherwise. A Type Number
Three either doesn't understand or doesn't want to understand that he always acts in his own self-interest. He
therefore feels very sincere when he tries to make you
believe he's thinking of you first.

But, regardless of their reasons or what they profess,
all three always do act in their own self-interest. And
that's the bottom line. A Type One tries to deceive no
one; a Type Two tries to deceive you; a Type Three
deceives himself first and unconsciously tries to deceive
you second.

The least that a lack of understanding of the Three

Type Theory can lead to is continual shock and disappointment—disappointment over the fact that people don't (actually can't) act unselfishly as you might think they ought to.

Put in proper perspective, selfishness is neither bad nor good; it's simply a reality. When you engage in irrationally selfish acts, you can hurt yourself and others. By contrast, when your behavior is rationally selfish, you increase your chances for getting a piece of the pie, and others will usually benefit as a result of your actions. So doing what's best for you does not preclude its also being in the best interests of other people. While it is possible to act in the best interests of others, the important thing to understand is that that will never be your primary objective.

From this day forward, no more cringing at the words *selfishness* and *self-interest*.

Human-Nature Reality No. 2: The Definition Game

Ah, the games people play. They never cease to fascinate me. Here's one we all play, whether we realize it or not.

DEFINITION-GAME THEORY

Every word, every act and every situation is defined by each human being subjectively, usually in such a way as to fit in comfortably with his actions and/or the circumstances of the moment.

We all are involuntary participants in the Definition Game. Because each of us is a unique human being with varying desires, tastes, prejudices, experiences and personality traits, we see things differently. The most prudent way of proceeding in life is to assume that everyone, consciously or unconsciously, uses a definition guide that looks something like this:

Good is what I do; bad is what you do.

Right is what I do; wrong is what you do.

Honest is what I do; dishonest is what you do.

Fair is what I do; unfair is what you do.

Moral is what I do; immoral is what you do.

Ethical is what I do; unethical is what you do.

And on and on the game goes. If you have an insight into how the Definition Game is played, you'll be better equipped to look out for Number One. That's because you won't delude yourself into assuming that everyone else is in tune with you when you think you're having a perfectly harmonious discussion. The story of life is filled with people nodding their heads in agreement, shaking hands, then facing each other in court somewhere down the road. No doubt there were many occasions when two cavemen grunted affirmatively and walked away apparently satisfied, only to end up clubbing it out a short time later when they realized they had misunderstood each other's grunts. The two big advantages they had over us were that there were no attorneys around to make matters worse and they didn't have to wait two or three years for their cases to come to court.

What further complicates the game is that people have a habit of changing their definitions as they go along. This is usually the result of one's established definitions becoming incompatible with his current actions. When you play the game with an Absolute Moralist, for example, the going can really get sticky. The Absolute Moralist, in his unceasing efforts to convert you to his moral standards, plays the game with unmatched fervor. If he can coerce you into accepting his definitions, he's laid the groundwork for getting you to act in his best interest rather than your own.

SCREWOR-SCREWEE THEORY

In essence, this a theory within a theory. Simply stated,

the screwor is always the other guy; the screwee is always you. Screwing is something the other person does to you; it's never what you do to him.

I once was involved in some business dealings with a man whose tactics were a little hard-nosed, to say the least. Compared to this guy, Al Capone looked like the Flying Nun. During one of our meetings, as this man characteristically argued over some penny-ante point, he bellowed, "My wife is right. She's always telling me I'm too easygoing—a soft touch—that I let people step all over me."

Now the nicest thing this fellow ever did was mumble "sorry" after flicking ashes in my coffee. But having cleared the way by portraying himself as a man who was perennially bullied, he could justify taking dead aim at my scrotum with every weapon in his Definition Bag.

You may not like it; I may not like it; but the reality is that the perpetrator can always justify his actions.

THE BOOK THAT DEFINES NOTHING: THE DICTIONARY

Most words in a dictionary are technically defined in several ways, which only encourages people to use their own definitions instead. But even if you use the dictionary's definition of a word and follow it through by in turn looking up the definition of those words used to define the original word, you'll always arrive at the same conclusion: the dictionary leaves the real definition up to each individual.

Take a favorite Definition-Game word like *right*. Looking only at the first definition given in the dictionary, this is what you see:

Right: "in accordance with what is *just* or good"

Just: "in accordance with what is *right*"

You've reached an impasse immediately. Right is in accordance with what is just and just is in accordance with what is right. Webster in effect has said to us, "I don't want to get involved. You guys fight it out." The solution? The Definition Game—each person defines every word to mean what he wants it to mean. What's your definition of right? Or your neighbor's? Or your lover's?

FOR SHAME

Then there are the "shame words," used effectively as intimidation tools by Absolute Moralists. Shame on you if you're not "patriotic"; shame on you if you're an "anarchist"; shame, shame, shame.

The dictionary defines a patriot as "one who loves his country and zealously supports its authority and interests." An anarchist is "one who rebels against any authority, established order, or ruling power." Therefore, if you lived in Germany in the early forties and supported the Third Reich, you were patriotic. But if you rebelled against the totalitarian orders of that police state, you were an anarchist. Those who led the rebellion against England in 1776 were considered patriots on this side of the ocean, but to the English they were anarchists and traitors of the worst kind. Keep these examples in mind the next time someone calls an individual an anarchist or tries to tongue-lash you for being unpatriotic. You needn't feel compelled to support any immoral government action because of the fear of being called unpatriotic.

Does it really matter to you if people, particularly those who advocate doctrines which you consider immoral, call you names? These are not sticks and stones we're talking about; they're merely words. As such, you should never allow them to hurt or intimidate you. Above all, don't waste time trying to explain yourself to a name-caller. He won't understand, because he is not able to think logically and rationally. If you train yourself to ignore him, however, he eventually will go away and leave you to continue your peaceful pursuit of looking out for Number One.

In a *Newsweek* article, Memphis prosecutor Larry Parrish brilliantly stated, "There is absolutely no question that there is such a thing as obscenity. The Supreme Court has said that there is and Congress has said that there is."[3] I realize it's a little hard to contain your laughter, but honest, folks, that's a verbatim quote.

Sure there's such a thing as obscenity, and I'll tell you exactly what it is. It's what you think is obscene. Mr. Parrish evidently believes that *Deep Throat* is obscene; someone else might think it's obscene for a government to enslave an individual and force him into a situation where he must either murder strangers or be murdered himself. (The government refers to this as being drafted into the armed forces and given the opportunity to defend your country.) Again, it's all in the eyes of the beholder.

When you say someone is "dishonest," what you really mean is that you and he differ in your definitions of honesty. This doesn't mean his moral standards are lower than yours; they're simply not the same. And if that person thinks your moral standards are lower than his, that's his problem. It's not your job to look out for him; your job is to look out for Number One. Your only concern, therefore, is to make sure that your head is on straight. Your moral standards should be what you define them to be. Don't allow others to be so presumptuous as to set them for you.

Human-Nature Reality No. 3: The Line-Drawing Game

The Line-Drawing Game is a sort of corollary of the Definition Game. Not only do people define words to justify their actions, they also define words *by* their actions. When, for example, a man steals groceries because he believes he's "entitled" to them, this action reveals his definition of the word *entitled*. Every individual arbitrarily draws a line between right and wrong, conveniently placing it so that his actions lie to the "right" side of his line. Where the other guy draws his lines may not seem rational by your standards, but the man who thinks for himself is not particularly concerned with your opinions, especially if he disagrees with most of the values you espouse.

LINE-DRAWING-GAME THEORY

Every person subjectively draws his own lines concerning what is and is not proper action, based either on his own moral standards, the moral standards of others, or what is convenient for him at the time of the action. The net result is that his actions, to one extent or another, express his definitions of words. As with the Definition Game, every human being is a participant in the Line-Drawing Game whether or not he chooses to be. Through his every action (or inaction) he advertises to the world on which side of which lines he stands.

The conflicts arise when Absolute Moralists begin drawing lines for people other than themselves. Since billions of individuals can never agree on all things at all times (a slight understatement, to say the least), a statement like "someone has to draw the line somewhere" is utter nonsense—meaningless political rhetoric. The obvious response to such an unrealistic and dangerous statement is, "But who shall be the one to draw it?" Unfortunately, there has never been a scarcity of crusaders, bureaucrats and would-be dictators willing to step forth and draw lines for everyone. And since the reality is that all members of a society can never agree simultaneously on even *one* thing, any line drawn by others—under the guise of a commandment, a law or any other facade—is destined to make many people unhappy.

Though we have no choice but to participate in the Game, it is within our power to be satisfied drawing lines only for ourselves and resisting the urge to draw them for others.

I'LL OBEY YOUR EVERY COMMAND; JUST DON'T MESS WITH MY GUCCIS.

Recently I attended a dinner party and happened to sit opposite a middle-aged woman dressed in a chic Gucci outfit. Throughout dinner, she rambled on about "the good of society" and doing what was "in the best interests of the people." After about an hour of this, I decided that the Marx Brothers made more sense to me than she, particularly Harpo. As she extended her unsolicited lecture into the area of moral standards, I bravely fought off the urge to regurgitate on my Rock Cornish game hen. Carried away by her own rhetoric, she finally declared that the world (she wasn't satisfied with a mere city, state or country; she was going for the whole ball of wax) had to have some moral code for everyone to live by, else we would all be doomed.

I thought about that statement for a moment, scratched my head, took a sip of wine and watched it dribble down my tie, then concluded: "We're all doomed."

What that woman really meant was that lines should be drawn for everyone according to *her* standards. I can assure you that she would have hollered loudly had the Worldwide Line Drawer arbitrarily decided that people should not have the right to wear diamonds or Gucci clothing while millions were living in poverty.

AND GOD SAID, "LET THERE BE SMOKE. . . ."

A good friend of mine is, by his definition, an "orthodox" Jew. As such, it always struck me as rather strange that this man, who would not smoke on the Jewish Sabbath, had no hesitation about using his car. According to Jewish "law," both riding and smoking are forbidden on the Sabbath.

I finally realized that it was a simple case of line drawing. On this particular issue, my friend's line was conveniently situated right between smoking and driving.

Had he been an exercise buff who was addicted to smoking, perhaps he would have reversed the position of the two. To him, riding was more important than smoking, so "orthodox" was made to fit in with, and was defined by, his priorities.

CAN JUST ONE A DAY KEEP THE GUILT PANGS AWAY?

Adultery, a subject close to the hearts of many, lends itself especially well to the Line-Drawing Game. I know people who draw the line at thinking but not touching. Others just indulge in a little hanky-panky in the office now and then, but draw the line at that. Then there's the really adept Line Drawer who feels he's honorable because he only cheats on his wife "now and then."

At the far end of the spectrum are those who practice adultery with the same zealousness as religious fanatics. But even among those who practice it as though it were a vocation, there are a variety of lines drawn. One guy feels he's not doing anything immoral because he restricts his extracurricular activities to the daytime (even if it's one a day). Another man's morals are protected by the fact that he only goes to bed with "classy women." The philosophy of a third individual is, "The hell with class, I'm shooting for records." Where do you draw your line?

LINE DRAWING BY ANY OTHER NAME

Property rights are an area where actual, physical lines are drawn. How far back do you go to determine who originally occupied a piece of land? If you're in control of an area of land today, then you draw a line which assures that your ownership is valid. But if the land was taken from you by force a hundred years ago, you wouldn't be inclined to go along with the maxim that possession is nine-tenths of the law.

Court fights over rightful land title are common, with title companies employed to trace ownership back to "original" owners. The only problem with title searches in the United States is that they go back only to the point where the line was arbitrarily drawn by its conquerors. That line appears just *before* the American Indians owned the land.

You might wonder how we can arbitrarily draw the line there, how we can ignore the fact that European settlers blatantly took land from Indian tribes who had occupied it long before they arrived. The answer, of course, is that we do it by playing the Line-Drawing Game.

Here's specifically how our "forefathers" (are we supposed to feel responsible for the actions of human beings we didn't even know?) rationalized drawing the line on land ownership. They conveniently invented something called (are you ready for this?) Manifest Destiny. According to them, "the Europeans and their descendants were *ordained by destiny* to rule all of America." [4]

I mean, really, you can't help but chuckle at the thought that grown men, educated and undoubtedly brimming over with feelings of personal integrity and honesty, looked at each other with straight faces and tried to act as though they seriously believed that. But apparently they did, because whenever the Boys in D.C. needed to break a promise made to the Indians, they just moved the line over a little and passed something called a new "law."

Today we simply ignore the facts and begin all discussions of property rights on the premise that the original owner of a given piece of land was the first owner *after* it was confiscated from the Indians. Our "ancestors" were pretty adept at playing the Line-Drawing Game, don't you think? And we're not doing too badly ourselves at keeping this ruse, and many others, alive. When one talks of the American Indians' rightful ownership of land today, he's likely to encounter one of three things: 1) non-acknowledgement, 2) patronizing smirks or chuckles, or 3) a prominent place on some government list labeling him a potential troublemaker.

But what happened hundreds of years ago is no longer relevant, even if you or I think it *ought to* be. The important point is that "Manifest Destiny" exists today—in *your* life. Do you allow people continually to infest your brain with fancy line-drawing phrases the equivalent of Manifest Destiny? If you don't acknowledge the reality that the Line-Drawing Game is being played right now— by everyone—people will continue sticking their Manifest Destinies in your ear until you no longer possess the ability to make your own moral judgments.

A BLESSING FROM GOD AND A MESSAGE FROM MICHAEL

And who can forget *The Godfather?* In a dramatic sequence near the movie's end, as Michael "stood god-father" at the baptism of his sister's son, his henchmen were rubbing out all the bad guys who might challenge his authority. There was Michael, in church, asking God's blessing on his nephew, while simultaneously spilling the blood of those who had "crossed" him. You and I may not draw our lines where Michael did, but we do draw them where needed to justify our own particular behavior. Those *Godfather* scenes were not only a message to all of us, they were a message *about* all of us. Michael murders; an orthodox Jew rides on Saturday; governments invent Manifest Destiny. We all play the game.

Now you know the answer to that age-old question, "But who shall draw the line?" The answer is: everybody. Everybody has always conveniently drawn his own lines to fit his particular circumstances. Whether or not you or I happen to like that fact is not relevant. It's simply a reality of the Human Nature Group.

As with the Definition Game, what considerably complicates the matter is that, in addition to the fact that everyone draws his lines subjectively, people also are constantly erasing lines and drawing new ones to fit their changing circumstances. A majority of people, I would venture to say, have not rationally and logically analyzed the moral standards they wish to live by. As a result, when something they want happens to be on the wrong side of one of their lines, they simply relocate that line so that the desired item or end falls on the "right" side.

Don't be intimidated by the line drawing of others. How they wish to play the Line-Drawing Game is their business, so long as their lines don't infringe on you. Likewise, make sure they understand that you require no help in deciding where to place your lines, either.

The People Hurdle

Damn it, why can't life be easy? If it were, I could have been vacationing in Rio instead of writing this book. And you wouldn't feel the need to read it; instead, you could be living the carefree, glamorous life that Madison Avenue depicts for us on television.

But alas, life is not as Madison Avenue portrays it. It's not a gentleman in a tuxedo lounging before a fireplace on a bearskin rug, sipping cognac with a sensuous playmate in a chic black satin gown. (Do they ever work? Or fight for parking spaces? Or spill their cognac?) Life is not your friendly neighborhood insurance agent appearing at your side, like a genie out of a bottle, whenever a little problem arises.

Yes, life *ought to* be an eternal tiptoeing through the tulips, but it's not. You and I know better, because we've been there. Life is Janis Ian's "At Seventeen":

> *To those of us who knew the pain*
> *of valentines that never came*

and those whose names were never called
when choosing sides for basketball
It was long ago, and far away
The world was younger than today
and dreams were all they gave for free
to ugly duckling girls like me[1]

Let's face it, my friend: life can be a ball-buster.

And there's one driving force at the root of most of life's hassles. That force is a living creature. Thousands of years of recorded history have shown that he is directly or indirectly the cause of most of the problems which surround us daily. To make it interesting, let's see if you can guess the culprit from the multiple choices below:

A) Reindeer   C) Baboon   E) Man
B) Zebra   D) Caterpillar

If you guessed reindeer or zebra, give yourself a *GT* for Good Try. You get an *NC* for caterpillar—Not Close. In the event you checked baboon, you were warm; you earn a grade of *AR* for Almost Right. But if you picked man as your answer, take a bow; you're very perceptive.

All it took was a little rational analysis. You've never seen a reindeer, zebra, caterpillar or baboon try to impose his moral standards on others, have you? There's no escaping it: what the world has are People Problems. They're the source of most of life's frustrations and complications. If you can learn to deal effectively with the neuroses of human beings, you will have cleared a gigantic hurdle in your path. But as with all realities, you have to identify them before they can be properly handled.

NATURE OF MAN

What makes man tick? Why is he so troublesome? What, exactly, is he? Let's first define him by process of elimination. What man isn't is what you want him to be.

It's back to "Is's" versus "Ought To's": no individual is what you think he ought to be; he is what he is. To try to believe that a person is something other than what he really is—a very common error—is to lie. Worst of all, you're lying to yourself (and maybe to the person you've stamped with the "ought-to" tag).

What else do we know about man? That he is automatically selfish and that he plays the Definition Game and Line-Drawing Game. We also know that these traits are neither good nor bad, that they are just realities and will cause you problems only if you allow them to.

We have also seen that there are three general types of people in the world: a Type Number One—the honest, straightforward individual who makes no pretense about always acting in his own best interest; a Type Number Two—the guy who tries to deceive you into believing he's looking out for your well-being first, thus encouraging you to drop your guard; and a Type Number Three—the Ostrich or Mr. Magoo—who either doesn't understand or refuses to face the reality that he's out for himself, which can cause you to feel unduly relaxed in his presence.

A characteristic we haven't discussed, but which is extremely important to understand, is that man is imperfect. The failure to remember this reality can cause you endless frustration and disappointment. We want so badly for people to be perfect (if not our enemies, then at least our friends) that we often hurt ourselves by expecting too much of them.

Once you recognize the reality of man's imperfection, you'll realize that people don't hurt you; you *allow* them to. This hurt often is not only the result of your inability to cope with man's imperfection, but of your taking it upon yourself to make a person into something he's not. If you insist upon engaging in this self-appointed duty, you're guaranteed to experience the inevitable futility of tampering with the impossible.

This futility is especially evident in dealing with those who are closest to you. Friends, lovers, parents and children are people, too. They're all subject to the same human imperfections, but because of their relationship to you, they're in a position to cause you more grief than others—*if* you let them. Since people are at the root of most of life's complications, it's understandable that those closest to you have the potential to do the most damage. It doesn't mean they have to or that they will; it's just that they have the potential.

Listing the characteristics of human beings is a little like discussing reality in that the scope is infinite. But to clear the People Hurdle, it's not necessary to attempt to identify every human characteristic. To begin with, we can eliminate all positive human qualities, not to play down the good side of man, but because it's usually his negative points which do the damage. All his pleasant attributes—his ability to be humane, to show kindness, to express love—are bonuses. When you get them, they're welcome additions; but by not sitting around and waiting for them to show up, you'll be taking charge of your own happiness instead of leaving it to the mercy of others.

For this reason, I'll focus my attention only on characteristics which have the potential to block your path to a better life. Eliminating People Problems requires that you face the reality that people possess an unlimited number of potentially harmful traits, that you learn the art of spotting these qualities, and—the supreme test—that you develop the ability and self-discipline either to ignore such actions or, in extreme cases, eliminate from your life those individuals responsible for them. You qualify for your doctorate on the subject when you convert the energy once used for hassling with such characters into attracting individuals who can add happiness to your life. When you've reached that point, Number One is well on his way to a better life.

In this chapter I've restricted my discussion to a mere handful of potentially devastating human peculiarities. If you were to believe that every person in the world possessed each of the upcoming traits to the same neurotic degree, you'd probably be booking passage on the first space shuttle to Mars. Granted, the world at times seems to be one gigantic insane asylum, but it's not that insane.

Most human qualities appear in a broad range among different individuals. Each of us possesses every trait, and while certain of them are undetectable in some persons, they're a dominant part of the personalities of others. That, more than anything else, is what makes human beings exciting—their uniqueness. And it also makes your odds very good. There are over four billion individuals in the People Store and you need only select a handful of the right ones to fill your companionship needs. Seen from that perspective, the odds are overwhelmingly in your favor—*if* you know what you're looking for and have the determination to settle for nothing less. But because the majority of people you encounter will not be among that select group, you'll never find the roses unless you keep the weeds cut down to size.

The weeds which grow most out of control are known as neurotics. A neurotic is a person who has an emotional disorder. This covers a lot of ground—probably everyone you and I know, to one extent or another and at various times. Each of us is a little neurotic in certain areas, or at least has been on occasion. But those people who consistently have either too many neuroses, or a single extreme neurosis, can seriously disrupt your life.

IRRATIONALITY

Irrationality is the most logical trait with which to begin, because it's usually the base from which other negative attributes spring. Your objective vis-à-vis irrationality should be twofold: to be able to spot it in others and to control your own thought processes so as to act in a rational manner as consistently as possible.

By *rational*, I mean the basing of one's words and actions on reason and logic. But since each individual's definition of reason and logic may vary, how can one be

"I have two Neurotics and a Weed in the car. I'd like to trade them in on a couple of Roses."

sure whose perception of rational action is correct? From a long-term standpoint, that's easy: the irrational person will fail to obtain his objectives, while the rational person will succeed.

As a simple guideline for making rational decisions, I suggest you develop the habit of asking yourself two questions:

1) Will my action have the potential to better my existence, either by bringing me pleasure or by eliminating pain?

2) Will my action in any way be forcibly interfering with the rights of anyone else?

Now we're back on familiar ground. To take action that is happiness oriented, you have to know what you're doing and why you're doing it, which means you must be aware of the facts (i.e., realities). Again we arrive at the inescapable starting point: correct perception of reality. If the things one does to enrich his life are contrary to the facts, he's acting irrationally. Whether he acts in opposition to reality because of a malfunction in his reasoning power or because he lies to himself is irrelevant. In either case, his conduct is irrational and, on a long-term basis, he will fail.

Ideally, then, facts alone should influence your actions. This can best be accomplished when intellect, rather than emotion, is in control. Take the time and make the effort to think through, in a logical manner, those philosophical issues which affect your life. Do this during periods of solitude, when there's nothing to distract your thoughts— when you're relaxed and unemotional.

Once that's done, you must have enough confidence in your analysis to remain steadfastly loyal to your rationally determined code of behavior, especially when encounters with irrational people arise. Be strong enough not to let emotion sway you. However, just because you're able to reason, don't make the mistake of assuming that the other guy will be logical, too. The path to a happy life is jammed with irrational people who are ready, willing and able to do numbers on your head if you can't spot them. Don't assume that all those with whom you come in contact will act rationally; they won't.

Spotting the Irrational Argument

How do you know when someone is being irrational? First you must learn to see past a person's statement to his basic assumption. Once you've identified his premise, you may find that you disagree with it. If, for example, a man argues that tax money should be spent for a purpose he thinks worthwhile, you inherently may feel that something is amiss in his argument. On analysis, you might conclude that the premise—the stealing of money from individual citizens under the label of taxation—is wrong by your standards. Therefore, *any* purpose for which he feels the funds should be earmarked is unjustified because the entire argument is based on his assumption that stealing is proper.

"You aren't really interested in helping others, are you?" This is the type of question I'm inevitably confronted with on radio and TV interviews.

I've no way of honestly responding to such a question without making the asker first define some of his words. If by *others* he is alluding to all people, then my answer is definitely no. There are rapists, murderers, Absolute Moralists, robbers (e.g., all people who draw government paychecks), and many others whom I don't wish to "help" in any way. But I do have very deep feelings for many people, namely those individuals who add something of value to my life and thus contribute to my happiness.

If by *helping* the questioner means giving others something for nothing, then I definitely am not interested in helping *anyone*. I am, however, happy to be able to "help" many people if it means doing something for individuals with whom I have value-for-value relationships. I have no desire to hand out love, friendship, money or any other valuable commodity indiscriminately to anyone who happens to cross my path. To do so would cheapen what I have to offer. Special things are for special people—those who really mean a lot to me. Neither do I wish to receive love, friendship, material gain or anything else from someone who hasn't received, or doesn't expect to receive, something of equal value from me.

You needn't answer any question until your questioner agrees to define his terms. If you find that a question is based on what you consider to be a false assumption, then any answer you give will be a dishonest one. I often find that when I unmask the premise, no question exists; instead, it becomes a hypothetical question. A question is a reality; a hypothetical question is a forced illusion. I don't have time to clutter my mind with hypothetical questions based on false premises, nor do you if you intend to spend the time and effort necessary to make your life an exciting journey.

The illogical person tips his hand in many other ways, but you must be alert to pick up the signs. Irrational people stray from the main point; they dwell on the irrelevant; they rely on nonfactual slogans; they're at their best when generalizing. The invalid analogy is another old trick of the irrational, while perhaps their favorite technique is to "prove" a point by restating it, in a veiled manner, as though it were fact. All of these employ the use of the magician's philosophy: distract the person's attention in order to pull the trick off with the hand that isn't being watched.

If none of these techniques works, the irrational person will often invoke "faith" as a last resort. If someone says that a particular belief is based solely on faith, then it's not a matter of his tipping his hand, but an *admission* that he is not employing his reasoning power. Faith is the antithesis of logic. To base your behavior on faith can be suicidal, much like the drunk who, having faith that he will not be harmed, attempts to cross a busy freeway. On the other hand, "faith" supported by fact is not faith at all; it's confidence. It's blind faith that poses the danger.

Perhaps the most common behavioral pattern of the irrational person is emotional excess. Whenever I feel strongly about making a point, I'm always reminded of Gertrude's telltale statement in *Hamlet:* "The lady doth protest too much, methinks." The more one belabors a point, the more skeptical I become; the louder one talks, the further I back off. Repetition raises doubts in the minds of those to whom you wish to make your point. The power of the understatement is enormous. Say it once; say it calmly; say it firmly. If your point is rational, state it rationally. Every statement beyond that is a step backward.

Fascination with this phenomenon has led me to formulate the

I'VE-GOT-MY-SHIT-TOGETHER THEORY

This theory is exemplified by the lady in *Hamlet* who protested too much. In the entertainment field, one has occasion to come in contact with a great many individuals who, shall we say, have a tendency to be a little "off balance." Ironically, one of the assertions most commonly heard among this segment is, "I've really got my shit together." It hasn't taken unusual perception on my part to notice that the people who most frequently and emphatically make statements of this kind are generally those who seem to be prime candidates for the cuckoo's nest.

If you pay close attention to the amazing consistency of this principle, you can astound friends with your fortune-telling abilities. The more someone dwells on a point (particularly if the information is volunteered for no apparent reason), the better your chances of being right if you assume the opposite. It's a matter of proper translation, and it goes something like this:

STATEMENT: I've really got my shit together now.

TRANSLATION: I'm so screwed up that I'm past the point of even acknowledging it.

STATEMENT: We've got the perfect marriage; we never argue; my husband never looks at another woman; I'm perfectly contented.

TRANSLATION: Our marriage is a bore; we don't talk; I know the bastard is cheating on me every night; I'm going for the jugular when I file for divorce.

STATEMENT: I'm making money hand over fist; pay for everything in hard cash; got it made.

TRANSLATION: The sheriff's one step behind me; my Mercedes is on a month-to-month lease; unless a miracle happens I'll be belly-up within a month.

Beware of the person who overstates his case. He's telling you something, but you have to be alert to hear the real message. And if you find *yourself* trying too hard to make a point, do a quick check on your reasoning. There's a good chance you may be acting irrationally.

INTIMIDATION

Intimidation—motivation through fear—is an ever-present head game played in a myriad of ways. If you give it some thought, you might be shocked to find that a large percentage of your actions are motivated by fear. You may be motivated by the fear of physical harm, the fear of losing someone's love, or the fear of being embarrassed, to name a few. Some of these fears are valid, but most are not. It's the preponderance of unfounded fears which unnecessarily disrupts your life.

Intimidation comes in a variety of packages and isn't easy to spot if one is not aware of the ways in which it's camouflaged. Whenever you have the feeling you're being intimidated, ask yourself one simple question: Why am I doing what I'm doing? Be honest in your answer. If you can trace the reason for your action to any kind of fear, you're being intimidated. The exception is when careful reasoning on your part has led you to conclude that the fear is well-founded—that it *is* in your best interest to do something you'd rather not do. In that case, since you're not acting out of blind fear, you're not being intimidated.

But by far the majority of the time, people are motivated by fears which have no real bases. All too often, we react like Pavlov's dogs and obey the commands of others at the mere sound of their voices. It can be a miserable existence; motivation through subtle intimidation can become such an accepted mode of life that an individual doesn't even realize he's a perpetual victim.

Intimidation through Posture

As The Tortoise has long emphasized, it's not what you say or do that counts, but what your posture is when you say or do it. This can be a very nice fact of life if you happen to be the one holding the posture aces, but if it's the other guy, he can intimidate you out of your shoes, your morals, and your concentration on looking out for Number One.

You may not be in a position to implement posture intimidation on a grand scale, nor do you necessarily have any desire to. But you do have the power to keep others from snowing *you*. Not that it's easy. It takes a cool head, a rational mind, and an understanding of the game of intimidation.

Size Power

Size alone can give a person an intimidating posture. It's hard to overcome the apparent disadvantage of having to look up to the person to whom you're speaking. But, assuming you're not in a situation where physical violence is expected, a person has no advantage simply because he happens to be bigger than you. Some people, however, consciously try to use their size to gain a psychological edge. Don't buy it; it's meaningless in all matters that do not involve physical strength.

MONEY POWER

Wealth can give an otherwise inept man a strong posture. The power of money can sometimes seem awesome. But as Washington continues to decrease the value of the dollar through counterfeit printing and bankruptcy spending, each dollar has less and less power. Illegal printing of money by the government, however, can't dilute the value of your capabilities. In a total crash of the economy, those who are educated in the game of life—who know how to use their wits—will survive.

In the meantime, while money manages to retain at least a small percentage of its original value, respect what power it holds, but don't let it overwhelm you. Don't be intimidated by wealth alone. Make a guy come up with something better than a balance sheet before conceding a good posture to him, and even then don't allow yourself to be intimidated.

MAGNANIMITY POWER

Most of us grow up in total awe of magnanimous individuals. To a child, such a person seems beyond reproach. But I'm not a child anymore, and I hope you aren't either. Magnanimity is a first cousin to self-righteousness. As you grow older and begin to observe more carefully, you begin noticing things that cause you to have doubts, sometimes carrying you beyond skepticism to cynicism.

Doesn't it often seem that humanitarian and church

awards are directly related to one's financial statement? The typical magnanimous person is usually someone who can afford to be magnanimous. I'll tell you one thing, it was a hell of a lot easier for me to be gracious after I became a bestselling author than when I was flat busted.

EXPERT POWER

What is an expert? He's just about anything you want him to be. Generally, he's a guy who can tell you all the reasons why *you* can't do something. Personally, I prefer to discover for myself what I am or am not capable of accomplishing.

Sometimes an expert is really nothing more than an ordinary guy from out of town who knows his job. I've had occasion to travel over the years, more than I care to remember, and I've always marveled at how an individual's status as an expert seems to increase with the distance he travels.

The printed word helps, too. Heck, for years I was saying many of the things I now write in books, but I didn't attract too many listeners. I don't want to make you feel bad, but if you'd been around a few years ago, you could have gotten most of the information in this book for free. In fact, I probably would have treated you to dinner just for listening.

I began developing a phobia about experts when I first read Aristotle. In his time, the man was what you'd call a pretty fair country expert, but he insisted, among other things, that the earth was the center of the universe and that seven planets, including the sun and moon, revolved around it. Based on the facts known at the time, his pronouncements were reasonable. But that's just the point: new evidence is always cropping up.

The Tortoise becomes an expert.

Just having the right tools can play a big part in

making an expert out of an otherwise ordinary guy. I found this out when I went broke. I was never very interested in learning how to fix things; in fact, I was a danger to myself when it came to repairs. I thought a hammer was something you stirred a pot of soup with. As far as I knew, nuts-and-bolts was the name of a new dance.

But when the roof caved in financially, I was forced to learn how to solve some of these mechanical mysteries myself. To my surprise, I became pretty good at it—mostly because I discovered that half the battle was having the right tools. A great revelation occurred the day I spent five hours trying to get a sticker off a piece of glass. I threw boiling water on it and almost scalded myself; I scraped it with a steak knife until I broke the tip of the knife; I cursed it and shook my fist at it, but the sticker continued to do its thing: stick.

In exasperation, I went to the hardware store and asked if they had a tool that was made to do the job. They did; it cost about a buck. It's a little metal gadget that holds a razor blade firmly in place with the entire edge of the blade exposed. It took me about thirteen seconds to remove the label, in perfect fashion, and with virtually no effort. After I got through crying, I stared at the little tool that had done the job so easily and muttered, "You little bastard, you've just made an expert out of a basket case." Now, whenever I undertake *any* task in life—not just those having to do with repairs—I make certain that I have the right "tools" before I begin.

A Quick Cure for Expert Fixationitis

If you wish to overcome your awe of experts quickly, consider the following true story. A director and an instructor in psychiatry, both from the University of Southern California medical school, teamed with an assistant professor of medical education at Southern Illinois University to conduct a rather unusual experiment. They arranged to have a Dr. Myron L. Fox, purportedly an authority on the application of mathematics to human behavior, speak to a group of fifty-five educators, school administrators, psychiatrists, psychologists and social workers. His topic was "mathematical game theory as applied to physician education."

It must have been a great speech, because forty-two of the fifty-five in attendance commented that the speaker's examples helped clarify the subject and that the material was well organized and the lecture stimulating. All of this was fine, except for one small matter: "Dr. Fox" was a hired actor and his "lecture" was never meant to be anything but pure double-talk.

God help us all if our fate is to be left in the hands of anyone who happens to claim the title of expert!

Even experts get fooled by experts.

But don't feel embarrassed if you've been taken in by experts in the past. It happens to the best—even those who are supposed to be experts themselves.

You may remember NBC's out-of-court settlement with a little television station in Lincoln, Nebraska. After coming out with a brand new logo, NBC discovered, much to its chagrin, that the Nebraska Educational Television network had already been using the logo for quite some time. In the settlement, NBC paid the small Nebraska station $55,000 in cash and $500,000 in used equipment in exchange for the rights to the trademark. Not a bad settlement, considering the fact that it had cost the Lincoln network less than $100 to have one of its own staff members develop the logo.

Oh, by the way—NBC spent about $750,000 to have specialists develop virtually the same logo; experts don't come cheap, you know.

I wanted to retire and play golf, but Legalman saved me.

The expert of all experts, of course, is Legalman (still

referred to by some people as: the attorney). If you're not familiar with this astounding character, allow me to reintroduce him. When things are going well for you—particularly if you're about to close a worthwhile deal—Legalman is the guy who leaps onto the stage in the final act, brandishing his satchel full of little deal-killing goodies, just in time to bring down the curtain (on everyone involved).

I never saw Legalman in better form than on one occasion when I was still fumbling around in the corporate world, trying to make acquisitions. I'd been contacted by the wealthy founder and controlling stockholder of an American Stock Exchange company, a tired-looking man who had come to the conclusion that there must be more to life than just working and getting old. He had decided that he'd rather play golf in the Bahamas for the rest of his life than continue to oversee his widget factory.

And he damn near got his wish. I was ready with the cash; he was ready with the stock. But Legalman—that omnipresent defender of the nonexistent problems of people—was ready, too, with his bag of deal-killing goodies.

Onto the scene he dashed, just in time to blurt out his standard opening line: "I want you to know that I'm not one of those attorneys who kills deals, so you can relax. It's up to my client to make his own decisions." He then grabbed his victim (er, client) by the throat and dragged him out of the room for "a few words in private."

Whatever went on in the other room must have been a takeoff on *The Manchurian Candidate*. All I know is that he didn't sell his company to me. The owner became thoroughly "convinced" that he really hadn't wanted to play golf after all. Legalman had saved him from the horrors of a relaxing life in the Bahamas, making it possible for him to continue slaving away in his widget factory until either he died or the government decided to outlaw widgets. His job completed, Legalman then picked up his goodies bag, spread his cape, and disappeared into the suburbs to enjoy his evening martini.

A Real, Personal God

Millions of people believe in a personal God—not just a symbolic, abstract cosmic force, but a sort of supernatural man. You may or may not agree with them, although to my knowledge no one has conclusively proven otherwise. Still, there are limits to what I can accept as possibilities. To picture God running around with a stethoscope and tongue depressor is pushing it a little too far.

Therein lies the difference between law school and medical school. A law student is taught how to find or create problems and then assert himself as an expert intimidator; a medical student is taught that he's God! Not all doctors buy the story, but I've met plenty of them who apparently did.

Many years ago a physician informed me that I was the victim of an abnormal growth, painting an extremely bleak picture. He told me that the chances for a malignancy were high and that it was in the worst possible area —one conducive to a rapid spread throughout the body. He urged immediate surgery.

I was frantic. It looked like my game was going to be over in the early innings. It never occurred to me, at that young age, that a doctor might just be completely wrong in his diagnosis; I was too impressed by his expert status to question his opinion. I was scared; I was in awe of his stature; I didn't want to "offend" him by seeking a second opinion; I was in the throes of intimidation by an expert.

Next to a legaldectomy, my operation was the most painful thing I had ever endured. The discomfort, the blood, the stay in the hospital, the time and money lost— it was a lesson you didn't soon forget. It took me a year to recover fully from the side effects, and it still causes me discomfort at times. What did the medical expert find when he cut me open? Nothing!

Months later, after I talked to two outside doctors, I became a little bitter, to say the least. Both of them said that, given the facts, including the available X rays, they would not have operated. That hurt almost as much as the operation itself. I had really paid my dues—in blood —and I would never again accept the word of an expert without further investigation.

If ever you should find yourself in such a situation, don't agree to something as serious as surgery without obtaining at least one other professional opinion. If this insults your doctor, feel fortunate to be rid of him; he's telling you something about himself. Your physician might be the most ethical and qualified man in the world, but the reality is that you're just one of many "deals" to him. He may have good intentions every time he does his thing, but he's *not* God; he's human. In the event he's too neurotic to understand that, make damn sure that you aren't.

Remember, in your life you're the *only* deal. You blow it and you don't get back in the ballpark; it's all over. Maybe you can't take matters into your own hands to the extent of operating on yourself, but you certainly can get a second, or even third, qualified opinion. Doctors make mistakes, and they're entitled to; they're human. Just make certain that you aren't one of their mistakes. If you don't, looking out for Number One can become an academic matter very quickly.

Experts, Experts, and More Experts

On and on they go, and where they stop, nobody knows. Throughout history, experts have been intimidating people into making plans based on their scientific predictions for the future. But the future is arriving so fast these days—proving the experts wrong more quickly

"Let there be turtle soup."

than in the past—that only a fool would rely blindly on the forecasts of an expert.

In 1976 *The Wall Street Journal* ran a series of articles entitled "The Future Revised," in which it outlined how drastically the so-called experts, over the past ten years, had changed their prognostications for the year 2000. Although each article delved into a different area of expert miscalculation—everything from world hunger to population growth to the economy—the subject was summed up (for me, at least) in the first article of the series. An economist at the National Planning Association confessed that "There's not much interest in long-range forecasts around here any more. We've been wrong too often." [2] (Even experts can be Type Number Ones.)

How does expert intimidation affect *your* life? Do you purposely eat a big breakfast because the experts have hammered home to you that it's essential to good health? A couple of other experts—doctors, in fact—have concluded that a big breakfast is actually unhealthy because, among other things, it supplies unneeded calories, sets the fat-depositing, insulin-glucagon machinery in motion, can cause a craving for more starchy foods, and causes the blood to shift to the intestines at the expense of the brain and muscles.

Do experts have you worried over the energy shortage? I'll introduce you to other experts who either don't think the energy situation is of crisis proportions or don't believe it's a problem that can't be solved with relative ease. Your plumber says you need a whole new faucet unit? I'll get you one who will assure you it's only necessary to insert a new screw in the old unit. You're staying in a bad marriage because a marriage counselor has told you that the "right" thing to do is work it out? I'll find one who will tell you that it's more practical to cut the chain and get a fresh start. Are you shying away from a favorite food because a scientist has proven it causes cancer in worms?

With a little searching, I'll find one who claims it's the healthiest food you can eat.

Face it: "experts" don't have all the answers. At best, experts are people who are knowledgeable in their fields —knowledgeable, but not infallible. And the best ones will admit that openly. Kick the expert habit; don't make decisions based solely on the opinions of a purported expert. By all means, listen to what he has to say, but weigh it against all the other evidence available to you. Most important, weigh it against your reasoning power. Then make your final decisions accordingly. No expert can hold you captive against your will.

CREDENTIALS POWER

Credentials power is similar to expert power, but even more ludicrous. The emphasis here is strictly on a piece of paper or, in some cases, experience.

Don't be so naive as to believe that because a person has a license from the government, the Mafia, or any other gang that allows him to practice his profession without interference (it's sometimes known as buying "protection"), he knows all the answers. Nor is experience necessarily a relevant criterion. I've met many people new to a field of endeavor who instinctively had more knowledge than others who had been in the same business for thirty years. Seniority isn't relevant; ability and knowledge are.

No diploma, license or other piece of paper can take the place of knowledge of the facts. Don't try to impress me with your diplomas or your number of years on the job; instead, overwhelm me with your power to reason!

If you're in the dangerous habit of checking out a man's credentials for proof of his expertise, particularly if his only "credential" is a piece of paper issued by some bureaucratic institution, break it—now. Then get *in* the habit of checking a man's premise when he speaks. If his premise is rational, then and only then is it worthwhile to proceed and take into consideration—not accept as the last word—what the man has to say.

INTELLECTUAL-WORD POWER

Vocabulary intimidation is the ultimate weapon of the credentials-wielding expert. If his reputation and diplomas don't intimidate you, he'll cut you down to size with a dazzling array of stupefying words. But in reality it's a hoax, for if a person is talking over your head, it may well be that his points are not strong enough to stand on their own when stated in simple, straightforward language. Esoteric terms are often a smoke screen for an irrational or weak argument.

Many people allow themselves to be intimidated by the 24-carat vocabulary of the intellectual. In all too many situations, intellectual power gives a man the posture he needs to snow the other fellow. Don't allow yourself to be taken in by impressive words. Insist on facts—simple facts that are readily understandable.

In truth, so-called intellectuals are formally overeducated (I stress *formally* because it's impossible to be overeducated in its true sense). They're so involved in academic, technical and sometimes hypothetical matters that they know very little about the subject of living; they can't see the logic for the words.

Don't be hoodwinked. Refuse to allow intellectual illiterates to intimidate you through word games that evade the real issues.

Intimidation through Custom and Tradition

Custom and tradition play havoc with people's reasoning powers. It's not hard to see why. Men have been known to be a bit overzealous, to say the least, in protecting the cherished "good old ways." In the strictest sense, most people are conservative in that they lean toward a desire to preserve things as they are, feeling safer with established customs. The fear of change causes many individuals to resort to their irrational worst in defense of the status quo.

The reality, however, is that a tradition does not become more logical with age. The rationale behind it does not improve with the passing of time. The fact is that the seniority of a custom bears no relation at all to its rational validity. Those who revere the good old ways merely because they're old prove only one thing: they're good old fools.

Is Number One a good old fool? Are you a victim of unthinking obedience to the established order? If past ideas contradict reality, logic or current circumstances, they must be abandoned without ceremony. It usually takes nothing more than keen observation and common sense to dispense with the majority of irrational precepts.

Intimidation through custom and tradition infests many areas of life. It runs the gamut from law and religion to protocol at social gatherings and the proper setting of the dinner table. For centuries it has kept brilliant women darning socks and making pots sparkle; it has killed millions of young men who were thrilled at the chance to "serve their country"; it has sometimes forced males to strangle themselves with a thing called a tie when going to the office or out to dinner.

OLDIES BUT BADDIES

If an established practice is good for you—if it's logical and harms no one else—fine, then there's no reason to be concerned about it. But those practices which have no bases in fact, whose premises rest on quicksand, or no sand at all, must go. Since looking out for Number One requires a knowledge of what you're doing and why you're doing it—a rational effort—you should rid yourself of the oldies but baddies. The oldies but goodies can stay, but keep them under careful surveillance at all times and make them stand the test of changing circumstances.

I had a fantastic idea about inventing a new game that would make millions. Unfortunately, after thinking about it for a while, I realized that everybody already had one. Yours is in your brain, adjacent to your Weight-and-Balance Happiness Scale. When you play the Electronic Thought-Particle Game and lose, irrational thoughts flow into your Weight-and-Balance Happiness Scale, causing it to malfunction.

The game is tough. It's played on an imaginary TV screen, much like the games you see in arcades. When you have a rational thought, it automatically activates the machine. Irrational custom-and-tradition particles begin flowing from left to right on your screen, while the lone rational particle starts to make its way from right to left. The object of the game is to maneuver that single rational thought-particle through the maze of irrational custom-and-tradition particles without a collision.

You'll know when there's a smashup: the symptoms are nervousness, frustration, headaches, sleepless nights and guilt feelings, among others. These discomforts are the result of rational thought's having collided with irrational conventions and practices. The collisions manifest themselves as mental conflicts between doing the right thing and doing the instinctive thing. The Pavlovian instinct in you wants to bark like a good little doggie; the human ability to reason wants you to do that which is in your rational best interest.

It takes a good deal of practice to play the game effectively, but a good player reaps the reward of self-esteem—the self-esteem which comes from knowing who you are, what you stand for and where you're going in life.

A Tip to the Wise

People often make the mistake of expending time and energy doing "the proper thing" because they believe their actions will be appreciated. It's nice when they are, but I'd sure hate to depend on someone's gratitude as a basis for my actions.

YOU-WON'T-GET-CREDIT-FOR-IT THEORY

Simply stated, don't do something for the reason that it's "the right thing to do" if there's no benefit to be derived from it. You're a big loser in the Electronic Thought-Particle Game when you irrationally yield to "time-tested" codes of conduct, only to find that people not only don't appreciate your actions, but may even dislike you for them. That's the You-Won't-Get-Credit-For-It Theory at its extreme.

You've seen this theory in action if you've ever begrudgingly tipped a waiter who's given you bad service. It's an established custom to leave tips in restaurants, so when a waiter serves you cold food, snarls at you, and makes you wait twenty minutes for a glass of water, your thought-particles begin colliding. Should you leave a tip or shouldn't you?

Finally, because you're intimidated (by the fear of being embarrassed) into leaving a tip, you boldly decide to make it a small one to show your displeasure. Zap! Custom and tradition have intimidated you into making an irrational decision that *you won't get credit for*. You didn't enjoy your meal, the waiter hates you because you gave him less than he expected (he may even disrespect you for not having had the courage not to tip him at all), and—bring on the Excedrin—you're also out the money you left him!

In the ancient language of hieroglyphics, you are what is commonly known as a S-C-H-M-U-C-K. But take heart. If you eat out much, the money you save in tips alone during the next year should pay for the cost of this book many times over.

What if you rented expensive crystal and nobody cared?

Have you ever found yourself worrying about the "proper" way to do something, yet at the same time wondering why it mattered? It doesn't happen to me too often anymore, but it certainly has in the past. The pivotal episode on this subject produced what I call the

PLASTIC GLASS THEORY

I've been known to throw a party or two in my time, and I've never heard complaints from anyone who has indulged himself in my food, liquor and entertainment. Prior to one particular party, however, I happened to be dating a young woman who was very protocol and etiquette conscious. Although she herself had never had the opportunity to give a party, she knew all the proper things to do. She admonished me severely for having used disposable plastic glasses at a previous party, chiding me with the rather tender remark, "You've got no class." I argued (which immediately displayed my stupidity) that, first of all, since most of the activity would be outdoors, it was more practical to use unbreakable glasses, and, secondly, the bartender would not have to be bothered with rinsing them. Most important, though, I reasoned that anyone who would look upon me with disfavor because I committed the unthinkable—used plastic glasses—would be an individual I would not care to have in my house again anyway.

After hassling over this critical subject for a couple of weeks (which shows you how little we had to talk about), I was finally on the verge of renting some nice crystal glasses. My party was to be on Sunday, and by late Friday afternoon I was still wavering. Fortunately, I left the final decision for Saturday morning.

That evening I went to another party, this one at the palatial estate of one of Los Angeles' wealthiest and most famous men. This particular celebrity doesn't throw

"Thanks for the tip, jerk. Are you sure you can afford it?"

parties in the normal sense of the word. His get-togethers are more like Roman feasts, with several hundred friends invited to enjoy the luxurious goodies and entertainment. But amidst this elaborate gathering, flowing with the finest wines, liquors, and indescribable delicacies—every detail reeking with good taste—what to my bloodshot eyes should appear? Plastic glasses! Had the man gone mad? Had he no class?

That was hardly the case. More likely, it was a simple matter of his having come to the conclusion that plastic glasses were more practical because they were unbreakable, the bartenders wouldn't have to waste time rinsing them, and, most important, anyone who didn't like his using plastic glasses would be welcome to eat and drink elsewhere the next time around.

Needless to say, I used plastic glasses on Sunday. But the heck with me; examine your own situation. Are you strutting rigidly through life using irrational "crystal" instead of rational "plastic" at every ring of the old custom-and-tradition bell? If so, are the people who insist that you do things the conventional way willing to pay for the crystal if it breaks? I can assure you they are not. You will be the one to pay—in the lost pleasure and increased pain which always accompany the lackadaisical mistake of being intimidated through custom and tradition.

There is no law of Nature that says you have to obey man-made rules, so long as you don't bother anyone else. Reasoning does not consist of trying to come up with arguments to support a long-established convention. Instead of using your energy to find new reasons for hanging onto old fallacies, search for truth via logic. It's an exciting and rewarding experience to break down the bars of your Custom-and-Tradition Cage and enjoy the freedom of the wide open spaces of the world of reason.

Intimidation through Conformity

Intimidation through conformity is an offshoot of

intimidation through custom and tradition. When you adhere to the established way of doing things, or when you're intimidated into going along with a new fad, a new idea that has gained wide acceptance, or the latest "in" thing, you're conforming. You're conforming whenever you do anything just for the reason that everybody else is doing it. You're being intimidated into taking action motivated by the fear of standing apart from the herd.

There's nothing necessarily wrong with the popular way of doing things. Just because something is in vogue doesn't make it good or bad, it only means that more people are doing it, wearing it or saying it. If you rationally decide upon a different course of action, however, that doesn't make you bad or stupid or crazy. It makes you unique.

The herd instinct in all of us makes conforming a natural tendency. But it may not be in your long-term best interest to do so. People may jeer you in the interim, but in the end they'll admire you for having had the courage to do what was right.

Avoid the inborn tendency to do something just because it's in style. While it may seem easier at the time, it can be very costly in the long run. Conforming, as the channel of least resistance, can carry a heavy price; the long-term cost may be a lack of self-respect.

THE THOUSANDUPLETS

I once took a drive down to Manhattan Beach to survey the social situation I had heard so much about. As I trudged across the sand toward one of the volleyball nets, vigorously sucking my thumb and performing dazzling loop-the-loops with my yo-yo, I became puzzled. It was like a weird dream, as though I had landed on a faraway planet.

There, in Manhattan Beach, I saw them: the Thousanduplets. It seemed there were a thousand identical twins standing around with cans of Schlitz in their right hands. Each of the Thousanduplets was tall, with a flat, muscular stomach, a dark tan and, of course, blond hair down to his shoulders. Cocked at just the right angle at the front of their blond mops, as you've already guessed, were sunglasses—the kind no one ever wears over his eyes.

No, this wasn't a commercial. These guys weren't grabbing for all the gusto they could get. They were concentrating on assuming "cool" poses and making sure their sunglasses didn't fall off. And the girls sitting around them were neither pretty nor smiling. I was not only perplexed, but depressed. Even if I were able to balance a pair of sunglasses at the top of my forehead, there was no way I could fit in. My hair wasn't blond, my stomach wasn't flat, I didn't like beer, and I knew I couldn't get a tan on a tortoise shell.

As I made my way back across the beach to my car, I looked back over my shoulder one last time, did two final loop-the-loops with my yo-yo, and thought to myself, "Amazing . . . absolutely amazing."

What an anonymous life, that of the Thousanduplet. Many unanswered questions still haunt me. Like what kind of woman gave birth to a thousand boys? How do they know they're in the right apartment at night? And if their sunglasses should fall off and break, are they exiled to Redondo Beach? Oh, the price of conformity.

MY MOM, THE PASSENGER

The airlines should give my mother special rates for being a model passenger, the way insurance companies give lower premiums to people who have good driving records.

Talk about conformity, my mother goes cross-country sitting at attention. She doesn't look to the right or the left; her eyes are focused straight ahead to make sure the pilot keeps his eyes on the road. She never violates Federal regulations by doing sinister things like having a

"Amazing...absolutely amazing."

briefcase out when the plane is ready to take off or not having her seat in an upright position fifteen minutes before landing.

When the stewardess, Miss Pleasant, finally gets around to bringing her a cup of coffee (at the usual time, five minutes after the passenger has finished the meal), Mom not only thanks her, but invariably turns to Dad with an afterthought like, "What a sweet young lady she is." Mom swears that she no longer asks permission to use the restroom, but Dad claims she still scours the entire bathroom before leaving because of the sign on the mirror suggesting you be considerate of the next passenger.

A sweetheart of a lady, my mother, but a conformist to the end. As for staying in line, she wouldn't know how to get out of it. I think the least the airlines or banks or supermarkets should do is give her a plaque. Many have tried, but few have come close to her record for conformity.

THE SELF-CONTAINED CONFORMITY FACTORY

Have you ever wondered why banks make so much money? It's because a bank is the ultimate self-contained conformity factory. Until I realized this, I'd always wondered what banks did. I knew they didn't lend money, so their true function was a great puzzle to me. A bank is like a giant nuclear reactor which, instead of converting atoms into nuclear molecules, converts people into robots. The next time you go into a bank (perhaps to give them the use of your money, interest free, in a checking account), look around. There are the Thousanduplets again, stripped of their bathing suits and forced to earn a living. No more flat stomachs, suntans or beer, but they still dress alike, act alike and talk alike. They start out behind a teller's cage, stacking and counting money in a precise banking manner, and, if they're lucky, eventually end up behind a cheap-but-new, sharp-edged wooden desk with gleaming metal legs. From there they spend five days a week perfecting their true function—the art of saying "no."

And it works—for the banks. But what about the robots who had once been human beings?

Intimidation through Slogan

By *slogan,* I refer to any phrase, saying or adage—new or old—intended to effect a knee-jerk response from the listener.

Whether the intended purpose of the slogan is good or bad by your moral standards, the fact remains that all slogans are irrational to the extent one tries to use them as a basis of argument. Most, in fact, are intended to keep you in line.

WAR IS PEACE
FREEDOM IS SLAVERY
IGNORANCE IS STRENGTH

Thus reads Big Brother's slogan in George Orwell's frightening novel, *1984.* It is intended to be the ultimate in irrational slogans. Orwell demonstrates that people can be made to believe anything if they hear it often enough. Through slogans backed by traditional government force, all citizens in *1984* are whipped into line, conforming to the point where they're virtually mindless—ready to accept any slogan as fact.

Governments, of course, are the masters of intimidation through slogan, simply because they have the money, the manpower and, if needed, the guns to back them up. My candidate for the most intimidating government slogan ever tossed at the American public was John F. Kennedy's emotion-grabber: "And so, my fellow Americans, ask not what your country can do for you; ask what you can do for your country." The face was handsome, the personality pleasing, the smile captivating, but the words terrified me.

Let's analyze this brilliantly conceived slogan carefully and logically. First of all, what is a country? It's a geographical area composed of—in the case of the United States—over 200 million *individuals.* I've never asked 200 million people to do anything for me, except not to interfere with my right to live a peaceful life. Ask what you can do for your *country?* Does this mean asking each of the more than 200 million individuals what you can do for him?

No, individuals are not what Kennedy or any other politician has ever had in mind when using the word *country.* A country is an abstract entity, but in politicalese, it translates into "those in power." Restated in translated form, then, it becomes: "Ask not what those in power can do for you; ask what you can do for those in power." You wouldn't respond quite so eagerly if it were phrased in its true form, would you? On the contrary, you might laugh in disbelief.

In this way, government fraud continues each year, slowly but surely convincing the masses that hell is paradise via a never-ending stream of clouded or meaningless phrases and slogans: the good (?) of "society," your duty (?) to your "country," the "general" welfare (?). Of course, they have a few "Edsels" they've given up on and put into storage. Remember the WIN buttons (Whip Inflation Now)? We were supposed to believe that badges and words would somehow negate the government's practice of pumping counterfeit bills into our money supply (the only true cause of inflation).

"Better dead than red": Immediately we grab our pitchforks and lynching ropes and begin hunting for "communists" under our beds and behind our garbage cans.

"All men are created equal": Equal how? I won't insult your intelligence by explaining the obvious absurdity of this statement.

"There's strength in numbers": Maybe so, but I've found that in most cases I have much better control over my destiny if I don't consult others before acting.

"A penny saved is a penny earned": Who made this one up, the U.S. Savings and Loan League? A penny saved is a penny's less enjoyment or a penny that isn't invested profitably. The fact is that you don't earn anything when you save; when money is put in a bank or savings and loan, you *lose*. Your rate of interest is almost always less than the real inflation rate (not the rate published by the government, though it's usually lower than that one, too).

"Don't be fuelish": Immediately you lower your living standards by easing up on fuel consumption, right? But do you really have firsthand knowledge of the worldwide fuel situation or are you just going by what you read in the papers? Did it ever occur to you that fuel companies and/or governments might have ulterior motives for inundating you with slogans to get you to sacrifice?

"Give until it hurts": Hurts who? How much hurt? Why?

Never allow yourself to be intimidated by a slogan. Whether its intended meaning is good or bad by your standards is not the issue; a slogan is not, of and by itself, a valid reason for taking, or not taking, action. A rational man bases his behavior on facts. More often than not, the real purpose of a slogan is to keep you in line—to prevent you from looking out for Number One.

Intimidation through Guilt

Notice how the various types of intimidation tie together? Someone wants you to conform to his way of thinking, so he uses a slogan on you. Through the use of slogans and other weapons, he hopes to stir up feelings of guilt, thus motivating you to do what *he* thinks is right.

Guilt is a state of mind you needn't endure. Through rational analysis, *you* must decide what is right and wrong for you. Once you have, there's no reason to feel guilty for acting in a manner considered improper by someone else's standards.

If you do engage in behavior that you later decide is wrong by your standards, guilt still is not the solution. If they are in order, make the necessary apologies in a straightforward manner—one time. You're a human being, and you must accept the fact that you're not perfect. Like all of us, you make mistakes. No matter how great your error, simple logic tells you that a guilty state of mind will do nothing whatsoever to help the situation. The most practical solution is to remember the lesson learned, then forget about your mistake and concentrate on not repeating it the next time around.

THE HARASSMENT GAME

People probably wouldn't have the opportunity to trap you in their guilt snares if they weren't meddling in your life in the first place. Many individuals have an uncanny knack for taking the liberty to invite themselves into your private world. As Eric Hoffer explains, "A man is likely to mind his own business when it is worth minding. When it is not, he takes his mind off his own meaningless affairs by minding other people's business."[8] The Absolute Moralist, whom we've already unmasked, is an interminable meddler. Heaven help you if you're guilt prone. Absolute Moralists will swarm around you like vultures around a carcass in the desert.

The scary reality about the Absolute Moralist is that, because he's convinced that his view of morality is right for everyone, he can justify any method necessary to convert others to his way of thinking. Consequently, he shackles himself with no restraints when it comes to meddling in the lives of others. He's a master at intimidating people into conforming by inducing guilt feelings.

You see him all around you. He's the self-appointed guardian of the law—the guy who shakes his fist and honks his horn at you for a full block after you've accidentally gone through a yellow light. It's his moral duty to make sure you understand that you've violated a law.

The "energy crisis" has been a welcome addition to his meddling bag. Don't think you can get away with wasting fuel; he's always watching, always protecting the "public" from violators.

One time he caught me burning spotlights outside my house all night. Instead of confronting me personally, he left a newspaper article in my mailbox. The clipping urged citizens to sacrifice their use of electrical power because of the supposed energy crisis. If this particular Absolute Moralist was convinced that there was an energy shortage and wanted to contribute to saving power, no one was stopping him from cutting back on his own use of electricity to any extent he desired. Speaking for myself, I would not have objected had he unplugged his refrigerator and stove. His horizons, however, were too broad for that. He would not be fully performing his duty unless he were able to force his conclusions (which may or may not have been correct) on others.

Morality is a very personal matter; others can't decide your moral code for you. *You* make the decisions regarding your own moral standards, using an honest and rational approach, then never again allow anyone else's opinion on the subject to evoke feelings of guilt. Because that's just what it will be—*his* opinion.

THE EGO TRIP OF THE SELF-RIGHTEOUS

The self-righteous individual has a big ego problem. The irony is that when a person dwells on his righteousness, you're on pretty safe ground if you assume there's a guilty conscience lurking behind his saintly veneer. What you see and what you get can be quite different, as Thoreau guessed: "There are nine hundred and ninety-nine patrons of virtue to one virtuous man."[4] Be wary of the person who states his virtuous case in such a manner as to make you feel guilty for being "beneath" his standards.

MISCELLANEOUS GUILT GARBAGE

There's no end to the number of guilt games some people can play. The burdens which others would like you to bear are both incredible and endless.

Given the opening, there are individuals who will gladly criticize and blame you for everything from losing their jobs to passing up opportunities for better jobs. Don't be so ready to accept criticism and blame and, whether justified or not, don't waste time feeling guilty. If you're guilty, say so, apologize, then forget it. If you're not guilty, skip the apology and just forget it.

You must overcome the fear of being condemned for refusing to do what others want you to do. Don't accept a responsibility just because someone thinks you should. An important rule to remember in clearing the People Hurdle is:

Learn to say no politely and pleasantly, but immediately and firmly.

Most important, don't feel guilty about looking out for Number One. On the contrary, make certain your actions are as consistent as possible with your objective of looking out for Number One. To the extent you allow other people to sap your energy by engendering guilt, you'll be hurting your chances for getting your share of life's goodies.

Oh, one other thing. Make sure you don't try to do guilt numbers on other people, either. It cuts both ways; no one has any duty to you.

Intimidation through Slander

*If you can keep your head when all about you
Are losing theirs and blaming it on you . . .*

If you don't understand your accuser's neuroses, slander can be a very intimidating device. Because human beings do possess, to varying degrees, such unpleasant traits as jealousy, hate, sadism and cruelty, a tool like slander is used widely for the venting of emotions.

If you can bear to hear the truth you've spoken
Twisted by knaves to make a trap for fools . . .

When someone tries to twist your words, change your meanings or restate your intentions, you instinctively want to lash out and defend yourself. There's a natural inclination to want to prove to the world that what's been said about you is false. Everything else becomes secondary to righting the terrible wrong that has been committed against you. When your emotions reach that stage, the slanderer has won.

Why would someone have a desire to hurt you? There could be any number of reasons. He may envy you because of your achievements; he may be frustrated over his own low station in life; or he may be unfortunate enough to possess the traits of hatred, sadism or cruelty to an excessive degree. Whatever his reason, the effects on you will be the same if you're vulnerable to bad-mouthing. The moment you begin analyzing your tormentor's intentions, you've already taken a step in the wrong direction.

Or being hated don't give way to hating . . .

Hatred can be frightening at times. It can be especially shocking to an individual who minds his own business and concerns himself with his own happiness. Pascal insisted that all men by nature hate each other. While I don't agree, I can understand whence his conclusions were derived. As you make your way through and around the irrational people in life's path, the hatred they exude can be astounding. There is so much bitterness due to feelings of inadequacy, guilt, and failure, not to mention "self-sacrifice," that the neurotic individual sometimes feels he can vent his frustration only by hating.

Once, during a talk show I did in Miami, a woman called in to give me a piece of her mind. She ranted bitterly for nearly five minutes—in the most hateful tones—about how happy she was that she had spent her life helping others and had never thought of her own well-being. She chastised me severely for being a selfish person and insisted that I couldn't possibly be happy.

When her vitriolic tirade finally ended, I told her nicely that I couldn't take issue with anything she had said because it was so obvious she was a very happy woman. The interview host then cut the line and the "conversation" was over. But it's hard to forget the satanic hatred in that woman's voice. The only thing she did was confirm my fear that there are people running around out there who harbor irrational hatreds which are further fueled by the success of others.

Or, being lied about, don't deal in lies . . .

The hardest type of slander to swallow is the outright lie. It's like being shocked with a cattle prod. When it strikes, it throws you off balance, often leaving you undecided as to your best course of action.

What's hardest about an out-and-out lie is the horrible reality that there will always be some people who will believe it and others who will at least partially believe it (where there's smoke, there's fire). Therein lies its effectiveness as a weapon. But the potency of the lie is considerably diminished if you refuse to take the bait. The effects of a lie are temporary, even with irrational people, unless you cooperate by keeping it in the spotlight. And to rational men—the only ones with whom you should concern yourself in the first place—the lie is no more effective than any other statement unsupported by fact.

Face the reality that you are going to be slandered

from time to time. If you feel the necessity to defend yourself against a lie, the best approach is first to allow yourself to cool off. During the cooling-off period, analyze all the factors involved. After you've thought it through rationally, state your defense clearly, simply, and firmly—but only to those whose opinions you value. Avoid nasty adjectives and broad sweeping statements which tend to have the reverse effect and only succeed in discrediting you. Skip the extraneous and avoid repetition. The destruction of the lie in the eyes of those you care about will depend very much on how you handle yourself in the matter.

It's not a case of turning the other cheek, but, rather, of doing what's in your best interest. To feel compelled to expose the lie to every person you know is to dignify it. If it must be dignified, a defense that is too vehement only ensnares you in the trap of the Protesting Lady.

NEVER VOLUNTEER.

Since human beings seem to do quite well at slander on their own, never make the mistake of giving them added fuel. I know people who volunteer negative information about themselves as though they have a death wish. The bad apples out there have already made a believer of me, so I've slowly but surely learned the wisdom of the

SELF-INDICTMENT THEORY

Simply stated, don't undress yourself in public and don't wear your problems on your shirtsleeve. Never provide the would-be slanderer with something for nothing. Let him go ahead and tell his lies, let him work hard to dig up negatives about you, but don't make it easy for him. If you're occasionally afflicted with blabberitis, see a doctor, or use masking tape, or do whatever is necessary to put a stop to it. But never volunteer information about yourself which could be used against you by the neurotic slanderer.

If you're presently succeeding in most of your planned objectives, don't allow mudslinging or false accusations to throw you off course. And if you're down and out, you're in a position where you can least afford to let slander affect you. The most certain way of failing to move upward is to keep your ears constantly attuned to the verbal garbage that eventually finds its way to the bottom of the pile. Such garbage always filters downward because those who manage to stay at the top are adept at quickly discarding it.

The cosmic Economic Law of the Future—the long-term—guarantees that you will always be paid in kind for everything you produce. In the end, you'll get exactly what you deserve—no more and no less. Having so often seen people repaid commensurately for their actions, I've learned to become a very patient person. I call this phenomenon the

PINSPOTTER THEORY

Life is like a giant pinspotter in a goliath's bowling alley, with billions of humans relegated to the status of bowling pins. In the final analysis, the Pinspotter shakes us down into our proper slots and we end up exactly where we belong. If you're presently in a slot that displeases you, I suggest you begin doing whatever is necessary to work your way into a more favorable position before the Pinspotter clamps you firmly into place.

Work hard to ignore the dirt that people carelessly kick up. They'll find their proper slots in the Pinspotter, and you yours. In the meantime, keep concentrating on looking out for Number One.

Intimidation through Grouping and Tagging

People have a habit of creating fictitious entities out of large numbers of individuals. "Government," "the people," and "society" are typical examples. These are abstract terms that in themselves have no characteristics. Each individual within a group, however, does possess traits, and it's important to understand that no two individuals are exactly alike. If this were not the case, life would be rather dull.

Don't make the mistake of grouping or tagging people and don't be intimidated by those who do. When a person tells you he "likes people," his statement has no real meaning. He likes some people better than others, and some individuals he doesn't like at all. Show me the professed saint who "likes everyone," and I'll be happy to introduce him to a few human beings who will put his saintliness to a severe test.

Groups don't have qualities; people do. You're being unfair to a person, as well as to yourself, when you stamp him with a group label or tag. You're cheating yourself of what he, as a unique human being, has to offer.

THE ULTIMATE IRRATIONALITY OF GROUPING

What's convenient about tagging people is that it makes it easier to indulge irrational hatreds. When you combine bigotry with slander, you have the most irrational and dangerous of all weapons. Those who suffer from a lack of self-esteem need scapegoats. If they can vent their anger on others, they needn't search for causes within themselves.

There has always been prejudice. The word *barbarian* has been traced all the way back to Sanskrit, where it translates as "stammerer." In other words, if a person didn't speak your language and act like you, he was a stammerer—an ignoramus.

Since there wasn't much contact in the early centuries between different races, most bigotry was based on religion. You weren't a man; you were a Jew, a Christian or a heathen. Then again, you may have been a woman, which automatically saddled you with a number of traits you most likely didn't possess. Aristotle, scholar that he was, insisted that women (a term covering millions of unique individuals) had inconclusive reasoning powers and that their nature was, for the most part, inferior. In his judgment, "A man would be thought a coward who had no more courage than a courageous woman."[5] (Were he alive today, he'd have lost a lot of money on the Billie Jean King–Bobby Riggs match.)

THE PROGRESS OF CIVILIZATION

As centuries passed and the world grew smaller, the opportunities for bumping into human beings with different physical characteristics increased. And although millions of people still cling to other irrational methods of grouping and tagging, the phenomenon of different skin coloring made scapegoating a much simpler game to play. A person having feelings of inferiority and bitterness found it considerably easier to hate en masse.

As early as 1758, Carl von Linné, the famous Swedish botanist, made the characteristics of all black people "scientific fact." In working out a system of classifying every known living thing—which actually became a cornerstone for modern biology—Linné "scientifically" described the black African as "crafty, indolent, negligent and governed by caprice."[6] With science on its side, racism gained an air of respectability.

Later, in the land of the free and the home of the brave, all sorts of irrational occurrences continued to reaffirm Linné's scientific judgment. In 1857 Chief Justice Taney of the Supreme Court reasoned, in handing down the famed Dred Scott decision, that a black person "has no rights which a white man need respect."[7]

Then, finally, there was Abe. It's amazing what our history books never told us. In one of his well-publicized debates with Stephen Douglas, Lincoln stated:

107

I am not nor ever have been in favor of bringing about in any way the social and political equality of the white and black races. . . . there must be the position of superior and inferior, and I as much as any other man am in favor of having the superior position assigned to the white race.[8]

The Gangleader (President) tells it like it is.

But all the goodies weren't reserved for blacks. All you had to be was different and you qualified as a faceless and brainless member of a group. Before the days when presidents came to understand that it was safer to be Type Number Twos at all times, Teddy Roosevelt lovingly exclaimed:

I don't go as far as to think that the only good Indians are dead Indians, but I believe nine out of every ten are, and I shouldn't inquire too closely into the case of the tenth. The most vicious cowboy has more moral principle than the average Indian.[9]

Thank God Manifest Destiny existed or one might have thought Teddy prejudiced.

If Linné only knew . . .

One of the truly humorous aspects of all this irrational grouping and tagging is that there is some scientific speculation that we all started out black. Many anthropologists believe that Homo sapiens evolved somewhere in Africa, with racial differences developing only after various groups began migrating away from the tropics. If that's true, then Linné, by nature, also was crafty, indolent, negligent and governed by caprice. And so are you and I. Except for politicians, doesn't it seem a little absurd to stick any group of human beings with such tags?

WHY TAG YOURSELF?

The brainwashing of custom and tradition has taught
108

us to "be proud of our heritage." But why? You not only had nothing to do with the actions of your ancestors, you didn't even know them. What your ancestors accomplished is no feather in your cap; you should be proud of what *you* are. If your great-grandfather was a child molester or a horse thief, I can assure you that would not affect my opinion of you as a human being.

In a private conversation in *Guess Who's Coming to Dinner,* Sidney Poitier (as John) tries to make his father understand the irrationality of tagging himself. As Poitier puts it, "you think of yourself as a colored man, and I think of myself as a man."

Think of yourself as a man—not a black man, a Jewish man, a Republican man or an American man. Are you willing to be stuck with the characteristics of every other individual in any of these groups—or any other group?

Don't be intimidated by bigoted people. Don't take an irrational stand against any person—because of his race, religion or any other irrelevant factor—out of the fear that you may not be accepted by your peers. If your peers don't accept those who refuse to play the grouping-and-tagging game, the solution is not to appease them, but to find new peers.

Intimidation through Violence

The ultimate manifestation of intimidation through slander or tagging is intimidation through violence—motivating a person to act out of the fear of physical harm. As with all forms of intimidation, such fear may be either well-founded or baseless. To look out for Number One, you must learn to distinguish between the two.

You may not believe a law is moral, but it might be wise to obey it out of the rational fear of what might happen to you if you didn't. Laws themselves don't keep people in line (except through intimidating slogans such as "your duty," "law-abiding citizen," etc.); it's the threat of violence—the guns behind those laws—that do the job. Therefore, it's perfectly rational to obey an immoral law if you feel your chances of getting caught are great enough, and the punishment duly severe, to warrant it.

There are varying degrees of violence, of course, so you have to become astute at determining the real extent of the threat. When I was six years old, I was followed to school one day by a dog who had his sniffer tuned to my lunch bag. Since my parents had convinced me that all dogs had rabies, I increased my pace rapidly, only to have this intimidating four-legged beast break into a trot behind me. There's no doubt about it: he was the intimidator and I was the intimidatee. I dropped my brown bag, which made it a glorious day for the dog, and ran the remaining two blocks to school. Today I would simply speak to the dog in a harsh tone and he'd skip off in another direction, looking for more accessible goodies. But at the time, I was intimidated by an unreasonable fear.

THE TOUGH GUY

From time to time, you may have occasion to run into a weird humanoid known as the Tough Guy. He's a fellow who suffers either from delusions of physical grandeur or the misguided notion that demonstrations of "toughness" engender respect and admiration. It's a dangerous neurosis, and one you can't afford to indulge. Use your intellect. Realize that when the Tough Guy tries to goad you into a fight, one of three things can happen: either you get hurt (which is definitely bad), he gets hurt (which, hopefully, would not give you pleasure), or you both get hurt (which means everybody loses). Hardly what you'd call attractive alternatives. On top of all this, in the eyes of sensible people you both will be making fools of yourselves.

It seems to me that if being tough were important, dinosaurs would not only be ruling the earth today, they would all be wealthy. Physical prowess, obviously, is not something you can afford to waste time on since it's totally irrelevant to your pursuit of happiness. Don't threaten others with it, avoid those you believe are neurotic enough actually to use it on you, and don't be intimidated by those you know are *not* in a position to use it. Being intimidated into a physical confrontation could destroy a lifetime of near-perfection at looking out for Number One. It's not rational and it's not worth it.

CLEANING HOUSE

I think we've examined enough of the negative traits human beings possess, to one degree or another, to appreciate why clearing the People Hurdle is essential to looking out for Number One. Although you may be a bit shaken by some of the characteristics we've put under the microscope, the fact remains that we've only dissected a small sampling. You and I couldn't complete the list if we had a lifetime in which to do it. Nor is it necessary for our purposes. If those we've discussed have struck a chord of understanding, you're in a position to lay down workable guidelines on how to handle almost any snow job a guy might try on you.

You may not know it, but you have a weapon at your disposal that can wipe out, in one shot, his entire arsenal: ignore him.

ANTI-NEUROTIC THEORY

Ignore all neurotic remarks and actions of normal people and *all* remarks and actions of neurotic people. In cases where a neurotic person persists, notwithstanding your lack of attention, take swift and positive action to eliminate him from your life altogether.

You have no obligation to deal with irrational people. You needn't accept nagging or coercion for the sake of keeping the peace. You have a right to live your life as you please, so long as you're not bothering anyone else. To the extent you allow others to bother you, however, your life will be filled with frustration and aggravation.

Talking, arguing and/or begging don't work with irrational people. Attempting to persuade them through logical argument will only wear you out. Dealing with an irrational person is a can't-win situation. If he's adept at mind games, you often will find yourself boxed into being "damned if you do and damned if you don't." Always go out of your way to avoid can't-win situations. When someone surrounds you on all sides with irrational points, don't stand for it. Exit through the top, if necessary, but get out. When every side you turn to leads to trouble, you're in a can't-win situation.

Ironically, the surest way to create foes is to allow neurotic people to remain in your life. When you argue with an irrational person, you're inviting an enemy. When you ignore him, he may pout for a while, but chances are good that he'll eventually go away and leave you alone. He'd rather devote his attentions to someone who is more willing to waste time arguing.

Total Ignore

Ignoring isn't a matter of just refusing to acknowledge the individual who's trying to harass you. It means totally ignoring—disregarding his words and actions, as well as him.

Have you ever had a person pull something off that is so unbelievable you have an urge to pick up the telephone and describe the incredible details to everyone you know? Have you ever been so frustrated by the neurotic actions of another individual that you feel like running up and down the street explaining it to everyone you see?

If what the person did was so unbelievable, that's

reason enough not to try explaining it to everyone. You'll only succeed in further aggravating yourself. A little analysis will tell you that if it's so unbelievable, it really might be difficult for others to understand. The rational way to handle such a situation is to ignore it. When your instinct is to rant and rave and work yourself into a frenzy, it's hard to keep your mouth shut and blank the matter out of your mind. If you can do it, however, I'll assure you of this: you'll love yourself in the morning.

But what if they won't let you ignore them?

If a troublemaker refuses to be ignored, should you do nothing about it? Is a compromise the right approach? Or is it best to talk it out until you agree on who's right?

You certainly know that doing nothing is not the answer, because looking out for Number One involves effort; to remain stagnant makes you a sitting duck, waiting to be controlled by others. Let's look at the other two alternatives.

THE COMPROMISE

If you wish to make certain that a person will continue to act irrationally, all you have to do to encourage him is give in to his neurosis. And when you compromise, even if it's 1%, you're giving in. To cite a previous example, if you "compromise" by answering a question based on a false premise, you're giving in—you're taking the bait. You've given the other person hope by acknowledging his premise.

The problem with encouraging irrationality is that it only prolongs the inevitable moment down the road when you *are* going to have to draw the line. And like all problems whose permanent solutions are postponed, when that moment arrives it will be even harder to put your foot down, because the passage of time will have given the neurotic the illusion that there is strength to his argument.

THE DEBATE

The second alternative—talking about it—would be fine if you were dealing with a person capable of reasoning. There's nothing wrong with a discussion, so long as it remains a discussion. But when a discussion reaches an impasse or the other person refuses to employ logic, you begin to enter the dangerous area of The Debate. And The Debate is an exercise in futility. When The Debate enters, that's your cue to exit.

In using the word *discussion*, I refer to a calm, rational, verbal coexamination of the facts. By *debate*, I mean an irrational exchange of words in which at least one party either clings to a false premise, tries to use slogans, broad sweeping statements or slanderous words as some sort of "proof," or talks in a loud or harsh tone as though he believes it will somehow drown out the facts. Intimidators love to debate, because through debating all things are possible. It gives hope to the wounded neurotic. It's a miraculous channel through which the illusion can be created that logic and reason do not exist.

The professional debater can dangle an irresistible carrot under your nose. He might say something so illogical that you'll have trouble avoiding the temptation to prove him wrong. But wait; it's only a trick on his part. Since he isn't going to use logic or acknowledge reality, he'll escape your reasoning trap simply by jumping from one ill-founded premise to another.

It takes self-discipline to ignore those who would intimidate you into debating. But the first time you turn your back on an absurd situation and walk away, you'll experience a wonderful feeling of self-respect—a self-respect that can only come from knowing that you refused to dignify an irrational statement.

114

If ignoring, refusing to compromise and refusing to debate aren't enough to send an irrational pest scurrying off in search of greener pastures, then you're left with only one alternative: completely eliminate him from your life.

What this means is that you must dare to precipitate a crisis. You have to have the courage to confront him, in a civil but straightforward manner, and make your desire crystal clear. If he calls you names, don't return the favor. If he becomes so insulted that he wants to resort to fisticuffs, refuse to partake—even if he's half your size. State your case in a calm, civilized, candid and firm manner, being as pleasant as circumstances will allow. Then excuse yourself and make your exit. As long as you allow neurotics to remain in your life, you're in danger of becoming a victim of the

I'M CRAZY/YOU'RE SANE THEORY

It's my contention that if you attempt to carry on a relationship with an irrational person long enough, it's only a matter of time until you begin wondering if day really isn't night and $2 + 2$ really doesn't equal 5. Given enough time, an irrational individual can make you think that you're the one who's neurotic. Don't let that happen. Can you imagine a more terrible nightmare than rattling the bars of your cage and having peanuts tossed to you by a neurotic person you carelessly allowed to remain in your life?

When you eliminate an aggravating individual from your private world, you're effecting a long-term solution; it's a cure. Humoring (compromising) is only a short-term patching job—the equivalent of taking an aspirin. Handled effectively, the neurotic will not only leave you alone, but probably will forget about you. It's when you allow him to remain, and try to get him to "see the light" through facts and logic, that he *can't* forget about you.

Remember: *People will bother you until you no longer let them!*

YOU CAN'T LIVE WITH THEM AND YOU CAN'T LIVE WITHOUT THEM.

It might be simpler if you could just eliminate all human beings from your life, but that's obviously not a desirable alternative. Man was not made to live as a hermit. The fact is that many people have wonderful qualities to offer and can add a great deal to your happiness. But that doesn't mean you have to allow *everyone* access to the one precious life you possess. Those people who display negative traits on a basis consistent enough to cause you complications should be eliminated from your life; those who display rational, positive qualities on a regular basis should be looked upon as welcome additions.

Above all, don't try to change a neurotic person. Like you, he has a right to live as he desires, without any interference from others. That, however, does not mean that his cause is hopeless. It's possible he may get well on his own, and then—who knows?—at some future time he could become a pleasant addition to your life. Until then, however, spare yourself the aggravation— and save him the use of an additional crutch that will only prolong his problem—by steering clear. After all, the best way to handle an irrational person is to avoid him in the first place, which is a luxury you can afford when you're completely engrossed in looking out for Number One.

Decide how you want to live your life, then proceed accordingly as though there were no irrational people to bother you. If you allow neurotic individuals to have an effect on your decisions, you'll be out of control—a

"Hee, hee—2 + 2 equals 5...yuk, yuk, yuk—2 + 2 equals 5."

position totally untenable with your main objective. You've cleared the People Hurdle when others have a minimum effect on your efforts to look out for Number One.

5

The Crusade Hurdle

By *crusade,* I refer to any group—regardless of its purported objective—whose platform calls for aggressive action to advance an idea or eliminate an existing idea or circumstance. You may be involved in a group right now which you've never considered a crusade, but which may, in fact, be a hindrance to a better life.

Because I have never been able to think of a rational reason for becoming involved in group action, I've studied and analyzed many organizations and crusades in an effort to see if perhaps I had overlooked a significant advantage. I've talked with many hardcore crusaders and even attended meetings to observe the methods of group leaders.

I have definitely received something of value from all this study and observation. What I've specifically gained is a reaffirmation of the existence of a peculiar human trait.

LIFE-COMPLICATION THEORY

People seem to have a tendency to seek ways to complicate their lives. Given a choice between an easy way to do something and a more complicated way, a person will often opt to proceed along the more cumbersome route. Why this is so, I can't say. Perhaps it's simply that it's irrational, and most people do not lead rational lives. In any case, it's a source of unending astonishment to note the lengths to which individuals will go either to find new entanglements or to invent ingenious methods to avoid eliminating old complications from their lives.

A crusade, movement, cause, or group action of any kind is a hurdle which can complicate your life. Yet it doesn't have to if you understand that the concept of group action is unrealistic and if you have the self-discipline to ward off the intimidating pressures to become involved. To do this, we will, as always, have to place crusades under the microscope and carefully examine their components.

THE GROUPING-AND-TAGGING GAME WITH AN OFFICIAL STAMP

All crusades tag people, which is reason enough to avoid them. But, unlike general grouping and tagging, crusades are organized and puffed up in stature by the use of official names. A common cause—whether rational or irrational—unites those involved. The problem with this is that it's erroneously assumed by a great many people that because you support a cause, its leader speaks on your behalf. You therefore involuntarily lose a certain degree of individuality the moment you take part in group action.

Organizations themselves would be innocuous to nonmembers, were it not for the fact that all too often they become heated campaigns. A poker club, for example, is a perfectly harmless group so long as its members stick to playing poker with one another. But if they go berserk and decide it's their duty to make everyone in the world play poker, embarking on a campaign to solicit new members through pressure tactics, they suddenly become a poker crusade.

That's how a seemingly inoffensive group transforms itself into a crusade: when its members begin interfering in the lives of others by pressuring them to join or by attempting to force them to do, or stop doing, something. That's the point at which the game threatens to become a dangerous hurdle to you.

I'D LOVE TO SACRIFICE MY TIME, BUT WHERE DO I START?

Crusades are an area where there are so many irrational choices, one doesn't know where to begin. There are as many causes as there are people in the world. How do you know which one (or ones) to sign up for?

There are crusades for and against just about everything: abortion, big business, the CIA, communism, drugs, energy conservation, gun ownership, homosexuality, pollution control, pornography, the reopening of assassination investigations, segregation, smoking, and voting, to mention just a handful. There are movements which espouse seemingly reasonable objectives and some which promote the zaniest projects one can imagine. There are even campaigns to persecute specific individuals.

The Diaper Corps (comprised of people under twenty-one years of age—or those over thirty who still play with rattles) is responsible for many of the really far-out movements. Were they not given heavy publicity in an effort to sell newspapers and magazines, most of their would-be causes would die natural deaths even more quickly. Kids can be militant about Zen Buddhism one day, socialism the next, then—who knows?—the merits of backgammon or the mating of humans with giraffes.

Whether a crusade is created by the Diaper Corps or

by irrational adults, its merits should be judged only on the basis of logic, reality and fact. And even if its stated purpose does pass the test of reason, the movement is still immoral in nature (by my standards) if it interferes with the lives of nonmembers.

THE GAME'S THE SAME.

What's fascinating about crusades is that, no matter what they purport to believe in, their structures are remarkably similar.

One thing that seems to be present in virtually every movement is the distortion or deletion of relevant facts. The guy or guys promoting a crusade quite naturally paint only one side of the picture, so don't be particularly impressed with the seeming worthiness of any cause or the soundness of any group's sales pitch. Always remember that you're only getting their side of the story.

Emphasis on the future has been a common but important tool of crusaders for centuries. As long as the reward is somewhere down the road, dedication to the cause can be justified. The less a movement offers in the present, and the more it offers in the future, the better its chances of success. Most crusades would go out of business quickly if they promised immediate results. Therefore, if you intend to start a movement of your own (heaven forbid), may I suggest you give your enlistees a specific time at which you expect results to be achieved. The year 2128 would be a nice target date. Just to be on the safe side, however, tell them that if worst comes to worst, results could be delayed till as late as 2133. On that basis, and all other things being equal, you've got an excellent chance of keeping your members in line.

Another factor critical to the success of crusades is the degree to which they are corporately organized. The reason for this is obvious: the better the planning and structure of a group, the more it gives the illusion of being a living entity; that in turn makes it easier to strip the followers of their own identities. Individual characteristics always pose a danger to the "group objective" (which is really nothing more than the objective of the leader), so the better organized the movement, the more overwhelmed the individual members. A well-organized crusade also makes it easier to violate the rights of others, because such interference is not being perpetrated by a human being, but by a "group"—and usually in the name of "the public good."

Our old friend, intimidation through slogan, is another common denominator of most movements. As a general rule, the less a slogan actually says, the greater the popularity of its basic "philosophy" and the more people to whom it has the potential of appealing. Slogans are used because, to the unthinking individual, they appear on the surface to be interchangeable with fact. "Don't be fuelish" makes it a *fact* that there is an energy shortage. "Love it or leave it" makes it a *fact* that the country belongs to those making the statement and that you're under an obligation either to agree with their moral standards and political views or else move to another country. In truth, the more clever the slogan, the less the crusader need concern himself with facts.

The spectacle goes hand in hand with the slogan in stirring the emotions for group campaigns. From the smallest protest marches to the biggest parade or ceremony, spectacles are an essential element of the crusade—often the very glue that holds together an irrational structure which would otherwise crumble. When reality threatens to shatter a group member's faith, a spectacular ritual, however meaningless, can be the drug needed to keep him on a false high. The bigger the spectacle, the more effective its use.

I was well acquainted with an individual who devoted an enormous amount of time to a group whose stated purpose was "world peace." Observing from the sidelines and listening to his talk about the group's activities, I realized that what he was really doing was spending his time contributing free labor to the preparation of a gigantic yearly spectacular. Anticipation of the annual "celebration" was, by itself, enough to work the group's members into a frenzy. To the best of my knowledge, these folks haven't stopped any wars, but they have put on some great shows. The spectacle is a vehicle for pretending; it's an escape from reality.

Most mass movements also find it necessary to create a "devil." If a movement is trying to "preserve the coastline," the devil is the individual who doesn't want his beach property confiscated for "the public good." If it's a crusade to end smoking in public places, the devil is the smoker. Throughout history, the crusades may have changed, but their basic characteristics have remained the same. "Heretics" were the Inquisition's devil; Jews were Hitler's; today, if no other devil is convenient, the group leader is forced just to settle for the guy who doesn't belong to the movement. The good guys are those involved; the bad guys are those who haven't "seen the light."

One of the most disturbing similarities among crusades is that they always seem to become ends in themselves. The official objective of the group somehow gets lost in the rearranging of the facts, the emphasis on the future, the endless bureaucracy of its corporate structure, its obsession with slogans, the spectacles it creates, and its never-ending beratement of its foes. The crusade never quite seems to get around to its stated purpose. That's why the "all-or-nothing" approach is usually used; you must accept the tenets of the group in toto. Mass-movement leaders throughout history have been well aware that outside interests detract from the energies needed to keep a movement going full steam.

A group may dwell endlessly on how it's going to help you become a happier individual, but its claims are meaningless since the very premise of group action negates that possibility. Whenever you contribute time and subordinate your interests to those of an organization, you lose not only your individuality, but irreplaceable hours which could have been spent confronting the specific obstacles in your own life. This is one of the main reasons for an emphasis on the future. The farther off the promised results, the more obvious it becomes that perpetuation of the group itself is the real objective of the leader.

Finally, their most dangerous characteristic: most crusades try to achieve their aims through the use of force. Possible exceptions might be self-improvement groups (such as transcendental meditation) and charitable organizations (although these, too, often become a little overzealous).

I'm not speaking here just of religious crusades or ideological movements like communism, but any cause which involves forcible interference in the lives of others. The use of force includes the attempt to get new laws passed (laws really being dictums which are forced upon a given number of individuals and backed by guns and manpower). Whenever a group is formed for the purpose of inducing government leaders to create a law, what it amounts to—when stripped of fancy words and pretenses—is that certain people are asking the government to impose their personal desires on others.

WHO STARTS ALL THESE COMMOTIONS?

The promoter of a crusade is a special type of character. Although he may not seem very different from others you may already have flushed from your life, the leader of a movement—in addition to being a guy with problems—usually possesses an insatiable ego. He irrationally believes that his self-esteem can be upgraded by being "helpful" to others. But rest assured that if his personal problems could be solved, his burning convictions for the cause would fizzle out rather quickly.

The leaders of so-called mass movements, in particular, have a tremendous need to have their egos assuaged. A study of mass-movement leaders of the past reveals a distinct pattern: rejection in other fields of endeavor, usually resulting in frustration and self-contempt, which in turn manifest themselves in hatred of others, an attraction to martyrdom, extreme vanity and, above all, absolute moralitis.

Because of the jumbled mental state of the reform chief, one has to look carefully beyond the slogans and rituals for his real motives. All too often the head of a movement feeds his own glory and power at the expense of his followers. "Needs" can be created to keep an organization going, if necessary. As Napoleon perceived, "Vanity made the revolution; liberty was only a pretext." If a reform leader is clever enough, he can mask the truth in such a way as to appear the champion of the people—to make it seem that his actions are aimed at improving "the welfare of society."

Above all, most big cheeses in crusades find it easy to be harsh with others and are usually intolerant and cruel toward those who do not see things their way. In truth, the would-be reformer is a vain individual who is presumptuous enough to believe that everyone else should agree with his views.

The crusade leader, when scrutinized by an unemotional, rational individual, is really just an Absolute Moralist with a banner.

PROFILE OF A HABITUAL JOINER

Without followers, the head honcho of a crusade wouldn't get too many thrills. To snare his disciples he has to compete with all the other crusade chiefs for the available talent, because a joiner is a joiner is a joiner. Although the joiner himself doesn't recognize it, the cause is really secondary to him.

To keep the recruiting ferocity down, crusade leaders should agree to hold an annual draft, much like the owners of professional sports teams, and divvy up each year's crop. As teenyboppers come of age, the Diaper Corps is perpetually restocked with new talent.

The joiner is a person who needs to be needed to an excessive degree; he's a very frustrated individual. He usually feels abnormal self-contempt, which makes it easy for him to join his leader in expressing contempt of others; previous failure makes him wish to remove the burden of personal responsibility from his shoulders (by getting lost in the group, the pressure for personal success is lifted); and, of course, he's a natural for the role of Absolute Moralist.

It's a kind of paradox that while the frustrated are prime candidates for group action because of their desire to see things changed, they also are ideal followers because of their willingness to focus their efforts on the future. The follower allows this seeming contradiction to exist because the promised glory of the "future" is precisely what takes his mind off his current misery. The group is like a narcotic for him; it temporarily eases the pain.

The professional crusader also finds it safer to vent his feelings of hostility under the banner of a group. When lost in the faceless depths of a movement, it's not he, but the group, who is interfering with others. Cruelty and hatred become justifiable; because of his own "sacrifices," he can be tougher on his fellow man. One attains great freedom as part of a crusade—the freedom to be harsh and intolerant, the freedom to pressure others, and the freedom to interfere in people's lives without guilt.

Above all, the pathological joiner must have the ability to ignore any rational argument that threatens to undermine "the cause." Such Magooism or Ostrichism gives him the strength needed to confront the obstacles and contradictions which constantly arise. By refusing to see or hear them, such problems simply fail to exist. Thus the most successful crusades have been those most effective at keeping their followers separated from reality.

Because all crusades have so much in common, the

chronic joiner finds it easy to jump from one to another. After all, if the basic characteristics of most groups are indistinguishable and the traits of their members similar, a switch isn't very difficult to justify. I'm sure you're acquainted with at least one person who is group addicted. How many times has he jumped on a new bandwagon, proclaiming that "this is the answer"?

But it's *your* bandwagon that you should be concerned about. To stay firmly aboard it, don't be tempted to jump on each new crusade that comes rolling along. An easy way to check yourself against vulnerability to the Crusade Hurdle is to examine the number of times you've hopped on new causes, as well as how fast and how radically you've made those hops. Habitual joiners jump often, quickly and radically because they are victims of the

CONFUSED-THINKING THEORY

This theory maintains that when a person's philosophy takes a sudden and dramatic shift in an opposite direction, his reasoning is suspect, because:

1) If his previous beliefs were foreign to his present ideas, his thinking must have been confused where his former ideology was concerned; therefore, how can he trust his reasoning power with regard to his new ideology?

2) On the other hand, if his original thinking was sound, his old philosophy should have been correct; therefore, his reasons for joining the new crusade must be incorrect.

The Confused-Thinking Theory applies, to one degree or another, to most shifts in philosophy, but it is most clearly demonstrated in cases where people swing from one extreme to another.

While the outward characteristics of all movements are similar (slogans, ceremonies, emphasis on the future, etc.), the stated objectives can be completely opposite in nature. If you're experiencing radical swings in your basic beliefs, the Crusade Hurdle is still in your path. If you're on the right track and thinking rationally, you'll be growing and evolving constantly, but the growth and evolvement will be in the same general direction. Beware of your emotions when you stumble onto a new group or movement which stirs up your enthusiasm—particularly if it makes you feel that it is *the* answer.

Wanted: Habitual Joiners and Other Confused Thinkers

As the champions of various causes jockey to make the best possible impression on the pool of available group followers, they employ many motivational techniques for appealing to a wide variety of desires and emotional traits. It's essential that they understand the would-be follower's range of motives for joining. Among these are companionship, boredom, a desire to conform, ego satisfaction, escape from personal responsibility for success and happiness, or even a genuine belief in the worthiness of the crusade (or at least the belief that he believes).

But more important than any of these motives is a lack of knowledge and/or rational thought. If everyone who joined a movement, cause or crusade throughout history had carefully analyzed the realities, it's very possible that every group action ever undertaken might well have become a one-man crusade. There are many reasons why group action is irrational from the individual's standpoint, including the following:

1) The group may never accomplish its intended purpose, in which case the individual might someday feel very bitter over the time and energy wasted—time and energy which could have been supplying fuel needed to better his own life. In other words, the joiner has to be completely ignorant of the realities of Murphy's Law. This explains why the hardcore followers of many crusades are young people. Once you've been out there in the Jungle, you become a believer—in Murphy's Law—and

you're not as quick to commit those rapidly vanishing seconds of your life to some cause which others happen to believe is worthy.

2) In many respects, there is weakness in numbers, not strength. Another old adage shot to hell. Suppose I want to help "the poor." Rather than waste time getting involved in the muddled bureaucracy of some organization, where I would have to confer with others over such questions as who qualifies as poor and what should be done for them, would it not be easier, faster, and more effective to make all necessary decisions unilaterally and take immediate action myself? All I'd need to do is decide which person or people I deem to be poor, determine which type of help would be most effective, then take prompt action—without having to stop and consult anyone else.

Since it's easy to help others if you really wish to, I'm highly skeptical of the motives of do-gooders who form organizations to carry out charitable and "public-good" projects. The first thing I look for in such people is a big ego; the second is an ulterior motive behind the supposed real intent of the group.

3) Even if the project is "successful," you have no way of knowing that you'll live long enough to enjoy the results. To work on a crusade all your life and then not be around to see its fruition would be real salt in the old energy-waster wound. From this perspective, the crusade's emphasis on the future can be seen for the negative it really is.

4) But there's an even worse fate possible. What if the group's stated purpose is accomplished in your lifetime, but the results turn out to be quite different than what you had in mind all those years you were busting your tail to help bring them about? Although most groups never come close to achieving their stated objectives, I would say that, of those which do, disillusionment is the rule rather than the exception. The reason for this is obvious. Because each person in an organization is unique,

the Definition Game guarantees that your picture of the group's purpose and the picture the leader sees—not to mention the view of every other member—will be quite different. You can be sure that the masses in the early years of the Communist Revolution in Russia were not envisioning the same results as the leaders who promised that communism would free them. They had no idea that, as in Orwell's *1984*, freedom would actually turn out to be slavery.

5) Another reality—the one hardest for the Diaper Corps to grasp—is that your own personal growth in knowledge and reasoning power may shed a whole new light on a cause you once thought worthwhile. Thus the Confused-Thinking Theory enters the picture, and the eager, impressionable youth is soon off in an entirely different direction. Remember, new facts will continue to pop up which may take the glitter off a once seemingly worthy cause.

6) And, finally, the cruelest reality of all (because it injures our delicate egos): *your participation is unlikely to make any difference.* In fact, it probably will retard the cause, since every additional body only adds to the divergence of opinion, the bureaucratic muddling and all the other time-wasting features of group action.

In my opinion, therefore, joining a group to accomplish any purpose is irrational. In reality, it actually slows your attempt to get things done. And if you're joining for other reasons, you're probably asking for disappointment. If you join just to conform, you're not acting rationally; if you join for companionship, you're being dishonest with the other members of the group (unless that's the group's only purpose); if you join for ego satisfaction, you're on dangerous ground (the more you feed your ego, the more it wants, thus leading you farther off the intended course); and if you're joining out of frustration, you're simply avoiding a real solution, not to mention inviting the further frustration which comes from wondering why everyone else can't see things your way.

ANSWERING INTIMIDATING SLOGANS

When people chide you for being "unpatriotic," "immoral" or "selfish" because you're not involved in civic activities, are using too much energy, or aren't "giving your fair share," don't be intimidated.

First of all, if you go along with a crusade because you've been pressured into believing it's "the right thing to do" or because it's "your duty," when will you have time to sleep, let alone pursue happiness? If you're going to be irrationally intimidated by such slogans, then shouldn't you do everything that *everybody* tells you is "right"? After all, how can you be sure who's right and who isn't when you're out of control and are basing your actions on the choice of others? Unless you make short shrift of such verbal nonsense, you're certainly not going to have much time for a life of your own.

Second, always remember that the sloganeer's statement is based on an assumption. If the assumption is incorrect, need I say more? And if it's to be taken on faith, then, again, in whose assumptions should you have faith? For example, if someone accuses you of wasting energy, there's an underlying assumption in his accusation that there is, in fact, an energy shortage. Maybe there is; but, then again, maybe there isn't. Do you have firsthand knowledge of such an energy shortage? Or firsthand knowledge of the extent of the purported shortage?

Needless to say, firsthand knowledge is not derived from newspaper articles or government reports. I certainly don't possess such knowledge, you most likely do not, and I seriously doubt that any one person has all the necessary facts at his disposal to make such flat statements. (Speaking of flat, remember that experts once assured us that such was the shape of the earth.)

My approach is the exact opposite, a method commonly referred to as: scientific. I assume that nothing I hear is true and try to maintain that state of mental integrity until I've seen proof with my own eyes. I don't have proof that there's an energy shortage; I don't have proof that there's a God; I don't have proof that every many who's behind bars is guilty of a crime; I don't have proof that the ozone layer of our atmosphere is endangered by aerosol sprays or supersonic jets.

But I do marvel that so many people can be absolutely certain of so many things about which they possess a complete lack of firsthand knowledge—and in many cases very little knowledge at all. In truth, so-called experts have been wrong so often that one really has to be very foolish to make rash, time-wasting decisions based only on what others say. When people pressure you to join a cause, forget the slogans and frills and, instead, check the underlying assumptions. This will help prevent you from being swept along unthinkingly by the group's nonfactual (often guilt-inducing) rhetoric.

TIME'S A-WASTIN'.

I classify crusades, movements, causes—group action of any kind—as members of the Energy Wasters Family. I consider all members of the Energy Wasters Family threats, because they have the potential to rob me of a precious, limited commodity: time. Crusades take time, divert energy and complicate what could be simple actions on your part. Worse, they often entail expending energy on the impossible—the attempt to change the nature of the way things are to the way certain people think they ought to be. And that's a hurdle that, hopefully, we've already crossed.

Also, remember there's a geometric-growth problem in time wasting. It's not just the hours or days spent on the cause itself, but the time lost in "winding down" your constructive projects and the time wasted getting yourself back into the swing of things. Time is an unyielding dimension; it's the fixed item in your life's equation. Unfortunately, you can't buy it at the store. You don't get what you ask for, you take what you get. Worst of all, you don't even know how much you get until it's too late—until you've run out of it. Do you know the amount of time you have left to enjoy the pleasures the world has to offer a rational individual? Then why take chances with your unknown, limited supply? There are no return privileges. You can't trade in used seconds, minutes or hours for new ones. When you've blown them, they're blown.

MAN WAS NOT MADE TO LIVE ALONE, BUT . . .

Even if you believed in the purpose of a group and did have firsthand knowledge of the facts, it still would be less complicated and more efficient to act on your own rather than in concert with others. In fact, the group is a danger because, as already pointed out, collective action really helps you avoid personal responsibility.

If you feel strongly about a cause, by acting alone you can start doing something about it immediately. But if your approach is to put together a sophisticated organization, you may never get around to your stated purpose. The nature of such organizing—endless politics, debates on differences of opinion, funding and other bureaucratic obstacles—can easily use up all your available time and energy. As often happens, the organizational effort then becomes an end in itself.

If you have promoter's blood in your veins, why not go out and invent a new kind of golf club? Or a delicious food that isn't fattening? Or perhaps the steam engine? Channel your efforts into something that will give you a feeling of personal achievement and you'll be helping more people on your own than any group ever could. Your product or service will be useful or valuable to others, you'll be creating jobs for men and women, and, best of all, you won't be harassing people with noble causes; you'll be too busy looking out for Number One.

I emphasize the part about not harassing others. If you feel the urge to take action for or against something, don't waste time trying to convert others to your way of thinking, if for no other reason than because you have no right to. If you happen to believe in a particular philosophy, you should be too busy living it to spend time trying to convert others. If you have a desire to have your ideas heard, then write a book about them or offer to lecture in return for proper remuneration.

This book, for example, is not an attempt to convert you to my way of thinking; it's a free-market transaction in which I'm exchanging ideas for money. It's no concern of mine how religiously you practice my philosophy. I'm more than satisfied if you enjoy reading what I have to say and/or feel that you gained enough knowledge to be a repeat customer. It's none of my business what you do with the material once you buy it.

Don't feel you have a moral obligation to make people "see the light." Concentrate on looking out for Number One. I'm sure you have enough problems of your own without worrying about "helping others." As is, life burdens us with too many nonproductive projects, such as brushing our teeth, getting haircuts, and other normal-course-of-living drags. Don't look for more.

A GLANCE AT WHAT YOU'LL BE AVOIDING AS YOU CLEAR THE CRUSADE HURDLE

I group crusades into categories ranging from world antidisaster movements to "non-causes." Let's start with the non-causes first.

Self-Improvement Crusades

Self-improvement crusades include groups which purport to teach the individual about things such as meditation, financial success and personality improvement. I refer to these as non-causes because their criteria really don't correspond to those of the run-of-the-mill crusade. Self-improvement groups become crusades only when their members become so enthusiastic that they run about spreading the word with the fanaticism usually reserved for mass movements.

Meditation-type groups are becoming increasingly popular—a sign that people are grasping for help. But meditation is thousands of years old—perhaps as old as mankind—and most meditation-group leaders will admit that it's more effective when practiced alone. Why, then, do meditation groups exist? As always, as a crutch—a way of avoiding personal action. Since many or most meditation groups are profit oriented, it's certainly no big mystery that perpetuation of the organization is the primary objective.

Common sense tells you that you don't need someone else's special words to meditate. When you use words, slogans or readings presented to you by others, they lose their effectiveness. I knew a person who belonged to a group that required its members to sit on their knees and "chant"—for several hours a day—facing a contraption that was supposed to represent their "true selves." Aside from all the other questions of irrationality involved, the most shocking thing to me was that this man's chanting consisted of rapidly reading sentences from a small book written in a language he did not understand! The writings had been phonetically converted to English (not translated) so they could be given proper pronunciation, but he had absolutely no idea what they meant. In defiance of that reality, however, he insisted that his chanting brought him miraculous results.

Within less than a year, this young man gave up his chanting—miraculous results and all—and turned to transcendental meditation. By the time this book is published—well, who knows?

True meditation, performed on your own, definitely can be effective. Scientific results have indicated that proper meditation does have beneficial effects on your health. I frequently engage in something I refer to as Factual Meditation—that is, a free-flowing of the facts.

As with any effective meditation, it is practiced in a quiet, relaxed atmosphere, with the initial objective being to blank the mind. Eventually, thoughts begin to wander in and out of your consciousness, and the idea is to grasp the rational ones and filter out those which aren't rational. Factual Meditation, to me, is a way of ferreting out—in a quiet, relaxed atmosphere—those things which reason tells me won't work and retaining those which will.

I suggest you try Factual Meditation sometime. It's been responsible for some of my most rewarding decisions. It can (and should) be practiced alone; it's not hard to learn; it's soothing; it's rational; it's rewarding; and, best of all, it doesn't cost anything.

Personality-improvement groups, not as in vogue as they once were, can be dispensed with quickly. They, too, provide false props. A bogus atmosphere is created which gives one a false sense of security (assuming he doesn't suffer a heart attack when called upon to speak before the group). Besides, everyone on the outside can spot all those who belong to such groups. Whenever a guy tries to maim you with the ferocity of his handshake and smiles with all thirty-two teeth showing, you know you've just bumped into a member.

Financial-success groups can be put aside just as promptly. Back in my post-graduate Diaper-Corps days, I tried a couple myself. As you'd expect, they accomplished the opposite of their stated purpose. These kinds of groups create hypnotic illusions. Because they're comprised of men who are terrified of facing the hard realities of the business-world jungle, nonconfident followers often develop an enthusiastic loyalty toward the group and its fatherlike leader. Enlistment of new members spells perpetuation of the group, which in turn translates into its fanatical followers having further excuses to avoid facing the challenge of success; instead, they can just continue talking about it. (It also means continued profits, of course, for the group founder.) If you desire financial success, go after it. Don't avoid getting ahead in life by hiding out in an enthusiastic group of "success-oriented" people.

Remember in whose home charity begins.

Charity is fine, so long as you can afford the time and/or money to engage in it. I must again emphasize, however, that the best way to help the poor is by not becoming one of them. If your own situation is cool, by all means work on charity if it brings you happiness. It's no one else's business how you derive selfish pleasure, and if you've come to the conclusion that working on charitable causes is rational, don't be dissuaded.

Whatever your reason for becoming involved—whether to feel magnanimous or to achieve the good feeling you expect to experience from alleviating the suffering of others—do make certain that it's *your* reason. And be doubly sure that you're being honest with yourself about your motives. Any rational motive is okay, just so you understand exactly what you're doing and why you're doing it.

Then all you need to be careful about is making sure you don't chastise others for not believing in or becoming involved in the same cause. How they spend their time and what they believe is none of your business. When you start being so presumptuous as to concern yourself with involving others, you're crusading.

The next time you're tempted to work for a charity, or even to contribute to one, ask yourself these questions: Do I know firsthand exactly how the money I'm raising or contributing is being spent? Can I be certain that it's being used to help those the group purports to be aiding? And, if so, do I really know what percentage of the money, after bureaucratic waste, actually goes to the designated recipients?

I'll tell you one way you can be absolutely sure of the answers to these questions. Let's go back to the example of your desire to help the "poor." Pick out a family *you* judge to be poor; *you* decide how much of *your* money you'd like them to receive; then *you* take it over to them personally. Having accomplished your purpose, you then can go on to other matters without harassing anyone else about your beliefs; leave well enough alone. Simple, efficient, immediate results—all but impossible through group action.

If you acted in precisely the above manner, I'd be inclined to believe you if you told me you had a desire to help the poor. But if you tried to solicit me to join a charitable organization, I'd look you over very carefully and ask a whole bunch of questions you probably either couldn't answer or would prefer not to.

Forcible-Interference Groups

Forcible-interference groups are dangerous. They consist of people who band together to bring about change through the threat of force (i.e., they pressure those in power to pass new "laws" to help them attain their objectives, knowing that the power-holders' guns and manpower will make certain that these objectives-turned-laws are enforced). It's much safer for a group of people to use the threat of government force to take something from others, or to force them to do something they don't want to do, than it is to use their own physical power against those in whose lives they wish to interfere. By employing the awesome threat of government gunpower, the group hopes to get its way without blood actually having to be spilled.

People basically cling together under two different types of forcible-interference banners. One is the grouping-and-tagging label, such as blacks, women, the elderly, gays, laborers or any other convenient handle which disregards individuality. The second type is the "worthy cause," in which everyone is invited to join.

You should steadfastly refuse to relinquish your individuality to any group of people just because they happen to have a particular characteristic in common with you, whether that characteristic is sex, skin color, religious affiliation or occupation. Understand where such people are coming from when they appeal to you as being "one of them."

"Women's liberation," for example, is for women who really don't want to be liberated at all. They're merely going from one type of subordination to another—from supposed exploitation by men to exploitation by corporately organized women's organizations.

Resist the intimidation of forcible-interference label groups. Insist on remaining an individual and showing the world what you, as a unique entity, have to offer. Have too much self-respect to accept the blanket characteristics of a group. If you're a woman, you're different than any other woman in the world; if you're an "elderly person," there's no other elderly person just like you; if your skin color is "black," there's not another black person in existence with the same traits you possess. If you're a human being, you're one of a kind. Don't let the Crusade Hurdle trip you up and take that away from you.

COMMITTING CRIMES THROUGH "WORTHY-CAUSE" GROUPS

You must also refuse to relinquish your individuality under pressure from groups of people who might all happen to desire a similar social change. As always, the same logic applies: the action of groups is inefficient, and since their means of gaining objectives requires the use of force, they are immoral by the standards of any rational man.

Worthy causes can range from petty undertakings, such

as antismoking or antisex lobbying, to potential world-disaster crusades, such as pollution control, energy conservation and overpopulation.

With regard to petty "causes"—such as wanting to force others to stop smoking because it bothers you—as always, immediate action can be taken on your own. Of course, you first have to begin with a rational premise. In the case of smoking, you simply don't have the right to force others to stop. I've heard people argue that they don't care if others smoke, just so they don't do it in "public places." So right off we have a Definition-Game problem.

A restaurant is commonly used by antismokers as an example of a public place. But a restaurant is not a public place. It's a privately owned enterprise, and as such the owner should have the sole right to decide whether or not he wishes to allow people to smoke in his establishment. If he chooses to allow it, and I'm bothered by smoke, I can take immediate steps to do something about it—on my own—by not frequenting his business. On the other hand, if the owner restricts smoking, and you're a heavy smoker, you can take equally swift action by going elsewhere.

The above example is something known as—hmm, let me think—ah, yes, the free enterprise system. If Absolute Moralists would just leave it alone, it would work out fine, automatically adjusting itself to meet consumer demands. When an owner sets a rule regarding his own retail establishment and that rule is too widely rejected, the workings of the free enterprise system will force him out of business. He doesn't need an outside law to go broke; he can do that on his own.

But the really cumbersome crusades are those which involve so-called world-disaster problems. Ironically, if every man were engrossed in looking out for Number One, we wouldn't have "world problems." Because, of course, the "world" doesn't have problems; the men who live in it do. And people who look out for Number One don't create problems for others. The reality, however, is that millions of individuals who have the potential to be happy, if left alone, must waste great amounts of time and energy fending off those who are constantly trying to interfere in their lives through crusades.

That potential world disasters exist is a reality. But you don't need crusaders out there to remind you of it. Watching the six o'clock news makes it obvious that Chicken Little was a bit off the mark. While she insisted that the sky was falling, in truth the whole world was crumbling beneath her feet. You and I have been reading about and observing these potential disasters all our lives.

You should acknowledge the potential of problems which are of worldwide significance, because a man of reason never tries to shield himself from the facts. But do realize that they are potentials—not knowns. More important, remember that the same rules apply: group action is still a problem avoider, not a problem solver.

The existence of potential problems of world-disaster proportions can, however, have a positive influence on your thinking, in two respects. First of all, they help keep your day-to-day problems in proper perspective, and, secondly, they're the best reason of all to look out for Number One. If I were convinced the world were coming to an end tomorrow, I'd sure want to enjoy myself as much as possible today.

Energy Crisis: Real, Imagined or Created?

I've been very interested in studying the purported energy crisis, because it can so easily affect one's rational efforts to act in his own best interest. Realistically, one can't ignore it, because he's inundated with energy "data" and slogans every day.

But it seems to me that there are two very important unknowns which energy-conservation crusaders fail to acknowledge:

1) Most of the news we're fed is one-sided, coming

from sources (industry and government) that almost always have ulterior motives. How can any of us know to what extent the "news" is distorted on this subject and to what degree it's being handed down out of context? I'm an incurable, stubborn realist; as always, I want proof. Therefore, the key question is: Am I willing to accept added discomfort based on a crisis for which I have no proof? To me, that's a fair, reasonable and rational question.

2) Even if an energy crisis does exist, it does so only in the light of current knowledge. But new ideas—not to mention new resource discoveries—constantly render old "proofs" obsolete. I'd hate to spend the next thirty years shivering in my own house because of a desire to be a "responsible citizen"—keeping my heat turned down to a temperature the gas company tells me is "fair"—only to hear the good news, on my deathbed, that new gas resources have been discovered which are expected to last the earth's population for another 500 years. As I slowly faded into my final slumber, I think I'd be pretty ticked off—at myself!

About ten years ago, for example, a new deposit of iron ore was discovered in Brazil which was estimated to be large enough to supply the world for at least the next three centuries. In fact, many of those involved in the project have expressed the opinion that the full potential of the extent of this deposit has barely been scratched. What's next? Oil in Omaha? Coal in Yonkers? Who can say?

It's back to the same old question of which experts to believe. They're all over the place, predicting energy shortages of every kind, but you can also find plenty of them who don't agree. The doomsayers might be absolutely correct, but so might their critics—like a team of economists, headed by Nobel Prizewinner Wassily Leontif, who concluded that world resources were plentiful enough to last far into the twenty-first century. At that point it becomes academic; frankly, I don't have any great hopes of being around then, anyway.

As an individual trying to act in your rational best interest, it's imperative to understand that there are no conclusive proofs, that new ideas and discoveries are constantly arising and that the experts continue to contradict one another. Let them have their academic and intellectual battles over whether oil will last until the end of this century or for another 500 years. Just make sure you don't blindly and unnecessarily complicate your own life by becoming involved in an energy-conservation crusade on the basis of "expert" predictions.

The real energy crisis is the irresponsible waste of your body's limited supply of it.

Overpopulation: The Potential Body-Odor Crisis

I don't like crowds, so overpopulation does concern me. But not enough to join an organization of Absolute Moralists who would like the government to force their neighbors to stop making babies. All the same anticrusade logic still applies, so I won't bother to repeat it. But since you'll be hearing speeches about it the rest of your life, and since it could even affect your decision to have or not to have children, I think it's worthwhile to scan the overall picture.

Barring outside interference, the population of a species increases in geometric proportions. Giving the majority of expert opinion the benefit of the doubt (and plenty of latitude), this has resulted in man's proliferating to a population of ten million in a span of somewhere between one million and three million years, then increasing his numbers to *four billion* in just the next ten thousand years. What this boils down to is that the world's population is supposedly increasing at the rate of two little duffers per second. If there's any truth to these scientific guesstimates, it's enough to make one start to itch.

The future prospects of population growth tend to give one a slight case of claustrophobia. As best I can decipher, the going bet is that we'll hit seven billion people by the year 2000 and about fourteen billion by the middle of the next century (if we make it that far). Where does it all end? Good news! There is one limiting factor: space. The mathematicians tell us that if we continue at our present rate (2% per annum population increase), in about 650 years the people then living will be faced with the rather awkward dilemma of having one individual for each square foot of land on earth! Now that's what I call too close for comfort. I can envision body deodorants being in greater demand than gold or silver. Can you imagine the hassle of getting in and out of a pay toilet? Certainly some unique problems would be created.

I don't think you need an expert to tell you that other factors would obviously intervene long before things got that out of hand. And it wouldn't be the intervention of crusade groups; they've been at it for a long time, but the fact remains that in countries where the problem is most serious, population growth continues almost unchecked.

You can spend the rest of your life speculating on the outcome, but that's just what it would be: speculation. And circumstances will change faster than you can come up with new speculations. In addition, the disagreement of experts will only continue to make it certain that nothing is certain. An interesting illustration of this is the prospect of colonizing other planets. I heard one scientist discuss it as though he were talking about relocating company employees to a different part of the country. He was "certain" that this would be the ultimate answer.

But another physicist hypothesized that the spaceship necessary to make just one such journey would have to be pretty damn big. He had calculated that by the time it reached the nearest planet with environmental conditions resembling Earth's (meaning, I assume, smog, Big Mac wrappers lying in the gutters, etc.)—traveling at the speed of light—the population of the spaceship (assuming it had departed with three people aboard) would equal that which it had left behind on our planet!

Who knows? Who are you to believe? Do you want to spend the rest of your life debating it or, worse yet, crusading? How can you crusade when you're not even certain what you should be proposing? Why not give yourself a break and go have a little fun instead. If it will make you feel better, abstain from having children, but don't be naive enough to think it's going to make a dent in the purported problem of overpopulation.

Pollution: The Price Tag for the Goodies No One Is Willing to Give Up

Is pollution another potential world disaster? Yes, but the same realities are there to challenge it—differing expert opinion, the disadvantages of group action, the immorality of forcing people to relinquish more of their freedom, and so on. Face the reality that there's little you can do about the world's pollution problems and that group action only makes them worse. After coming to such a rational conclusion, you can then get back to something you can control: looking out for Number One.

There's reasonable evidence that the earth is already ecologically out of balance, and, as population increases, more and more pollutants will be poured into the air and water and scattered over the landscape. Our planet apparently is not equipped to recycle the amount of waste we're now feeding it.

Maybe there's a pollution crisis; maybe there isn't. As usual, no one person has even a small percentage of the facts, and the facts themselves will continue to change with each new discovery. Don't waste your life conjecturing on the ultimate outcome or, even worse, joining in the banner waving and bungling of organizations that "know" they're right.

If you're really worried about pollution, the next time someone commits the unforgivable sin of swerving in

147

front of you, don't honk your horn and shake your fist; noise pollution drives me bananas. On second thought, if it helps get your rocks off, you can do the fist-shaking part, without the horn honking; then no one will be watching, anyway, and you can shake to your heart's content.

Flappin'-in-the-Breeze Crusades

It's only fitting that the finale to clearing the Crusade Hurdle include those crusades in which your participation is not only insignificant, but completely meaningless. The two I'm going to explore with you are of such a nature that if you spent the rest of your life working on them, it would have about the same effect as using all my efforts to try to move the Empire State Building to the east side of Fifth Avenue.

THE INDEFINABLE CRUSADES: WORLD-PEACE MOVEMENTS

I've never paid much attention to so-called world-peace crusades. This is probably due to the fact that, in my lifetime—notwithstanding the increased efforts of "world-peace" movements—hostility and war among nations has continued to increase. What I'd never stopped to think about, however, was the reason there had always been war and why world peace was seemingly unattainable.

The problem is the mixing of the Definition Game with a little bit (or lots) of absolute morality. One guy's definition of world peace is to be left alone on his ranch. Another man's idea of world peace is forcibly splitting up the first fellow's ranch into a thousand plots and giving them away to those he deems to be in need of them. As long as these two men hold such incompatible views, the chances for peace are about as great as the odds against governments' putting an end to taxation.

World-peace movements don't work for the same reason that laws intended to regulate emotions don't work. You can't unilaterally decide what constitutes world peace, then go around cramming it down everyone's throat. The cause the would-be crusader for world peace really is espousing is having four billion people accept *his* idea of what constitutes world peace. I don't like people deciding what's right, then trying to force me to accept it. My idea of world peace is everybody leaving everybody else alone —each man being free to live his life as he so desires and not interfering in the lives of others. My fear of peace crusaders is summed up in Eric Hoffer's statement, ". . . when men league themselves mightily together to promote tolerance and peace on earth, they are likely to be violently intolerant toward those not of a like mind." [1]

Don't be intimidated by idealistic abstract phrases like "world peace." Everyone has a different idea of what it is, and there's no way that any group is going to get four billion people to agree to do anything—except through force. And forcing people to do things they don't want to do is not peace; it's something known as war.

DON'T WORRY, OUR LEADERS HAVE EVERYTHING UNDER CONTROL.

Flappin'-in-the-breeze crusade number two—the ultimate worthwhile cause—is something that's been sloganized as "Ban the Bomb." If it came down to it, I'd rather spend my time on the Empire State Building project. Perhaps I could take it apart brick by brick and rebuild it across the street—with the help of an army, a thousand slaves and a hundred million dollars (to be used partially for bribing city officials). That would be a realistic proposition compared to my attempting to stop the use of nuclear weapons.

The Bomb is the most ominous reality of the world in which we live. It's the "X" factor in the formula of our times. No previous generation was blessed with it (assuming that man has not evolved and subsequently destroyed himself many times over the millennia). The Bomb is the ultimate weapon, not that the technology of future generations wouldn't be capable of creating more awesome nuclear weapons, but because the destruction of mankind is a limiting factor. The first time a device was invented which had the capability of wiping us out—in toto—that was the ultimate. Improved weapons are academic once you've killed everybody. The only significance of the arms race is that it creates ways to kill more people faster, but does that really matter? You can only be blown to pieces once.

When the first Dr. Strangelove figured out how to rearrange the inside of an atom, The Bomb became a reality, and it changed the whole game. From that day forward, the world could never be the same.

Ah, for the days of Walton's Mountain. Things were so simple then. You chopped a little wood, made a trip to the general store, and occasionally there might even be some excitement—like catching revenooers poking around your barn. What did John-Boy know from nuclear war? Why, up until then, all we had experienced in the way of mass murder were several thousand Christians being thrown to the lions, the annihilation of a few bothersome Indians, a handful of inquisitions, and the normal succession of hand-to-hand, sword-to-sword, and gun-to-gun slaughters—all just part of man's simple way of life.

But let's not waste time daydreaming about Walton's Mountain. It's gone forever. The advent of The Bomb gave mankind's future a new dimension. He soon found that he couldn't live with it and couldn't live without it. Once the first government gang got its hands on one, all the other governments had to have The Bomb to "protect" themselves.

Now it's the "in" thing to do. If you're a nation who doesn't have it, you're out to lunch. It's estimated that at least forty countries will have the capability to produce The Bomb within less than ten years. We long ago got over the shock of discovering that China and India have it. And even little Taiwan purchased a research reactor from Canada for a mere $35 million—an amount which many individuals and hundreds of corporations can easily afford! You're kidding yourself if you think Taiwan is going to sit around and scratch its head while big bad ~~mainland~~ China looks down on it like an overstuffed cat waiting to pounce on a mouse. One of my nuclear predictions is that the first time the Big Red Machine tries to take its show on the road against itty-bitty Taiwan, it's going to get a whole bunch of plutonium right in its greedy face.

And on and on it goes: Israel and the Arabs, India and Pakistan, and so many countries in Africa mad at each other that it's impossible to keep track of who's on whose side and what they're all mad about. In the meantime, Peking keeps passing out brilliant political advice, urging so-called Third-World nations to arm themselves with nuclear weapons against the two "super powers."

And the super powers? Did you ever start something and then wish you hadn't? The Moscow and Washington mobs would like to call the whole thing off and play some other game, but it's too late. All they can do now is keep adding to their own arsenals. While it's true that they rule us, they also know that they've started something this time that could interfere with *their* lives.

But—have no fear—everything's under control. According to an article in *Saturday Review*, a young Air Force launch officer said that he was "scared as hell" by the fact that he and three other officers could, if they chose, unofficially launch up to fifty missiles without orders from anyone. His fright stemmed from his quite logical assumption that there were nervous young Russian officers in identical positions of authority over yonder. Pleasant dreams.

Don't worry that you might miss The Bomb Party just because you happen to be at sea. The United States has now developed a nasty little creature they've fondly named Captor. Like something out of a science-fiction movie, Captor "sleeps" on the ocean floor until it hears an enemy ship approach. Jarred from its snooze, the torpedo —with its little nuclear warhead tucked away in its belly —sets out in pursuit of the bungling vessel. Escape? Forget it. No one escapes Captor. Do you think the government would waste your tax dollars on a piece of junk? No, even if it screws up and misses the first time, it's programmed to keep chasing the enemy ship until it makes contact and destroys it.

You're wondering how the little fellow knows the difference between one of "us" and one of "them," right? That's no problem, either; its computer is designed to differentiate between the engine sounds. (Now I'm getting scared.) Oh, by the way, the Navy has asked the political Godfathers on Capitol Hill for enough taxpayer loot to build 500 more Captors. (Now I'm really getting scared.)

It's not that I don't have faith in computers, but with 500 nuclear warheads lying around on the ocean floor, how can one feel safe even taking his boat out on a Sunday afternoon? What if one of the computers happens to malfunction and thinks you're an enemy ship? If you thought Jaws was a neurotic shark, can you imagine being chased around the marina by a psychotic nuclear torpedo?

Oh, John-Boy, where have you gone?

Enter the nonpolitical mob.

One of the realities of the world marketplace is that the moment a commodity becomes valuable, it's only a matter of time until nonpolitical gangsters try to cash in on it. The political felons—always making certain to label the nonpolitical criminals with unpatriotic-sounding tags—refer to this as "the black market." At $10,000 per kilogram, plutonium now sells for about five times the cost of heroin and ten times the cost of gold.

What that means is that thousands of individuals can afford to buy, on the black market, the five kilograms necessary to build at least one small A-bomb. With the vast amounts of plutonium that are now being produced worldwide, we could begin having arms races between major corporations or wealthy individuals—a kind of minor-league farm system for the major-league version being played among the political powers.

It's easier to get than a good Havana cigar.

The last of the hairy thoughts in this living nightmare is that, in addition to the black market, there seems to be plenty of evidence that it's not the most difficult thing in the world for one to get one's hands on the materials necessary for manufacturing The Bomb. Plutonium is stocked in minute .05-ounce pellets, so a worker in a nuclear plant, by grabbing a handful a day, could accumulate enough material to make The Bomb within about 160 days.

No one knows for sure just how much plutonium has been stolen up to now, but there have been a great number of official reports of nuclear plant thefts and "missing inventories" over a period of many years. In some cases, plant workers have been caught in the act. Whose hands now hold all the rest of the missing plutonium is anybody's guess.

That the plutonium is out there—somewhere—is fairly certain, so that leaves only one step: converting it into The Bomb. And in this day and age, it doesn't take much to locate your friendly little neighborhood bombmaker. Don't be surprised one day if you're looking through the classified section of the newspaper and come across a want ad that reads, "Nut with 5 kilograms plutonium looking for partner with knowledge to build The Bomb."

If you have talents along this line, the *World Book* is supposedly one of the many excellent sources of instruction for producing one. So are several U.S. Government publications which are readily available to the public.

"Er, Fred, I think we're being followed."

In fact, using primarily government literature and widely distributed nuclear-engineering textbooks, a twenty-one-year-old Princeton student designed a version of The Bomb in 1976 that purportedly was more sophisticated, though less powerful, than the one dropped on Hiroshima in 1945. Among other comforting things, the student said he'd wanted it to be "simple, inexpensive and easy to build. . . . The idea was not to use any classified information." His parting reassurance was: "It is very simple. Any undergraduate physics major could have done what I did." [3] (We can pause for a moment if you'd like to take a breather and throw down a couple of aspirins.)

The Bottom Line of the Ultimate Flappin'-in-the-Breeze Crusade

Okay, enough's enough. By now you're probably asking yourself, "Why is this guy trying to scare the hell out of me with his assurances that sooner or later I'm probably going to be blown into little pieces?" The answer is that I'm not. What I'm attempting to do is face reality—that indispensable ingredient in looking out for Number One.

Given the availability of plutonium, bomb-production hardware and technology, it's not very realistic to assume that various versions of The Bomb won't be falling somewhere at some future date. With egomaniacs in control of The Bomb in international capitals throughout the world, terrorist groups running rampant, college students able to build homemade versions, and nervous young military men sitting with their fingers on nuclear buttons, I believe I'm making quite an understatement when I say that one has to be a blind optimist to believe that it will somehow all work out.

In a way, though, it's true. It will all work out, but perhaps not as you or I would like it to. The important reality you should have perceived from this little dissertation on The Bomb is that no group—with or without your efforts or mine—will have any effect on *how* it works out (other than the possibility that the button might be pushed sooner, rather than later, due to the meddling and harassment of various "peace" organizations and "Ban the Bomb" groups).

This book is about your life, and that's the paradigm within which you must relate these realities. How can they affect your life? Can they deter you from spending your remaining days experiencing primarily joy and happiness? Obviously, sitting around and worrying about the realities of The Bomb won't help your own cause at all. And to join others in a crusade to convince four billion people that The Bomb never should be used is absurd. Thousands of men, with intellectual and verbal capacities far exceeding yours and mine, are already engaged in such a task. But they're wasting their time, because the guy who is eventually going to push the button isn't interested in what they're saying. Furthermore, they don't know who he is or what his motive will be when he finally does it.

Being aware of the realities of The Bomb and being obsessed with them produce two entirely different results. Being aware helps to keep your own life in proper perspective and makes the philosophy of enjoying all that life has to offer—in the present—a very rational proposition. Being obsessed blinds you to life's great joys, robbing you of the happiness that is obtainable during your lifetime. Forget about Walton's Mountain; it's gone forever. The reality is that you're living in the age of The Bomb. Face that reality, then put it on the back shelf—out of your way—and go about clearing the Crusade Hurdle.

Naturally there will be the usual number of self-righteous world saviors who will be bothered by this attitude, either because they're frustrated over personal failures or actually have been intimidated by the words and actions of other Absolute Moralists. But understand that when you acknowledge the realities of The Bomb, yet choose to turn your back on it and seek a life of pleasure, you are not being indifferent to the potential horrors. What you're displaying is intelligence and the capacity to be rational. You're being realistic and honest enough to acknowledge that neither your efforts nor those of any group will affect the outcome in any way. What's more, by taking this realistic and honest attitude, you're not interfering with anyone else—not even those who do choose to join "Ban the Bomb" crusades.

An accurate perception of reality, as always, is healthy. If you refused to accept The Bomb as a reality —not to mention the possibility of disastrous consequences from such things as overpopulation, pollution and energy shortages—you might plan your life according to one set of guidelines. But by taking them into consideration (not being obsessed with them), you can make the adjustments necessary to achieve your purpose of looking out for Number One.

Your values don't change; only your plans do. That which brings you pleasure without infringing on the rights of others is still good; that which brings you pain is still bad. And it's precisely because your values don't change that your game plan has to be adjusted to cope with changing circumstances. You must learn to flow with the tide in order to preserve your values and achieve your objectives.

Regardless of what happens—heck, we've still had a better run than *The Sound of Music*. Some scientists believe that man has been here for more than a million years. According to them, most other species didn't make it much past 600,000; in fact, about 498 million of the estimated 500 million forms of life that have tried their acts on our planet have been long gone.

A HAPPY ENDING

If you're thoroughly depressed by now, you shouldn't be. If you're mad at me for telling it like it is—well, what can I say? And if I didn't even faze you, you either already knew it all or you've got a pretty tough skin.

But now it's time for the dessert. There's one great reality which supersedes all the potential world-disaster and flappin'-in-the-breeze crises. That's the reality that you can still lead an exciting, fulfilling, joyous life— starting right now. Disasters which may or may not come in your lifetime—or ever—cannot forcibly rob you of this opportunity nor can those who run around crusading for or against them.

As always, looking out for Number One must be the result of your maintaining control over your own actions —not relinquishing control to the desires of a group. Don't be emotionally swept along by herd instinct, the rhetoric of Absolute Moralists, or the slogans of anyone. Do your own thing. Crusades are not compatible with looking out for Number One.

And for watching over your own nest, rather than being so presumptuous as to try to solve the problems of others, I wish to extend my personal thanks to you for eliminating yourself as a burden to the rest of mankind.

6

The Financial Hurdle

I was almost tempted to take the lazy way out and tell you just to go back, reread the first five chapters—paying particular attention to the Reality and People Hurdles—and apply the same principles to your financial affairs. Finances—both personal and business—are just another facet of the game of life, and all of life involves reality and people.

My orientation here will be strictly gut-level, with an emphasis on skipping all the flowery nonsense and irrelevant "ought to's" and getting down to the way the Financial Hurdle really is.

WHO CARES ABOUT MAKING MONEY?

Who cares about making money? Apparently, everybody. A recent world poll attempted to find a nation—anywhere in the world—whose people were poor but happy. To quote one of the pollsters, George Gallup, "We

159

didn't find such a place." [1] What they did find was that nearly half the human beings on this earth are literally struggling for survival.

But everything is relative. Although you might not be on the verge of starvation, you may be struggling for financial survival on your own level; expenses have a way of increasing right along with rising income, the result being that few people ever achieve financial peace of mind.

There are those who protest that making money shouldn't be that important—that there are other things in life far more rewarding than money. In a way, they're right, but they're missing part of the picture. I'm more fortunate than most, because I've been there before. Where? At every level: the top, the middle, and lower than any low you can imagine (if you're lucky). Having made the journey more than once, I'm in a position to report that there's much truth to the rumor you've heard so often: money really and truly doesn't buy happiness.

Having been at both ends of the financial spectrum, I must admit that one of the most surprising discoveries from it all is the fact that some of the best things in life actually *are* free. But there's a catch to it: money *is* a means to an end—a vehicle for putting you in a better position to lead a more pleasurable life.

The hard reality is that if you're under constant financial pressure, it's hard to enjoy the beautiful, free things life has to offer. If your mind is cluttered with thoughts of financial insecurity, unpaid bills and lack of achievement, it tends to blind you to the goodies that are out there. In today's tension-filled world, I think it's impractical for the average person to maintain hopes for abundant happiness without achieving some degree of financial success.

The most important thing I've found that money can buy is freedom. I'm not unrealistic enough to believe it can buy total freedom, because that, of course, is impossible so long as governments exist. But, even so, you can enjoy more freedom with money than without it. Just having peace of mind is a great liberation in itself—being free to think pleasant thoughts instead of mentally hassling over financial problems.

Only you can be the judge of how much financial success it will take to obtain the freedom you desire. Clearing the Financial Hurdle, therefore, means succeeding in a conscious, rational effort to achieve the financial success necessary to do what you want to do in life; but it also means that the effort to achieve it should not make life a living hell in the process. It means giving you the freedom to concentrate on looking out for Number One, the freedom to act out of your choice instead of chance or the choice of others. For one person this might mean making $5,000 a year; for another it could mean being a millionaire. How much it takes to "buy" the kind of freedom which will make you happy is strictly up to you.

The one thing you must guard against from the outset is setting yourself up for a big disillusionment. If you've made considerable sums of money in the past, you already know that it doesn't buy happiness; if you haven't yet made it, I hope, for your sake, that you'll take my word for it before you get there. It's like the person who makes the mistake of expecting more from people than they are able to give. People who don't have money, but dream about the day when they'll hit it big, all too often are expecting something from financial success that it can't bring them.

I made this mistake the first time up the slope. The climb was slippery and exhausting, fraught with every imaginable obstacle, but I finally got there. When I arrived, however, what I found—instead of the fantasyland I had envisioned—was the real world all over again, but on a higher financial level. I was disillusioned and tried to compensate in other ways, but that only made matters worse. At the time I didn't realize that what I was really after was happiness and that money was just an *aid* to getting it.

The last time I made the climb, I finally got it straight in my head. I realized that the pot at the end of the rainbow was not filled with magic gold—which somehow could be converted into happiness—but with freedom. I also acknowledged that time was my limiting factor, so it was no longer good enough just to work toward the day when I would have enough money to obtain the freedom I was after. As much happiness as possible had to be achieved *while* I was making the climb. That was a big turning point for me—the day when I mentally transformed the climb itself from a struggle into a joy.

If you lose sight of the reality that money only represents a means to an end—an aid to your looking out for Number One—you'll probably never really be free to enjoy life. It becomes a vicious cycle. You seek more and more success, without stopping to figure out what you're actually after. It's like a self-imprisonment in which you prevent yourself from experiencing the unlimited joys life has to offer. As a summary of one of Buddha's teachings explains:

> . . . excessive desire makes us slaves of whatever we crave. Everyone has seen this principle in operation—a craving for food, a craving for popularity, a craving for success. All make us lose our freedom to choose wisely.[2]

Yes, making money does matter. But before we embark on the project of solving the money puzzle, I hope I've succeeded in putting it in proper perspective for you. Money is great; it's great because it rids you of many burdens which can sap your limited supply of time and energy, thus freeing you to concentrate on the pleasantries of life.

A MELANCHOLY STROLL DOWN LOSER'S LANE

Let's start at the bottom and work our way up. Perhaps you've been there—or might even be there now. If you've never experienced the misery of failure, the chances are good that you haven't tried hard enough to succeed. If you've made it to the top without ever having experienced the bitterness of defeat, my hat's off to you; I've never met anyone who's done it (and stayed there).

Failure, in fact, is a good indicator (though certainly not the only one) of both the effort you've expended and your willingness to pay the price of financial success. Disraeli was right when he said "There's no education like adversity." I've acquired a certain amount of knowledge from my successes—and there's no question they've been more fun—but they haven't taught me nearly as much as my many devastating, temporary setbacks.

What it really boils down to is the simple law of averages. It's the

ONE-IN-THE-SACK-IS-WORTH-A-HUNDRED-IN-THE-FACE THEORY

Everyone old enough to be reading this book knows the old joke about the guy who stands on the street corner, asking each gal who walks by if she'd like to make it with him. He gets his face slapped a lot, but he also gets his share of "scores." The moral, of course, is that if you aren't willing to make the effort and pay the price—ask for and be prepared to take the inevitable bumps and bruises—you've boxed yourself into a corner where the odds against your succeeding are about 100 to 0. It might pay you to check your face for slap marks; if you don't see many, you probably haven't left the starting gate yet.

Is poverty obscene?

If you haven't already cleared the Financial Hurdle, I think a few remarks about my own experiences down there in the pits might inspire you. There's no way I could describe all my stumbles in less than ten volumes, and some of them are so messy that, in this age of government absolute moralitis, Washington might even classify them as pornographic.

A description of The Bottom—that point on the financial ladder where I was so low I could easily crawl back and forth under any convenient rock—should suffice for relativity purposes. No matter where you are on the financial ladder today, you should be able to gain a better perspective of your own situation by comparing it to some tales of The Tortoise at his lowest ebb. Elaboration on my own devastation and humiliation hopefully will lead you to conclude that you, too, can clear the Financial Hurdle through the exercise of a little rational thinking, a lot of self-discipline and the application of a number of other principles spelled out for you in the pages ahead.

THE BOTTOM OF ALL BOTTOMS

After dabbling in the record and film businesses for a while, as well as a number of other masochistic enterprises intended to fatten the ego and slim the wallet, I awoke one morning to find myself in the rather awkward position of having to face the following quadrangle of financial facts: 1) an overhead of about $30,000 a month; 2) an income of zero; 3) a bank balance of $11.37; 4) debts in the area of $500,000.

Suicide suddenly seemed a rather attractive solution. I tried hanging myself, but the rope broke; an attempt was made at self-immolation, but I was sweating so much I kept putting out the fire; using a gun was out—I had one, but I couldn't afford bullets.

Since nothing seemed to work, I settled for relaxing on a chaise lounge next to my swimming pool, allowing my mind to drift into Factual Meditation as I gazed out over Jack Warner's estate. (Since I had the only second-floor swimming pool in Beverly Hills, I had the advantage of enjoying the view of Warner's massive grounds—including his private golf course—while sitting around my pool

164

area; living right next door, I was able to enjoy his acres of plush landscaping free of charge.)

Meditating didn't take me long. I came to the brilliant conclusion that I had a serious problem. I finally got around to facing the "is's" of the situation and left my "ought to's" for dead. Reality was once again in the driver's seat; as always, it had ignored my desires and incorrect perceptions and had maintained itself as an immovable force.

The worst reality of all? I was facing imminent eviction from both my home and business premises—where I had put a fortune into a suite of penthouse offices that made me look like Cecil B. DeJerk. As I departed the patio and walked through my bedroom, I couldn't help remembering part of the sales pitch given to me at the time I was considering the house. It was all very exciting then —the story that Marilyn Monroe had once lived there (which I was never able to verify); how Mickey Rooney used to dive out the bedroom window, into the pool, at the height of those old-time Hollywood parties—all the glamour and festivities of yesteryear. Exciting, but insane. At the time I concluded the deal, Nature must have been looking over my shoulder, saying, "Boy, am I ever going to stick it to you. Nobody, but nobody, violates my laws and gets away with it." Next thing you knew, her old Pinspotter had my testicles caught firmly beneath the #7 pin.

To express it in the simplest of clichés, the ball game was over. I had a total of three Mercedeses and a Fleetwood. One by one, all were repossessed. I was down to living in a mansion, with no wheels to get anywhere. Can you imagine living in Los Angeles without a car? I couldn't afford groceries either; I was getting panicky— to the point of eyeing the cat food left in the pantry. I started selling off what was left of my furniture, but the money was quickly swallowed up by alert creditors who were stalking me around the clock. The phones were

"(Gulp!) Have you guys heard the one about..."

disconnected and the gas and electric were ready to go any day.

What to do? Where to go? I even thought of climbing Warner's barbed-wire fence and camping out under some bushes at the edge of his estate, but he had a troop of guard dogs, each of which could have passed for King Kong. Then finally they came. Not Warner's dogs—the sheriffs. I'd been down and out before, but it had never gotten to this. I didn't know that when they came to hand you your walking papers, they arrived in pairs. When I opened the door, I was looking at two badges pinned to two gigantic chests. I gave them a warm hello, then threw out a couple of one-liners. No smiles—only cold stares. (Government employees never smile unless they're inflicting pain on citizens, and I don't think they realized that I was in a lot of pain.)

They handed me the papers, matter-of-factly spewed out some memorized legalese, then departed. The only thing they made perfectly clear to me was that they would be back in five days to check the premises and that if they found a tortoise around, he could expect to be booted out unceremoniously on his shell. I believed them. I always believe people who wear guns on their belts.

I managed to get ten cents on the dollar for a few more pieces of furniture and scraped together enough money to rent a truck. For the next five days I was in a stupor, walking back and forth through those mile-long hallways, going up and down the winding staircase, climbing into the back of the truck and trying to organize my worldly possessions into an 18-foot van. After a while all I wanted to do was sleep, but I was down to just 48 hours—then 36. Finally only 24 hours remained until the Wyatt Earps would be back on my doorstep searching for tortoises. Every once in a while I'd wake up in the middle of a room, quickly look at my watch and realize, to my horror, that I had inadvertently fallen asleep for an hour or two.

I never did get it all out. High noon arrived and I was forced to leave thousands of dollars in clothes and other

167

possessions behind. I still remember the last trip down from the second floor. I went through the back way to get one final look at the patio, the pool and the view of the lavish grounds Warner had so generously (and unknowingly) shared with me. As I looked out over the incredible beauty of it all for the last time—hangers of clothes draped over my back—two thoughts went through my mind. I believe that both proved to be my salvation in the long struggle that was to follow.

First, I had no hate in my heart for anyone (with the possible exception of Warner's dogs)—not for any of the Type Twos or Threes who had helped contribute to my downfall, not for any of my creditors, and not even for the government henchmen who were due to arrive at my door any moment. I did, however, have a great dislike for *myself*.

What a fool I had been. If anyone had ever proven the wisdom in Santayana's observation that "those who cannot remember the past are condemned to repeat it," it was The Tortoise. I had broken every principle I had worked so hard to develop—principles which I had proven produced results when religiously adhered to— refusing to acknowledge the reality that sooner or later Nature would return and hand me the bill. And here she was, presenting me with a tab so enormous I saw no way of ever being able to cope with it.

Second, I said to myself, "I'll be back, bigger and better than ever. I'll pay the price, whatever it has to be, but I'll be back. And next time, I won't allow myself to get in a position where anyone can take it away from me." With that, I descended the stairs for the last time, threw my clothes in the back of the truck and pulled away. As I chugged down the street, I couldn't help thinking of the contrast between the truck and the majestic homes, manicured lawns, and beautiful palm trees which surrounded me. The contrast was magnified when the sheriffs' car passed me, no more than a half-block from my home, going in the other direction. They may have been disappointed to find no one there, but, alas, everyone had abandoned the old homestead. Marilyn Monroe was dead; Mickey Rooney hadn't been in the pool for years, if at all; and The Tortoise had moved to his new home: a Ryder truck.

Leprosy in Beverly Hills

When you go broke in Omaha or Des Moines or Memphis, you make for good cocktail-party stories. Naturally, most of your old acquaintances would just as soon not be seen with you and you get the usual black-balling, but there's very little spitting. In Beverly Hills, it's different: they actually spit.

God forbid you should go broke in Beverly Hills. In the Golden Ghetto, bankruptcy is synonymous with leprosy. No one talks about you at cocktail parties. You're yesterday's news; you're dead. If you would just stay off the streets, they'd leave you alone. Beverly Hills has nothing against disease, the residents just don't like lepers crudding up the view of their swanky shops and chic boutiques.

Since the degradation and humiliation are impossible to describe, I won't attempt to. Let it just suffice to say that Loser's Lane in Beverly Hills is the loneliest, most humbling, most demeaning road in all the world.

Like so many things that are healthy for you, suffering is not something you would choose if you could avoid it. But the truth is that it's stimulating. By necessity, it forces you to use your wits. I remember a friend of mine—a well-known entertainer—philosophically laying it on me when I hit bottom. He'd been there too and he assured me that being down and out brings forth one's greatest creativity; that's how so many of the music greats had obtained that special charisma, that "soul" which their audiences could sense. It comes from having been there. It was hard to be consoled at the time, but as it turned

out, he was absolutely right. It was the best thing that ever happened to me.

When you're down there—all the way down—you either roll over and die or you fight back. One thing you know for certain is that you can't solve your problems by running from them. Every guy who's been at The Bottom knows exactly what it means: it's showdown time. Or, once again, in the words of Kipling:

> *Or watch the things you gave your life to, broken,*
> *And stoop and build 'em up with worn-out tools . . .*

As creditors scoured the bushes for me, things really began to heat up. The one thing which stands out most in my memory is the sadistic enthusiasm of many of the creditors and virtually all of the collection agents (including those who operated under the guise of attorneys). For some of them, it became a crusade. When you're the one being chased, you sometimes get the impression that you've become the focal point of every collection agent's life.

Every now and then Legalman managed to succeed in serving me with papers, which usually led to a default judgment. But that was only a dead end for him. Whether a deposition was being taken or a default judgment was being entered, Legalman, much to his dismay, was forced to face the hard reality that the bare bones of a financial corpse couldn't be converted into dollars at his command. As a result, his sadistic zeal usually turned to bewilderment very quickly. To give you an idea of Legalman's frustration, I quote verbatim from the transcript of one such deposition:

LEGALMAN: Mr. Ringer, where do you now live?
TORTOISE: Right now I'm living on a truck.
LEGALMAN: Could you be a little more specific about that?
TORTOISE: It's a Ryder truck—R-y-d-e-r.

LEGALMAN: Who owns the truck?

TORTOISE: The Ryder Company, I guess. I leased it from them.

LEGALMAN: When did you do that?

TORTOISE: I did that I guess about two days ago when the Sheriff put me out of my house.

If it was possible to experience joy in the midst of financial devastation, it might have been at that moment—when Legalman scratched his head and, peeping over the rim of his glasses, gave his client a look of complete hopelessness. And he was right; it was hopeless. He believed that I had cleverly devised some sinister plan for hiding untold piles of gold. Unfortunately for both of us, he was wrong. The cupboards truly were bare, and when there's no smell of money, Legalman quickly loses interest. That fact was a great aid to me in keeping the harassment down to near-humane levels during many delicate moments over the next couple of years.

The You-Won't-Get-Credit-For-It Theory strikes again.

Tipping waiters and not getting credit for it is one thing, but violating the reality of this theory in my predicament was nearly fatal. I was in a state of turmoil—the worst frame of mind for thinking rationally. The result was that I allowed myself to be a victim of intimidation through custom and tradition. I had always heard that "an honorable man pays his debts," so I was determined not to declare bankruptcy—an act which would have wiped the slate clean once and for all and given me a fresh start. The following was the result of my self-imposed intimidation:

1) I spent years hassling with creditors and drained myself of creative energy by worrying about bill collectors, shark-toothed collection attorneys and the ever-present sheriff. I robbed myself of valuable time which

could have been used on constructive projects to improve my life.

2) I paid creditors many thousands of dollars, which not only kept my standard of living at the suffering level for a long time, but which made it harder to get on with a creative undertaking that could have ended my treading water and started moving me forward.

3) Instead of having one simple, compact line—*bankrupt*—on my credit record, I had a list of collections, suits and judgments which made me look like a deadbeat. In reality, I was simply a guy who had made some financial mistakes and run out of chips.

4) The coup de grace was that I didn't even get a pat on the head for being a good little American tortoise and refusing to take "the easy way out." On the contrary, in cases where I made settlements for less than a hundred cents on the dollar, my creditors expressed a frightening, almost sadistic contempt for me. More astonishing, however, was that, after years of struggling, when I finally did pay off many creditors in full, they were at best indifferent and at worst hostile. They were convinced I had gotten away with something—that their bills had gone unpaid while I had substantial sums of money stashed away. Again, unfortunately, they were wrong.

It was the worst of all possible worlds. I had endured prolonged mental anguish, poured out thousands of dollars in hard-earned cash, developed an atrocious credit record, and still ended up the object of disdain. But I was supposed to feel good inside because, regardless of anything else, I had done "the right thing." Hogwash! I *didn't* feel good inside. I felt stupid. I had been intimidated through custom and tradition—intimidated into doing the instinctive thing rather than the right (rational) thing. It all sounded beautiful in theory, but in practice —well, you try it yourself and arrive at your own conclusions.

But I'm lucky. To make certain I learned my lesson, I

observed what happened to a friend of mine who had declared bankruptcy at about the same time I began having my financial problems. Once he did the deed—took "the easy way out"—it was over and done with. He was thus able to spend his time working on new projects, which not only produced great wealth for himself, but jobs and useful products for others. His credit record showed only one negative: bankruptcy. If you said the word fast enough, you hardly gave it a second thought. But the real salt in my custom-and-tradition wound: most people talked of my friend's bankruptcy in tones of sympathy. Instead of hating the guy, a majority of his creditors just shrugged it off as a tough break for him.

Don't do anything you won't get credit for! There's a wide disparity between the myth of "the proper thing to do" and the reality that awaits the man who unthinkingly follows such foundationless rhetoric. I got exactly what I deserved for allowing myself to be intimidated through custom and tradition; I did what *others* thought was right—but I, not they, had to bear the consequences.

PICKING UP THE PIECES

The purpose of describing my lowest ebb was to give you the advantage of a better perspective for your own financial situation. If you've been lower than what I just described, then certainly you've discovered literal Hell right here on earth. Hopefully, you haven't even come close to such a financial blitzkrieg, so as we approach the Financial Hurdle you already should have your own situation in a better frame of relativity.

I don't know where you're starting from right now. You may just be getting out of college; you may be a guy pushing forty and working ten or twelve hours a day at a job you hate; you may be a woman who's had it with being a slave to her house and family, longing to get into the business world; you may be an executive who makes big dollars and possesses all the material comforts of life, but who doesn't have time to really enjoy them.

Whatever your present situation, if you're not free, not able to do the things which inspire that irreplaceable feeling of joy (either not having the money necessary to do them, or having it, but not being able to enjoy it), there is a way out. There's a method for getting where you want to go. I did it from the most impossible set of circumstances imaginable; many others have done it; you can do it if you want it badly enough.

Rationality and Courage: Keys to the Prison Door

Whether you're facing total poverty or suburban poverty (high income offset by equally high overhead), the same principles apply. The first step is to convince yourself that you can wipe the slate clean and start over in another direction. Until you understand that, all other steps are meaningless.

A well-known actor, bitter at having spent most of his professional life in films rather than on Broadway, his first love, once said that the money in movies was so good, his lifestyle had expanded. Because of this, he was "forced" to continue to work in a medium he claimed to disdain; he felt he couldn't quit.

I have empathy for such situations, but I don't agree. It would be more appropriate to say that it's *hard* to quit. But there's a big difference between hard and impossible. If you're thinking rationally, your Weight-and-Balance Happiness Scale should be receiving good data. And with the right input, it will always feed you rational answers— answers that are in your best interest. When it's functioning properly, one logical point it will reaffirm is that you have only one life to live and that it is total nonsense to waste it doing something you don't enjoy. It should always be reminding you that in the final analysis you're the only one who possesses the unlimited power to hold back

Number One—to keep you from going after what you really want. Finally, it should be clearly spelling out the price you'll have to pay for a better way of life, so you can decide intelligently whether it's worth it to you.

The Road to Freedom

First off, keep calm, relax, and make sure you have your financial situation in proper perspective. No matter how dire on the surface, look at it for what it really is—a game. Sure, games are fun to win, but remember that when it's all over—no matter how many chips you accumulate—all you'll be taking with you is a quart of embalming fluid, anyway.

Next, rid yourself of those life-destroying "ought-to" thoughts and get down to the business of analyzing your "is's." Don't sit around and daydream about the way you wish things were; understand how they really are, then proceed with doing something about them. Honestly evaluate whether you like your present circumstances. If you do, then stay put, stop bitching, and enjoy what you're doing.

But if you don't really feel good about where you are financially, get out—whether it's an ordinary job, a profession, your own business, or unemployment. Don't spend the rest of your life griping and making excuses. It's only hard to quit—not impossible. To look out for Number One you have to make conscious, rational decisions, and it's simply not rational to spend the rest of your life working at something you find dull or unpleasant.

Salvation: Getting Mad at Number One

Remember that one of my final thoughts as I departed my home, with the sheriffs hot on my trail, was that I was mad at no one but myself. I've often told personal friends that that was my saving grace. I was the villain who had done in Number One; I was the culprit who had made the decisions that led to my own destruction.

Being bitter at others who "put it to you" is not only a waste of time and energy, it's a bore to everyone around you. Don't forget that the same guy you think did a number on you probably has a hundred reasons for thinking he was justified in doing it (the Screwor-Screwee Theory: each of you will believe it was the other guy who threw the kidney punch).

Many years ago, before I'd made it up the financial hill the first time, I taught myself to be grateful toward even the worst of the Type Number Twos who pilfered my chips. I always felt that if I got a real good screwing from someone, and was smart enough to apply the lesson learned, I really owed a debt of thanks to the screwor. I always try to radiate my hostilities inward—where they belong; I've never had any difficulty getting mad at myself. My adversary may have played the Definition or Line-Drawing Game cleverly with me, but that was to be expected; the rules never change. It was up to me to protect my flanks, and if I was too careless to do so, I suffered the inevitable consequences.

Forget about the guy you think caused your downfall. Don't waste time pouting and being mad at him. You did yourself in; he was merely a convenient tool you used to do the job. Why worry about him? The Pinspotter will be the judge of who did what to whom; you'll end up in your proper place, he in his. That is, if you'll just forget about him and work up a white heat of madness at yourself for goofing up. I can assure you I spent a lot of time in that damn truck browbeating myself to the point where I didn't think I could tolerate my own stupidity. The desire to succeed became a lot more than just making money; it meant proving that I could like myself again.

The same principle applies to being bitter at your friends for "letting you down." Such a focus only avoids the real issue. Sure, plenty of people forgot who I was when I hit bottom, but I could never see any particular reason to be offended by that. To forgive isn't divine, it's rational. I analyzed it this way:

1) Being bitter had no relevance whatsoever to the solving of my financial problems and therefore could not justify the expenditure of my time or energy.

2) Since my acquaintances were human beings, they were subject to human weakness; it seems to be a natural instinct for humans, as well as rats, to jump off sinking ships.

3) My friends had nothing whatsoever to do with my going broke, so why should they be involved in my misery?

4) Since friendships, as everything in life, should be based on value for value, I reasoned that I must not have had anything else of value to contribute to the relationships with those who vanished. Either that or I was guilty of making bad friendship choices in the first place.

5) Finally, when anyone performed a disappearing act, I figured it was his way of telling me that he didn't have confidence in my ability to make it back. And in that case, I lost confidence in his ability to make sound judgments, because I *knew* I'd be back. Therefore, I looked upon it as his loss and my gain; he had automatically flushed himself from my future by displaying his inadequate powers for sizing up the character and abilities of people.

The bottom line is to keep moving forward toward the solution of your problems. If others make mistakes in judging you, that's their problem. It's also not unusual; people make mistakes every day.

Don't confuse general bitterness with being mad at yourself. Being mad at the world is a waste of time; it will do absolutely nothing for your cause to sit around and be bitter. If you're making this error, put an immediate stop to it. Whether you're sixteen or sixty, every day spent concentrating on looking out for Number One, rather than on past mistakes, will be one more day which has the potential of being a plus when the debits and credits are tabulated on your life's chart.

EXCUSES: THE SAVIOR OF THE GUY UNWILLING TO PAY THE PRICE

If a person wishes to spend his time proving the profundity of the Life-Complication Theory, all he need do is concentrate on excuses rather than positive action. Nothing is as easy to dwell on as an excuse, and nothing complicates life more easily. An excuse may be justified, but it has nothing to do with improving your life in the future. Directly or indirectly, an excuse represents something out of the past.

The Favorite of All Excuses

The favorite standby, of course, is an offspring of old man Murphy, the "bad break." Is there such a thing as a bad break? Yes, and everyone has his share of them. Murphy doesn't play favorites; he treats us all sadistically. But there's a big difference in how each of us handles misfortune. One punter gets a bad snap from center, tries to get the punt off quickly and has it blocked; another player in the same situation sees that it's too late to kick, spots an opening around end and runs the ball for a first down. To the former, the bad snap from center proved to be a disaster; to the latter, the bad break was turned into a better play than the one that was planned.

People who dwell on bad breaks as excuses are often victims of the

WORLD-OWES-ME-A-LIVING THEORY

Those afflicted with this sickness not only are destined for a lifetime of failure, but tremendous bitterness and frustration as well. I really have no idea how individuals develop the absurd notion that anyone, particularly "the world," owes them anything. I do know, however, that until a person gets such a presumptuous notion out of his head, he'll never get out of the starting gate, much less succeed.

This attitude is often visible in show business. Thousands of would-be actresses, in particular, fail in Hollywood because they don't understand this simple law of Nature. The "lucky" ones are flown in from Peoria at the age of twenty, thrust into the makeup room, quickly emerge as Playmate of the Month, then sit back and wait for their next gift. The overnight attention, based on physical beauty, deludes them into thinking that people are waiting with bated breath to do their bidding.

But it doesn't work that way—not even in Hollywood. More often than not, after a few years of waiting, these girls erroneously conclude that they've been the victims of a series of bad breaks (when in reality each was handed an extraordinarily good break at the outset). The result of this is that they usually disappear from the scene rather quickly (although no one ever seems to know exactly where they go). Or, in some cases, the reality finally sets in that ability, self-discipline and the willingness to pay the price are the real determinants in the ultimate fame-and-money equation. But by that time, all too often, they're has-beens. It's a business which isn't known for its compassion.

Credentials—a Close Relative of the Bad Break

As already noted, there are two kinds of "credentials" accepted by the easily intimidated: "papers" (diplomas, licenses, etc.) and experience. But as also pointed out, neither are synonymous with knowledge of the facts. A lack of formal education or experience shouldn't hold you back any more than the possession of them can guarantee your success.

In fact, our educational factories have been the worst offenders at giving delusions of grandeur to the fuzzy-cheeked young men they turn out. Karl Hess, a former speech writer for Barry Goldwater, said, when asked why he didn't like education (he had dropped out of school at fifteen): "I *loved* education, which is why I spent as little time as possible in school . . . the only thing you have to do to get kids educated is abolish the school system." [8]

Where is one to gain all this education if not in the classroom? Just walk outside, keep your eyes and ears open and make sure your cranial computer is plugged in. You'll be amazed at how much you can learn and how quickly it can be absorbed. And without too much effort, you should be lucky enough to sustain a few setbacks, which are the quickest and best teachers. Believe me, I know. I earned my Masters in Disaster long ago.

Not having proper credentials in the form of experience is an excuse which won't stand up when it comes face to face with an individual who has already made up his mind that he's going to do it.

When all other excuses fail, label yourself.

Grouping and tagging certainly makes for a convenient excuse if you're desperate for one, but the facts prove it's not valid. If you're thinking rationally and are determined to look out for Number One, you won't get sucked into the label trap.

A woman actively engaged in making things happen for herself doesn't have time to get bogged down by cumbersome women's movements. In becoming part of such a "cause," she detracts from her own unique abilities. In the book industry, for example, a great many of the most prominent positions are held by women, many of whom I am personally acquainted with. All seem far too preoccupied with their careers to have time for carrying signs or marching on courthouses. And because they're proud of their achievements, I seriously doubt they would want to lose their identities by being grouped with others who happen to be of the same sex.

In response to this, I've heard such questions as, "That's

all right for the handful of women who have exceptional talent, but what about the rest of us?" This only avoids the issue—*your issue*. Stop worrying about others! It's not a question of whether you have as much ability as someone else. What's relevant is that you discover what your abilities are, then use them in the most effective manner possible. Waste no time in showing them off to the world. The same principles apply on all levels of the financial ladder.

And don't lower yourself to fight for the "right" to be where you're not wanted. Don't use government force or any other type of coercion or natural-law violation to get over the Financial Hurdle; it's not in your best interest in the long run. You'll never be able to use your creative abilities to their fullest extent if you work in an atmosphere of resentment.

Regardless of what you've been brainwashed into believing, there's an abundant supply of employers who are rationally selfish enough to obtain the best person available to fill a position, without considering sex or race. And certainly no rationally selfish capitalist would let irrelevant factors stand in the way of his making a buck, so if you're promoter oriented, seek out other rational promoters with whom to deal.

Remember that being black, female, Indian, elderly, handicapped or anything else is just one fact about you— probably the least relevant fact regarding your ability to do the job. How significant you allow just one factor to be in your quest to clear the Financial Hurdle will relate directly to your rationality, self-esteem and determination. You can dwell on the grouping-and-tagging excuse until you even manage to convince others that it's the primary deterrent to your success, but it still won't buy a loaf of bread at the supermarket. Instead of convincing your friends that you're being discriminated against, go out and convince some rational people that you can get results.

WHAT TO DO WHEN YOU'RE OUT OF EXCUSES

After all excuses have been set aside where they belong, the first question to ask yourself is what you really want to do in life. There are two factors to consider: one is how you can most efficiently use the talents you possess to obtain the financial success you desire in the shortest possible time; the other is choosing something you'll enjoy.

Nature conveniently works it out for us so that the two factors complement each other. Fortunately, if you're doing something you like, the odds of your obtaining what you're after more quickly are greatly increased. Which is why *you* have to be the judge; only you know what makes you happy. Two critical rules to follow when making this decision are:

1) Never pursue a career just because someone else wants you to. The person who advises you—whether it's your mother, husband, or a well-meaning friend—will not have to be the one to endure the frustration and dissatisfaction that come from working at something for which you have no enthusiasm. Don't try to be what someone else wants you to be; do what you enjoy and what you think you're capable of.

2) Never listen to anyone who tries to convince you that what you're contemplating is too unrealistic or too hard, or that it's too late for you to start. Bull! If it's what you've always wanted to do, do it. Which reminds me of a theory that is very much a part of the intimidation-through-conformity game:

OUT-OF-STEP THEORY

As a general rule, a person's chances for success will tend to increase the more he's out of step with "society." A la the old stock market axiom, the public is always wrong.

This theory applies to products and services just as it

does to friends and lovers. If you're offering what everyone else is touting, who needs you? Man, get with it: get *out* of step. Don't be intimidated by people who hit you with sarcastic statements like, "Sure, everyone's out of step but you." If you're lucky enough to hear this remark, it shouldn't throw you. Chances are good that you're doing the right thing rather than the instinctive thing. It's instinctive to follow the crowd, but the crowd is usually wrong.

Learn the Translation Game. Always try to determine where the other guy is coming from when he attempts to put you down. While the words are, "Sure, everyone's out of step but you," the probable translation is, "Sure, everyone else is doing the same old unimaginative things that get them nowhere, while you're kicking your spurs into life's hide and making it yield something better." Kick away; so long as you're not interfering with anyone else, why not? Your financial success, and thus your independence, may very well depend on your refusal to be intimidated into conforming.

Nature's Omnipresent Reality: Price Paying

If you're getting the feeling that there's a lot to making it over the Financial Hurdle, you're right. You've made the decision that you really can make a change if you want to; you've managed to forget those who did you in, as well as the friends who dropped you when you were down; you've succeeded in getting mad at yourself; you've cast aside all excuses; and you've managed to ignore the suggestions of others. Yet, you're barely getting started. Small wonder that so few people ever achieve financial peace of mind.

Price paying gets to be a pain in the neck after a while. You'd think it would eventually just go away and leave you alone. Forget that thought; it won't. Whether you like it or not, the Price-Paying Toll Machine will stand between you and everything you wish to obtain or accomplish all your life. And the damn thing never malfunctions. Either you pay its price, or it doesn't let you in; there are no exceptions.

After deciding what you'd really like to do, you have to get down to the hard realities of what it's going to cost. Don't play games with yourself and try to imagine you're going to get off easy. The only way it's going to be cheap is if what you're after is merely a cheap imitation of clearing the Financial Hurdle. The price you'll have to pay will depend on a number of individual circumstances, including your desire for things other than financial success, your emotional makeup, your background (which does not mean you have to have the right diploma or experience), and who else, if anyone, is intimately involved in your life.

Depending on these and many other factors, including the extent of your financial aspirations, you'll be required to pay varying prices in the form of time and energy, risk of capital, jealousy and resentment from others, less time for friends, lovers and/or family, and in the sacrifice of other things which may now be an important part of your life. This is where you need to do some serious Factual Meditation. You should analyze the total price, on your own, without verbal interference from others. If your Weight-and-Balance Happiness Scale is operating properly—meaning that you're feeding it honest data—it should correctly determine whether the price you'll have to pay is worth that which you hope to gain in return.

The extent of the price of many of the items mentioned above will depend a great deal on your decision to be a "promoter" or a "worker." When Karl Marx wrote *The Communist Manifesto*, he either had a bad hangover or had to be one of the great comedy writers of his age. The idea that "labor" produces everything is obviously absurd; it does you little good to be a skilled tradesman worth $20 an hour if there's nobody to hire you.

The truth is that both promoters and workers are necessary to any civilization. Promoters are people who not only come up with ideas, but put them into action by gambling time, energy and money in the hope of realizing greater financial rewards than might be expected by working for someone else. They have to hassle endlessly with illegal government interference, the financial pressures inherent in meeting monthly overhead, and a million and one other things with which someone drawing a paycheck need not concern himself.

The worker, on the other hand, escapes not only the pressure of the promoter, but accepts much less risk (particularly if he's good at what he does). Because of this, economic law dictates that the worker's financial potential be limited. Since the promoter theoretically isn't restricted by such a limitation, he must accept the other side of that economic reality: complete financial devastation if everything should go wrong.

It's the potential we're talking about here—not necessarily the reality of what usually happens. More often than not, top-salaried workers end up much better off than the average promoter. But what lures the promoter is the possibility of hitting the jackpot. In making your decision regarding this matter, be certain you have a clear understanding of the risks and potentials involved. As a worker, don't expect to make millions. As a promoter, don't expect to enjoy the same amount of extracurricular pleasures as the man who receives a weekly salary; it's simply not in the cards.

Whichever one you decide upon, the best use of your abilities will still be the major determinant in how far you go. The degree of your ability and the level on which you apply it are not the issue; the use of your ability is.

Before starting, recheck your luggage.

I haven't found the Financial Hurdle the easiest obstacle to handle, so the one thing you don't need is the excess baggage I refer to in "The Perspective Hurdle." You'll need to get rid of as many burdens as possible.

Lighten your load so you won't be fighting the sharks out there with one arm tied behind your back.

People obviously represent the greatest potential burdens. They can cause problems in a hundred different ways. If you're trying to support someone in luxury when your financial situation isn't up to the task, you're playing in quicksand. If you're married to or living with a person who isn't patient and understanding—who is not sympathetic to your cause—it's almost like having a traitor in your ranks. While you're busy trying to outmaneuver the other players on the field of battle, a nonsupportive domestic partner can be very detrimental, sapping you of valuable energy inside your own fortress. If you love the person who's purposely or inadvertently landing the inside blows, this may be one of your biggest price-paying decisions. Do you want what you're after enough to give him or her up? That again is something only you can decide.

There are a great many burdens in your life right now; there are in everyone's. Rid yourself of as many of them as possible. If you're serious about clearing the Financial Hurdle, you can't afford the extra weight. Take my word for it: it's tough to get up and over this one without tripping and falling flat on your face.

THE ACHILLES' HEEL AT WHICH THE DEVIL AIMS

The biggest burden of all can be your ego, particularly if it controls you rather than the other way around. In fact, it can be the most dangerous traitor in your camp. Everyone has an ego, so don't try to imagine you don't. It's far better to acknowledge that it's there and concentrate on keeping it under control. Unless you have very unusual capacities, you probably can't afford the price of both financial success and a bloated ego, because the cost of such an ego often *is* the foregoing of financial success.

The problem with an oversized ego is that it's like

having a dinosaur lying on your front lawn; if you don't continue to feed it, it might just step on your house. This feeding of the ego often manifests itself in perpetual movement of the tongue and mouth. Learn to be quiet and patient. The safest way to operate is behind the scenes, with a minimum of fuss. In my business, publicity goes with the territory, but I'm extremely secretive about my projects until they're completed.

Back in West Virginia where my daddy was born, they've got a saying that "if you can do what you say you can do, you ain't braggin'." That may be true, but from a pragmatic standpoint, there's not too much to gain by giving the world advance notice of your feats. If you achieve your desired end, people will know about it soon enough, and they may even think you're humble because you didn't shoot your mouth off about it. Knowing that Murphy is out there—just waiting to trip you up—should make you realize that you have a lot to lose by going on record ahead of time. At best, people will be impressed that you're able to back up your words, but they'll still resent your advance-notice attitude. That's hardly worth the risk of having one or more neurotic individuals trying to see to it that you end up dining on your own words some evening. The more you actually succeed, the more reason you have to feel secure, thus the less you should feel the urge to talk about what you're going to do.

The Devil's Helper

If Satan isn't alive and well on Planet Earth, then his chief aide certainly is. He's a little guy—'bout so tall— who carries around a miniature pitchfork and is always grinning. Next time you shoot off your mouth about a plan you have in the works, quickly turn your head to the left and you'll see him sitting on your shoulder, whispering in your ear. He's none other than the Pop-Off Mess-Up Man.

The Devil has assigned this little creep the eternal task

"One slip out of you, Greenie, and you'll be nursing a bad case of bursitis."

of urging incurable pop-offs to let everyone know about their upcoming goodies. How many times have you jumped the gun and talked about your plans prematurely, only to be embarrassed when they fell through? You'd better learn to respect this little fellow or he'll stick that pitchfork in your shoulder and hang on forever, snatching victory from your grasp, time and again, at the last moment. (I think that, unbeknownst to the Devil, Murphy has the Pop-Off Mess-Up Man on a commission basis on the side.)

The best way to let others know what you're going to do is to do it. And the better your chances for success really are, the less reason you have to risk messing things up. Your ego will be more than sufficiently assuaged, massaged and patted after you've actually achieved the triumph.

I think this principle is important enough to be a theory. It's a little long and complicated, but if you read carefully, I'm sure you can follow it:

ZIP THE LIP THEORY

If you've got something good going, *shut up!*

The Billionaire Babies

You've undoubtedly known at least one person in your life who was afflicted with the ego sickness of talking endlessly about million-dollar deals. Well, within the zany boundaries of Tinseltown, we can go you one better. Los Angeles doesn't fool around with millions; it has a whole army of Billionaire Babies. A Billionaire Baby doesn't concern himself with mere million-dollar discussions—everything involves billions. The first time you encounter a Billionaire Baby, you have the feeling he's putting you on. When you realize he's not, you start glancing around the room for possible exits of escape.

I once knew a seemingly intelligent young man who had

contracted a severe case of Billionaire Babyitis. He knew not one paltry millionaire; every person he was dealing with was worth billions. At first I thought it was just his way of figuratively expressing someone's wealth; later I became convinced that he actually believed there were carloads of billionaires running around our planet.

At various times, I had occasion to meet some of these "billionaires" he had referred to. One drove a magnificent Rolls Royce, which I later found out, quite by accident, was on a month-to-month lease. Another lived in a splendid mansion, but I discovered he was only a "front man" for a group of investors who had put up the money as venture capital for refurbishing and resale of the estate. A third was the biggest spender I'd ever met, and he was being chased all over town by collection agents.

So much for the Billionaire Babies. I've never met a billionaire, but I have had the opportunity to know many people in the $5 million to $100 million range, and there's one thing which stands out most in my mind about all of them: not only do they refrain from tossing money around loosely, they're even careful about the way they speak of it. There's respect in their voices at the mention of even $10.

This special kind of ego problem makes it timely to bring in another favorite of mine, the

TEND-TO THEORY

This simply states that most people have a tendency to believe their own bullshit and further warns of the dangers involved in your believing yours. It's one thing to put others on, but you're walking on thin ice when you start believing it yourself. When you think that every guy who flashes a hundred-dollar bill is loaded and, worse, when you begin imagining *you're* something you're not, you're in big trouble.

Megalomaniacs—people who suffer from delusions of greatness—are hopelessly caught in the Tend-To trap.

When you have occasion to meet one of them, don't stop to shake hands—run. A guy who believes his own bullshit is someone who makes decisions which rest on the landfill of the mind, and anything anchored to landfill is doomed to crumble at the slightest sign of a tremor. Make sure you're not around when that happens; it's dangerous to your health. Avoid getting sucked in by the Tend-To neuroses of others, and make sure the sickness doesn't afflict you, either. Don't try to be something you're not; avoid ego satisfactions; be totally honest—at least with yourself—at all times.

Telltale Signs of a Guy Headed for Egoruptcy

Egoruptcy is a form of bankruptcy caused primarily by the investment of too much time and capital in one's ego. Avoid business dealings with any person headed in that direction, because when he starts falling he's liable to pull you down with him. Feeding the ego is habit-forming and can lead the addict to dishonest acts in his attempts to get the "fix" he needs. Here are some signs to look for, though they're by no means foolproof; they're only indicators. If a person qualifies on several counts, however, the odds are good that you're in close proximity to someone who has the potential to hurt you financially.

1) The ego addict constantly lets you know that he's "got his shit together," although he may use phrases more appropriate to business than to Hollywood parties. Remember the Protesting-Lady Translation Game: the more someone volunteers a "fact" to you, the less reason you have to believe it.

2) He pops off incessantly about deals he's working on.

3) When not talking about current deals, he dwells on what he's accomplished in the past. Nobody's as interested in yesterday's news as the guy headed for egoruptcy.

4) Rapid expansion of offices (particularly when lavish in nature), staff or business in general are other signs,

192

none of them conclusive proof of the disease by itself, but all warranting a suspicious approach on your part.

5) Talking about what he owns is an almost embarrassing trait of the ego addict, yet he often resorts to this when desperate. What makes it embarrassing is that no one cares.

6) There's one that's even more embarrassing than that: talking about who he knows. When the disease reaches that stage, the ego addict's condition has deteriorated beyond hope. As is the custom when passing lepers in Beverly Hills, you should, at that point, shield your face to make certain the disease doesn't spread to you.

Standing on principle can be the equivalent of falling on ego.

Standing on principle is one of those custom-and-tradition-type dangers into which we frequently get trapped. More often than not, when a person makes an endless fuss over a relatively minor point, it's really just his ego interfering with his own best interest. I like to avoid confrontations, because they slow me down. If it's of monumental importance for a guy to win a business point that isn't significant to my overall objective, I'd just as soon give him the satisfaction. In fact, I'd prefer we concentrate on nothing *but* nonessential points. Let the other person think he's winning the battle, while you maintain your long-term game plan for winning the war.

Don't get sidetracked by irrelevant challenges. Disregard irritations that are unrelated to your main objective. When you argue for the sake of arguing, you're not acting in your rational self-interest; your ego is in control, which means you're out of control.

If you catch yourself trying to deal with associates or subordinates by instilling fear in them, that, too, is probably your ego guiding your actions—the subconscious motivation being similar to that of standing on principle. Never try to rule out of fear; it's another action which is not in your best interest. It also doesn't work, in the long run, because those you think you have under control will be precisely the ones who will fail to cooperate when you need them most. You need to be surrounded by competent people to succeed, and competent people don't need to be controlled with an iron fist.

As always, the best kind of associations are those based on value for value, whether they be employer-to-employee relationships, employee-to-employee relationships or promoter-to-promoter relationships.

The Ultimate Manifestation of the Inflated Ego: The Awards Game

Winning awards can be a pat on the head for not having succeeded commercially. What you must decide is whether you'd rather get patted or get paid. For obvious reasons, I talk of this in terms of the

FILM FESTIVAL THEORY

In the film business, as everyone knows, there's a bitter, snobbish element affectionately referred to as artistic strokers. These are film people who are so hopelessly out of touch with the desires of the consumer that they try to make themselves believe commercial success in films is irrelevant. And they're right; it is—so long as you prefer peanut butter and jelly sandwiches to filet mignon.

What helps keep them sane (?) is that they're "certain" they know the difference between an artistic film and garbage (garbage usually being defined as something like *Gone With the Wind, Love Story* or *The Godfather*). Actually, they're only succeeding in playing the Definition Game with themselves. What's artistic to them may be garbage to you or me. Not only are they out of touch with reality, but their condition seems to worsen with time.

194

"Artistic acclaim" is fine, but the plain fact is that awards are usually based on the opinions of only a handful of people—people whose opinions may not be important to most others. If you're interested in financial success, don't put too much emphasis on the critical acclaim of a small, elite group of individuals. That's not where the money lies; it's only where the ego seeks to be fed.

I've always had the suspicion that any film festival winner would gladly send his award back by air freight in exchange for just one *Jaws*.

Thinking Long-Term: The Road to Rational Decisions

I've already alluded many times to the wisdom of the long-term solution as opposed to short-term patching. If it should be emphasized anywhere, it's certainly here, in relation to the Financial Hurdle. I've been guilty of so many glaring errors in the past that it's difficult to award a place of honor to any one of them. But up there at the top of the list would have to be the destructive act of making decisions based on short-term results. Short-term patching is the catalyst for the proverbial act of jumping from the frying pan into the fire. When you're out of dough, the instinctive thing is to base your decisions on the expediency of the moment—which, of course, only makes matters worse.

The classic example of this is the largest bankrupt corporation in the world—the United States Government. When the government devalued the dollar, that was only an involuntary admission of bankruptcy; in truth, it has been bankrupt for decades. The main reason for the financial insolvency of the government, on top of its bungling, inefficiency and corruption, is precisely its insistence on the use of the short-term-patching approach. It simply doesn't work. This type of "solution" is like trying to use a bucket that's full of holes to bail water out of a sinking ship. The government keeps the public's attention focused on all the water it's throwing out of the boat, hiding the more important fact that the ship keeps sinking a little more each day.

The New Deal, minimum wage laws, counterfeiting ("inflation"), job programs (which, in fact, put some people out of work in order to "create" jobs for others), and an endless number of other panic moves are all examples of the disastrous consequences of the short-term thinker. In the case of the government, billions are spent on propaganda to make certain that the hood-winked masses see only the short-term effects, while the long-term catastrophic results are kept hidden in the closet.

To demonstrate just how bad the short-term-patching concept is, remember that the government's ever-increasing bankruptcy continues despite the fact that it operates on funds stolen from you. Don't you think that if you had the right to steal from your neighbors, print your own money, and operate with virtually no restraints, you could at least stay solvent? Even so, the government can't hack it—because short-term patching doesn't work.

It wasn't until I finally developed the self-discipline to think long-term that I began building a solid foundation for financial success. The irony is that I found, to my surprise, that long-term solutions actually turn out to be the most expedient. Because of this, I've come to refer to the long-term-solution approach as the "slow, fast way." Shame on any tortoise who couldn't grasp this concept much earlier. By solving a problem on a permanent basis—which may cause temporary discomfort and initially take a little longer—you never have to worry about it again. It's over and done with. You don't have to keep coming back to put out fires created by a haphazard, short-term solution.

Falsely assuaging the ego is a typical example of short-term patching's having ill-fated long-term consequences. If you buy a Rolls Royce you can't afford, just to feed that dinosaur on your front lawn, you may temporarily look like dynamite. But the long-term result could be that you'll end up riding a bicycle, instead. This doesn't mean you have to live like a beggar until some unspecified time in the future when you've accumulated a likewise-unspecified number of chips. One of the ground rules for clearing the Financial Hurdle is avoiding being miserable while working toward your financial objective. But it does mean you should acknowledge the realities of today—whatever they may be—and, based on such realities, make rational decisions which will prove to be in your best interest tomorrow. Ayn Rand framed it this way:

> A rational man . . . does not live his life short-range and does not drift like a bum pushed by the spur of the moment. It means that he does not regard any moment as cut off from the context of the rest of his life, and that he allows no conflicts or contradictions between his short-range and long-range interests. He does not become his own destroyer by pursuing a desire today which wipes out all his values tomorrow.[4]

CONSIDERING THE OTHER GUY'S DESIRES IS IN YOUR LONG-TERM BEST INTEREST.

Remember the reality of self-interest. If there's nothing in it for the other person, you may get in his pockets once, but in the long term you're going to lose a customer, client or business associate and will inherit a deserved black mark in the financial community.

It goes without saying that not everyone's desires should be important to you. But the desires of those with whom you deal in business are of paramount importance to your long-term success. Value for value is still the only formula I've found that works. There must be something in it for the other guy if you wish to keep dealing with him, and, as a bonus, he'll probably pass along the good word that you're a value-for-value type of person. Let the other fellow know you're a Type Number One (if you are)—that you're out to make the best possible deal for yourself, but not at the expense of losing a long-term relationship. No matter how much you try to make on any one situation, it most likely can't approach the amount that can be realized over a period of years during which you will be able to deal with the same person many times.

THE FALLACY OF GOAL SETTING

Goal setting is one of those great myths that have been handed down to us from a time and place unknown. I long ago came to the conclusion that setting goals, in the traditionally accepted context, is detrimental on a long-term basis. What originally caused me to take a closer look at goal setting was the fact that people who were among the most consistent failures I had known were forever setting newer and higher goals.

The trouble with setting a specific goal is that once you spell it out, you either reach it or you don't. If you fail to reach it, there are two alternatives open to you:

1) The acknowledgement that you failed to attain your objective, which could lead to a loss of faith in your ability to succeed, or

2) The failure to acknowledge the reality that you didn't achieve what you set out to do (the Ostrich approach), in which case you probably will go right ahead and set a new goal. But the new one will be meaningless, because you've already set a precedent by having let yourself off the hook the first time.

The other side of the coin is, what happens to you if you do reach your goal? The obvious thing is to set a new and higher one. And after you reach the new one, the same pattern follows. But wait. Aren't we forgetting someone? Mr. Murphy doesn't take kindly to being slighted. You can be sure he's hiding behind some innocent-looking bush along the road leading to your next goal. And under his arm is that unsettling reality of

Nature—a circumstance beyond your control. In other words, you simply aren't in a position to guarantee that you'll reach any specific goal. You can't even guarantee that you'll be alive tomorrow. All you can be sure of is that you'll give it your best shot; that, coupled with a little luck, may or may not be enough to overcome outside interference.

The bottom line is that sooner or later you won't reach a goal, which brings you right back to the two alternatives originally discussed. I went through this syndrome many times myself. I often had my moments of success, but more often I was clobbered by such things as the changing circumstances of others with whom I was involved, blind-side tackles by Type Twos and Threes, and various other Murphy ploys. In such cases, it took a lot of self-hyping to keep the faith.

But in order not to get sucked into the Ostrich trap of allowing goal setting to become a farce, I finally analyzed that, like so many other success myths which only make for interesting goody-two-shoes reading, it wasn't rational and therefore didn't work in actual practice. You do need something to aim for, but goals must have latitude in order to be practical and be taken seriously; otherwise, they're not long-term solutions.

That's not to say you should make your goals so general that they become meaningless. You shouldn't set a vague goal like: "I want to make lots of money." A more specific, yet realistic, goal—one which I myself set—might be: "Within five years I want to make enough money to be free to do what I please (within the limits of government interference) and go where I want to go (within the limits of government interference)." Because we're different people with different personalities and desires, such a goal would represent a different degree of financial success to you than to me.

But here's the most interesting thing about general goal setting. Though I wasn't unrealistically specific in my aim and was prepared to go even six or seven years if I didn't make it in five, by basing my decisions on long-term results—no matter how painful they were at the time—I actually reached my goal faster than anticipated. That, however, was possible only because I didn't use the generality of my aims as a cop-out. I truly gave it my best shot, and my long-term-solution orientation again proved to be the "slow, fast way." If you use the general approach to goal setting merely as an excuse to lie back, you're no better off than the person who sets unrealistic, specific goals.

THE LONG-TERM SOLUTION TO SECURITY

In a world that's crumbling under the financial chaos created by government counterfeiting and illegal deficit spending, it behooves one, as he enjoys the pleasures of today, to think long-term. As governments continue to inflate currencies and spend money they don't have, conditions will go from bad to worse. And since you can count on our government's short-term-patching approach to continue, it's only a question of how much longer it can avert total disaster by coming up with new schemes.

If you've attained a great deal of financial success, or plan to in the future, you must face the unfortunate reality that as the government (which is really just a giant crusade in which everyone is forced to join) continues to grasp for short-term solutions, it will come down harder and harder on its most convenient devil—"the rich." It must have a bad guy at which to point its soiled finger. It's been working on "the rich" (no one is quite sure exactly to whom the term is supposed to apply) for quite some time now. Of course, in reality the whole thing is total nonsense, like all other government rhetoric. As John Hospers points out, ". . . even if every millionaire were soaked 100% of his annual income, this wouldn't run the government for half a day out of the whole year." [5] Or, put in another perspective by Henry Hazlitt, if the government confiscated 100 percent of the income of every person who made over $50,000 a year and divided it up among the population, each citizen would receive the grand sum of $120.

Converting dollars into items which hold the best prospects for retaining a good portion of their values after the crash is one possible approach to the long-term problems the government continues to create. These items could be gold, silver, works of art—anything that might be in demand at a time when people refuse to take worthless paper in exchange for a loaf of bread. It's up to you personally to research such possibilities and come to your own conclusions. I try to avoid giving advice in this area, because I haven't yet studied all the available alternatives to my satisfaction.

The Felony Fund

If you're counting on Social Security as a future nest egg, forget it. There is no Social Security fund. The whole thing has been a short-term-patching fraud from the outset, just another government scheme to get its hands on more of your money in an effort to keep the sinking ship afloat. The "fund" is actually a $2.3 trillion I.O.U. backed by a bankrupt entity. It can be paid to the intended recipients only by stealing more money from you and other taxpayers in the future. In the land business, this scheme is known as pyramiding, and the same government which so blatantly practices it will put you in jail for a long, long time if you try to do the same.

Where are the Social Security resources? They're gone as soon as you pay them in. It's known as co-mingling of funds, another act for which you and I would go to prison. The money is used for putting out government fires elsewhere. What's most insulting to the intelligence of the average citizen is that the government doesn't even show the $2.3 trillion liability on its balance sheets (still another fraud for which you and I would go to jail). Though it is, by itself, five times greater than the admitted amount

201

of the national debt, it isn't even reported to the public as a liability!

Forget about Social Security and other government benefits. They probably won't be there when your turn comes, and even if they were, you'd be paid in dollars that would either be worthless or close to it.

If converting cash into other commodities is but an educated gamble, at best, and since Social Security doesn't really exist, is there any way to obtain financial security? Long-term, the only solution is your own ability. The best investment you can make is to improve your mind, your abilities, your worth to other people. If all else fails, those whose talents are still in demand will have the greatest trading power. At this point, at least, I don't see what the government can do to confiscate your abilities.

The Miracle of Simplicity

Looking back over the past, I'm amazed at how far out of my way I went to complicate my business dealings. The time and money spent on building large organizations, setting up complex corporate structures and operating coast to coast seem incomprehensible to me now. The result was that I never had time to do the one thing which really makes the big dollars—tap my creative abilities. All my hours were tied up in seeking ways to make things complicated.

Now, no one impresses me less than the guy who, with a telephone in each hand, madly shuffles papers as he talks, periodically interrupts his telephone conversations to blurt out orders to his secretary, and at the same time motions you to have a seat (with a wink which implies he'll "be with you in a minute"). More often than not, this is a sign of the "all-show-and-no-dough" syndrome of the ego addict.

Even when it's for real, you're looking at a fellow who's lost sight of what winning is all about. He may be making it financially, but he's forgotten that money is only a means to an end. I suppose you could argue that some people enjoy this, that frantic work makes them happy, and I guess that is possible. However, I know too many people (including myself) who thought they enjoyed that type of life at one time, only to wake up later and realize they didn't know what they'd been missing. In addition, operating in the classic hustle-bustle, harried-executive manner considerably decreases your odds of being around long enough to discover that money is only a means to an end.

After a couple of belly-ups, I realized that what applies to crusades applies to business as well: there is weakness, not strength, in numbers. The larger the organization, the more people there are who have to be consulted before decisions can be made, thus the greater the opportunities for bureaucratic bungling, time-wasting in-fighting, inefficiency and confusion. This is why—contrary to another popularly accepted myth—a large corporation can never effectively compete with a small, efficient, well-run company.

In large cities, for example, the nationwide supermarket chains never do as well as one or more of the local operations which are able to stay on top of their situations more effectively. That's why giant corporations are always backing "antitrust" and "antimonopoly" laws—still another government hoax. I think most people understand, by this time, that the purpose of most of these "laws" really is to *protect* big business against small competitors; the latter, because they're more efficient, cut into the profits of the giants.

The airlines, for example, howled when former President Ford suggested deregulation of the airline industry. They wanted to maintain government-fixed pricing and other controls, and they lobbied feverishly against opening the doors to competition. As always, you, the consumer, are the one to suffer. In this case, you're made to accept poor service, bad scheduling, fares arbitrarily fixed at a higher level than free competition would allow, and all the other discomforts which go along with the monopoly-protected airline industry. But the government won't protect your business, even if you want it to, because you aren't big enough.

I realized that my best protection lay in ridding myself of excess baggage, keeping things as simple as possible, and improving my skills. I lost the desire to be a high-priced baby-sitter, which is what you sometimes become when you have the responsibility for overseeing a large staff. It's a form of self-imprisonment. You have to consider everything from the clothes you wear to arriving at the office at a certain time, because others are looking to you to set an example.

The same goes for traveling. In the old days, I always believed the really great deals—"the isles beneath the winds where black trees grow"—were elsewhere, usually on the other side of the continent. Naturally, most of those deals turned out to be volcanic ash. All the while, I was wasting time and energy—not to mention thousands of dollars in traveling expenses—which could have been used for constructive projects right in my own back yard.

Keep things simple. Don't run all over the country tracking down deals which probably aren't as good as those right in front of you. It's amazing how much more efficient you can be in your own office, as opposed to an airplane or a hotel room. The only thing that can be stated with any degree of certainty regarding extensive business travel is that you'll probably date a lot of stewardesses, and that could be the most costly thing of all.

ESCAPING THE INSTITUTION(s)

Although your choice of occupation will somewhat determine the extent to which you can rid yourself of contact with big institutions, their absence from your life can go a long way toward simplifying your business dealings. I make far more money now than ever before, not only because I've reduced my operations to a skeletal staff, but because I no longer need to spend endless frustrating hours hassling with inefficient giant institutions like banks, insurance companies and regulatory agencies. When I was the head of a public company, I must have spent 95% of my time talking to the American Stock Exchange, the SEC (the Swift Execution Commission, a.k.a. the Securities and Exchange Commission), banks and other lethargic organizations, not to mention directors, brokers and stockholders. The other 5% of my time was used for performing the multitude of chores necessary to comply with government regulations. That spelled endless paper work, constant meetings with attorneys and accountants, and many other unpleasant tasks. I don't think anyone in a position of authority in a public company ever quite gets around to creating better products or services; there's simply no time for it.

BEWARE OF THE TURBANS.

Keeping things simple also means not working on a hundred deals at once. Being a writer has taught me the importance of not getting sidetracked, regardless of how good something else looks. I concur completely with General Patton in that you must be single-minded and drive for the one thing on which you've decided.

As I said earlier, you can't have all the candy in the store, so the sooner you face that reality, the quicker you can get down to the business of making money instead of chaos. I've stopped trying to be a jerk of all trades; I've become a believer in the principle of specialization. I'm willing to labor away at my books and leave all the other deals in the world to you.

I've become crotchety in my old age, to the point that I won't even talk to people about "deals." Maybe it's senility. There simply are too many "ifs" and "buts" and "maybes" that I don't understand anymore. Besides, they always involve dealing with more people, and I'm consciously trying to figure out how to deal with *fewer* people when it comes to money matters. People mean complications and complications mean roadblocks between me and the pot of freedom on the other side of the Financial Hurdle.

When I used to work for a living, probably every LSD Deal ever thought of crossed my desk. Condominiums in the Mohave Desert, bank charters in the Bahamas, converting cow dung into bricks in Bombay—you name it, I saw it. And the turbans—I still have nightmares about the waves of turbans coming at me. Always they came—wearing black business suits and turbans—talking about "Arab oil money" or representing "wealthy families in India." You know what? In all those years and through all the thousands of deals which came through my office, I never saw any Arab or Indian money change hands. It may be out there somewhere, but I can assure you that it's changing hands on a level far above your head or mine.

Forget about the fantasy deals that suck in the Billionaire-Baby types. Don't be impressed by every guy who walks into your office wearing a turban and a neatly pressed Robert Hall suit. We haven't cornered the market; the Arabs and Indians have their flakes, too. Remember, a man's status as an expert (along with his air of legitimacy) erroneously increases with the distance he travels from home. Place all your time and energy on one deal—preferably in your own city—that makes sense. Don't allow yourself to be sidetracked by all the other propositions that come floating by, whether they're presented by guys wearing turbans or bathing suits.

GIVE ME ONE HOUR OF CREATIVE THOUGHT TO A HUNDRED HOURS OF CONFUSION.

Remember the Life-Complication Theory and don't become a victim of the human tendency to make things difficult for yourself. Work hard at keeping your life uncomplicated. The more you simplify your financial affairs, the more time you have for the one thing that

makes the real money: creative thinking. Don't feel you have to be wheeling and dealing all the time, running around like a madman and talking to a hundred people a day about every financial situation that's out there in the bushes. That type of activity will only succeed in cluttering your mind. One good hour of creative thinking, by contrast, could literally be worth a million dollars to you. Get rid of all the garbage and excess baggage and get down to where it's all at: profit is directly related to the number of uncluttered, creative hours one has at his disposal.

Winning by Default

Organization and self-discipline go hand in hand with simplifying your money-making efforts. The nice part about it is that these two characteristics not only give you additional free time to engage in pleasurable activities, but allow you to enjoy more fully those nonworking hours. That's because you aren't consumed by guilt over something that's been left undone.

I believe I lead a very uncomplicated life and have more nonguilty free hours than the average person, chiefly because organization is my forte. In truth, I'm so disgustingly self-disciplined that it aggravates even me at times. But the result of organization and self-discipline is efficient use of time, which results in more creative hours—meaning less time is needed to get where you want to go financially.

I realize that not everyone has the same capacity for organization, but, again, it's the use of the ability you do possess that counts. One important aspect of the efficient use of time is learning to use both people and machines effectively. This holds true whether you're a promoter or a worker. The worker who understands how to expand his capacities through the intelligent utilization of people and machines makes himself a more valuable employee and thus increases the worth of his services.

Also realize that your personal life is automatically intertwined with your business life. The reality is that one affects the other. How well you do in business very much determines what you may or may not be free to do in your nonbusiness life. And if your personal life is disorganized or in turmoil, it most certainly will have a negative effect on your financial ambitions.

Friendship problems, friction with a mate or lover, sickness—any kind of personal turmoil can affect your ability to concentrate on business. The same is true of disorganization in your personal life; it, too, can take its toll on your dollar-seeking efforts. The reality is that you have to eat, sleep, see the dentist, and do many other things of a nonbusiness nature, and they all take time. If these nonbusiness items are not under control—if your personal life isn't properly organized—they'll put severe limitations on what you can accomplish financially.

Self-discipline comes into the picture because it's hard to stay organized unless you've got the willpower to avoid distractions. Earlier I discussed the geometric-growth problem in winding up and winding down one's work on constructive projects. You have to learn to say no—to both people and things. If you're looking for convenient excuses to avoid paying the price of success, you don't have to look far. There will always be an abundance of distractions around you—like the opposite sex, phone calls, spectator sports and TV.

You can even rationalize and convince yourself that a particular social gathering is necessary for business reasons, but I stopped buying that one long ago. The points are scored on the playing field, Monday through Friday, in your office or someone else's. I simply don't believe the guys who claim that their best business moves have been made at cocktail parties, golf games, or even business lunches (although, as per the Tend-To Theory, I think some of them really believe it).

I will admit I'm happy that most of the other players seem to think points can be scored outside the arena.

That's why I've often said that whenever I've succeeded, I considered it to be by default. While the other guy was having a "business" martini, I usually was working—behind closed doors—on my own. It's a much simpler way to win, and far more relaxing. I don't think of my past victories as head-to-head knockouts. Rather, I see them as my having ground the other guy into submission through self-discipline—usually while he was snoring away in his Dr. Dentons.

A good way to check yourself is this: if you're properly organized and good at self-discipline, most people will wonder how you got to the finish line "so fast." If they can't seem to figure it out, it's a good sign you rate high marks on the effective use of these two important tools.

Taking Hold of the Wheel

If there's one thing that makes me nervous, it's being a passenger in a car. I hate to drive, but I do so because I like being in control. We've been talking about acting out of choice rather than chance since the first page of this book, and that's only possible if you're in control of your actions. Organization and self-discipline afford you the base from which to control not only yourself, but the situations in which you're involved.

While it's true that there are endless factors beyond your control, there are many over which you do have power. If you've had some rough sledding in the past, you may find it hard to believe how many factors you have the power to control in a business situation.

First and foremost, you have the power to control your own awareness. No one can prevent you from being alert or from thinking rationally. Too many people are so convinced that they're dealing from a position of weakness that they fail to concentrate on what's going on around them. It's uncanny how the biggest events in a person's life stumble across his path when he's least expecting them.

The same type of mentality which can't understand that

everyone gets his share of bad breaks also has trouble comprehending that we all get a bushelful of good breaks in our lifetimes, too. The majority of people either are too unaware of what's going on around them, or too obsessed with bitterness over some misfortune they've endured, to recognize the opportunities which continually pop up. Of the few who do recognize these opportunities, only a small percentage have the alertness and/or courage to act on them in time. Finally, there's that very small number of men who not only are aware, but are ready and willing to plunge forward at the first sign of daylight. And if you're prepared, it doesn't take much of an opening. I like the way Gayle Sayers, former Chicago Bears running great, used to phrase it. He said that all he wanted was twelve inches of daylight (a "hole," as they say in football) and he'd do the rest. By contrast, people who fall into the first category I mentioned are victims of the

WAITING-TO-BE-DISCOVERED THEORY

There's not much difference between these unfortunate financial rejects and those who fall under the World-Owes-Me-a-Living Theory. The individual who thinks the world owes him a living usually has been a victim of some accidental good fortune which led him irrationally to believe that good things would continue happening to him with no effort on his part. As the inevitable number of bad breaks set in, such a person focuses on them and tries to believe that bad luck is the cause of his failure. He has been deluded by his early good fortune.

But the guy who's waiting to be discovered doesn't even have a reason for thinking that anyone is going to put his name in lights. I'd like to explain to you what causes this fantasy to develop in the minds of so many, but frankly I have no idea how such an absurd notion comes about. Just make certain that you're not waiting to be discovered, because you'll pay an enormous price (in the form of frustration and bitterness) for nothing. Getting discovered only happens in cheap novels and bad movies. Whenever you catch yourself falling into the mental lapse of sitting around and subconsciously waiting for it to occur, think about the following true story and it should inspire you to get off your tail.

A friend of mine decided to go into TV production after spending nearly ten years in totally unrelated fields. He had absolutely no experience in the business, had a degree in—of all things—metallurgy, and had spent a couple of years as a real estate salesman. He disliked selling real estate so much that he made the decision to quit—right then—without clinging to the traditional job-security excuse. For several months, he suffered among the ranks of the unemployed. But he had made up his mind that he wasn't going to waste any more years—that one way or another he was going to get into something he had really wanted to do for a long time.

The deciding factor? He began knocking on doors . . . and knocking . . . and knocking. He told the same story to everyone he approached: he had no experience, he wanted to get into TV production so badly that he was willing to do absolutely anything, and he didn't care what he was paid to start. In short, all he wanted was the opportunity to prove himself. The result of this attitude was that someone eventually was sufficiently impressed to give him a try.

It was a great vicarious thrill for me to witness his progress. As one production was finished, he was immediately hired for another; he seldom found himself out of work even for a day—a rarity in that business, particularly when just starting out.

By the time you read this, he'll be much farther down the road to financial success, and I'll be surprised if he doesn't make it all the way to the top. If so, it will primarily be because he didn't wait around to be discovered; *he* went out and did the discovering. Once he decided he wanted it badly enough to pay the necessary price, he went after it. The fact that the first fifty doors he knocked on were slammed in his face merely proved theories with which he was already familiar: the One-in-the-Sack-Is-Worth-a-Hundred-in-the-Face Theory and the Theory of Sustenance of a Positive Attitude through the Assumption of a Negative Result. Old man Murphy has a terrible time with fellows like him.

PAYING FOR CONTROL WITH LOSS OF INTEGRITY

One caution regarding the subject of control: don't do anything to gain the upper hand in a situation if it's going to cost you in the long run. Remember, rule that is derived through fear isn't lasting. If you bully or play dirty pool, it's likely to catch up with you.

Above all, don't compromise your integrity in exchange for control. I can't tell you how such an opportunity might arise in your case, because each situation is so different. But when your integrity is on the line, you'll know it—if you're awake. When speaking of integrity, of course, I'm referring to your definition of integrity—not someone else's. You be the one to set your own standards, then stick by them. If you make money, but lose respect for yourself, it's all for naught; you'll have trouble enjoying the rewards.

THE CONFUSION CRUTCH

Whether it's a decision as to which line of work to go into, when to make the move, or how to handle a specific financial problem, don't be vulnerable to the advice of others. Listening to too many people can be fatal to your financial aspirations. And that includes listening to so-called experts—that vague group of individuals we quite thoroughly dissected while clearing the People Hurdle.

There's an element in every industry which I refer to as the Discouragement Fraternity—people who will go to great lengths to try to convince you that you can't make it in their field. Because of their own insecurity, their philosophy is never to let you get out of the starting gate, thus avoiding the obstacle of yet another player with whom they are not equipped to compete.

Intimidation through credentials is often used to accomplish this end. The attitude is: "How dare you be so presumptuous as to think you can succeed in this business when you've never even done it before. You have no 'papers' (license, diploma, award, etc.) or track record. After you've had some experience (which we're trying to prevent you from obtaining), come back and you might have a chance." The absurdity is obvious: you have to start somewhere.

But don't expect people to help you get started. Assume the worst. Count on certain neurotic individuals to do everything they can to block your path; if it doesn't happen, just consider it a lucky break. Remember the pertinent theories that relate to this: no one owes you anything (and you can be sure they know it), and nobody is going to "discover" you (though many may try to see to it that you don't discover yourself).

It's up to you to decide when you're ready, and when you are—jump! I've previously described it as the

LEAPFROG THEORY

You don't need "credentials"; you don't need the approval of others; you don't need the crutch of reassurance from acquaintances (they don't know you as well as you know yourself), as this may only confuse you. What you do need is to be ready, and only you know when that is. If and when you are, simply ignore the Discouragement Fraternity, the rest of the pack, and everyone else. Leapfrog to exactly the point on the ladder where you think you belong.

But don't make the leap until you can handle it. It won't work if you're not ready. That doesn't mean you have to fight your way up "through the ranks" or let someone else decide when you've "paid your dues." We each pay our dues in our own ways, and again only you know when

214

you've paid yours. Paying one's dues isn't necessarily analogous to age or number of years of experience. Some people are ready at twenty; others aren't ready at seventy. Nobody knows what you've gone through to prepare yourself; by the same token, you should never be presumptuous enough to resent someone else's seemingly quick ascent to the top. You don't know what the other guy went through to get there.

If you're not sure that you're ready, you probably aren't. The moment the time comes, you'll instinctively know it. When it does arrive, don't waste precious moments fighting your way through the pack; leapfrog over it and begin operating on a new level that suits you.

PLAYING YOUR OWN GAME

Again, you may feel that you have a weak posture, but as I stated in crossing the People Hurdle, it's not what you say or do that counts, but what your posture is when you say or do it. As I've proven to my own satisfaction, a person can control his posture to a great extent. It does take guts and preparedness, however, particularly if you don't have the advantage of a big bankroll.

Guts means the courage to have things your way or be ready to go on to the next deal. A guy may have more financial strength than you, but he can't make you play marbles with him if you refuse to do so. A rational man, according to Ayn Rand, ". . . never leaves his interests at the mercy of any one person or single, specific concrete. He may need clients, but not any one particular client— he may need customers, but not any one particular customer—he may need a job, but not any one particular job." [6]

Some people call this the ability to bluff, but the fact is that you're not bluffing if you really mean it. I make it a flat rule never to bluff. I'm careful about throwing out ultimatums to people, because once I do, I follow through—always! You can afford this luxury only if you're prepared at your job; if you aren't good at what you're offering the world, being tough is an exercise in silliness.

You decide—within the bounds of reality—how you want to play the game, then find the right person or persons with whom to play it. An old adage in sports is to avoid getting sucked into playing the other guy's game. It's easy to play your game against a weak team, but the tougher the opponent, the more alert you have to be. You should be the one to set the tempo and guidelines, then steadfastly adhere to them.

Remember, you don't need any one particular person, client, customer or job. Part of your success in having a good posture will depend upon the parties with whom you choose to deal. Those guys out there in the business-world jungle are people and therefore possess all the human characteristics previously discussed. Beware of the neurotics and Type Twos and Threes. Learning to choose your playing partners wisely goes a long way toward determining how well you play.

If you're down and out financially, don't try to play with the big boys right off. Work up to it or you're asking to get spanked. The biggies have many secrets I had to learn through trial and error. One that particularly applies here is the

SCARED MONEY THEORY

If you're running scared—if you don't have the bucks to back up your talk—it shows, especially to the guy who's sitting pretty. The tone of your voice, the look in your eye—you can try hard, but there are tests that will give you away. (I've learned to administer many of these tests myself, and they work.) When you're operating on scared money—meaning money you can't afford to lose or no money at all—it's not only hard to be convincing, it's also difficult to make rational decisions; and it's almost impossible to avoid being intimidated by the player who does have financial strength behind him.

If necessity dictates your being involved with someone out of your league, there are only two ways I know to combat the negatives you're up against. One I've already discussed: be damn good at whatever it is you do. If you're prepared, the big boys can pick up on that, too. They may know you don't have financial staying power, but they'll respect you for your talent and may be willing to deal with you on a reasonable basis if what you have to offer is sufficiently appealing.

Ironically, the other weapon only works when you're completely down and out. When I was groveling around in the gutter, nursing my leper sores, I finally came to the conclusion that I had one advantage over just about every other player: I had everything to gain and absolutely nothing to lose. The result was that I not only got mad at myself, but mad in general. I wasn't mad at any specific individual; I had just had it with all the pushing, shoving and harassment. I fought back with unrestrained ferocity, because nothing mattered anymore. In simple terms, if you'll excuse my crudeness, I refused to take any more shit from anybody. I didn't need to; I was already as low as I could get.

This sincere renaissance in my attitude was very instrumental in helping me climb out of the gutter and shed my leper bandages. It managed to lift me back onto the sidewalk and allowed me to reenter the ballpark. As I continued to climb the financial ladder, I slowly dispensed with this weapon; that's because I reached a point where I did have something to lose.

Be sure to remember this principle when you're on top: never push a guy so far that he has nothing to lose. If you do, he's likely to recoil. It's one thing to keep him under control, but don't push him beyond the point of caring what happens. He might just decide to jump ship and pull you overboard with him.

There are an endless list of things you can do to control your posture, but you have to sit down and think about them vis-à-vis your own personality. Don't forget the Self-

Indictment Theory: you don't have to undress yourself in public. Learn to zip the lip about the bad things as well as the good ones. Another action which will taint your posture is trying to portray Phineas T. Bluster; don't get over-excited and blow things out of proportion. When you do, your strength and stability immediately become suspect.

Another controllable area is your choice of words. There are ways in which things can be expressed which are more likely to keep any given situation on a smoother keel. Don't talk in terms of "problems"; no one likes problems. The proper wording is "items to be worked out." "Contracts" scare people (and are an invitation for Legalman to enter the picture). You don't want the other guy to sign a contract; it's just a "simple understanding" you're placing in front of him. The English language affords you a wide range of choices; use that fact to your advantage.

The Bottom Line of Being in Control: Getting Paid

Controlling all the facets we've discussed is of course meaningless if you aren't properly remunerated in the end. The saddest picture in business is the guy who strokes himself by working on one big deal after another, but always ends up with little or no financial reward. Everything else you do is just a means to an end—that end being getting paid for your services. If you're a deal-maker, rather than a salaried person, your main focus should always be on the actual, physical, mechanical way in which funds will be transferred from someone else's hands to yours. It won't just happen by accident—and almost never without a great fuss. A last warning on this point: checks don't count until they've actually cleared the bank.

If you can't control the getting-paid aspect, then eliminate the guy who has to do the paying and find a more direct way to make sure you get what you earn. The only solution is to take matters into your own hands, which is exactly what I was forced to do after finishing my last book. Having been a student of the expert intimidation game for many years, I was not surprised to find that every major publisher I approached turned down *Winning Through Intimidation*. One small publisher, however, did show a slight interest. The editor-in-chief told me that if I would do considerable cutting and rewriting, acceptable to the company's editors, he might be willing to give me a $1,500 advance, with the idea of eventually putting the book on the market at $6.95. I appreciated his generous offer, but reasoned that if his company was looking for safety, it would be much better off putting its money in a savings and loan at 5% interest. In the meantime, I could preserve my integrity by leaving my work in its original form and publish the book myself at $9.95—which I had calculated to be about $3.00 more per book than $6.95. My reasoning was that if what I had to say wasn't worth $9.95, it wasn't worth $6.95, either.

About 200,000 hardback copies later—after I had published it myself at $9.95—*Publishers Weekly* announced that *Winning Through Intimidation* was the second biggest-selling hardback of 1975, a year in which some 39,372 new titles had been published.

All I really had done was recognize the right thing to do in this particular situation, instead of being intimidated into doing the instinctive thing. After the experts had spoken, the instinctive thing would have been to throw the manuscript in my top drawer and get a job as a short-order cook. The right thing was to take matters into my own hands, which is exactly what I did. This reaffirmed my faith in the

SURE THEORY

There's only one way to be sure that your objective will be given the best shot possible: *take matters into your own hands and don't expect any help from anyone.* When you proceed in this manner, you're in control; when you count on outside help, you're out of control and looking for salvation. So simple, yet so powerful and true. The instinctive thing is to listen to others; the right thing is to take control.

WHO ARE THE PLAYERS?

Once you've made it to the playing field, the next step is to understand exactly who your opponents are. Here, as I see it, are the main players in the game of business (hereafter referred to as The Game), each of whom has his own unique way of tripping you up before you can clear the Financial Hurdle:

1) Schmexperts
2) Competitors
3) Legalman
4) The government
5) Murphy's ghost

The Schmexpert: A Tongue Looking for a Home

Blind acceptance of the advice of a supposed expert is bad enough, but listening to the advice of anyone who happens to stumble by is masochistic. The expert, whether or not he deserves it, at least has a powerful posture. The nonexpert giver of advice—technically known as a schmexpert—is able to intimidate you only if he's a very good intimidator or you're a very good intimidatee.

You're particularly vulnerable when you have problems, because schmexperts, in their anxiety to hand out advice, tend to swarm on a troubled individual like a sea of locusts. When molded together, atoms of schmexpert advice form molecules of schmexpert stupidity, which, when readily digested, can quickly convert you into a *schmuck*-spert. Perhaps you know a schmuckspert—a person who is failing in life because he's constantly intimidated into listening to the advice of schmexperts.

Above all, make sure *you* aren't a schmexpert. If you succeed in looking out for Number One—leading a happy, meaningful life—you won't feel the need to falsely assuage your ego by offering unsolicited advice to others.

Even though he's on the field, the schmexpert should not be taken as a serious threat to you. So long as you're aware and in control, you should easily be able to spot and ignore him.

You might question how you can ever be sure of anything if you aren't willing to listen to others. The reality is that you never can be sure of anything in this world, regardless of how many other people you listen to. If you're waiting for a guarantee that your plans will succeed, you'll never get off dead center. If you're concerned that there might be people out there who have some helpful inputs to offer, how can you ever feel secure until you've listened to every person in the world? How do you know that some guy on the other side of the globe doesn't have an important tidbit of information for you? Why just listen to the handful of people who happen to volunteer advice? Don't assume that simply because a guy is in close proximity to you, he has something worthwhile to say (particularly if he's volunteering it). Even if you could talk to every person who had something meaningful to say about your situation, it wouldn't be practical because you couldn't possibly weigh every fact and plug it into your equation in an entire lifetime.

The only answer is to analyze the facts at your disposal—preferably on your own, but at most in conjunction with the opinions you *solicit* from one or two people you respect—then go forward with a decision on the basis of expecting the worst, hoping for the best, and being prepared to handle whatever happens.

Competitors: The Only Other Guys Who Really Belong in The Game

The legitimate players are tough enough, even without outside interference from those who have no business down on the playing field. What makes competitors (all the players legally competing for dollars by offering better products or services) worthy opponents is that each one is different. One guy plays by one set of rules, someone else by another. You can't rely on the same tactics against every opponent. The only thing you can count on is that each competitor will act in his own self-interest at all times.

It's not that I'm advocating an "anything-goes" philosophy in business. It's more a matter of my facing the reality that I have nothing to say about it; anything *does* go whether I like it or not. Each guy plays his own version of the Definition and Line-Drawing Games; whether he admits it or even realizes it is totally irrelevant.

UNDERSTANDING THE NATIVE TONGUE

Business has its own version of the Translation Game—many versions, in fact, because of the numerous differences in players. When I was still an active participant in The Game, I used the original Sanskrit version of Financialese to translate the remarks of others. Sanskrit Financialese is the safest approach when translating, because it assumes the worst—which, as you already know, all too often comes to pass. Some examples:

OPPONENT: Don't worry about a thing.
TRANSLATION: You'd better start worrying about everything.

OPPONENT: Let me know if there's anything I can do to help.
TRANSLATION: Don't bother me.

OPPONENT: I don't operate like that; life is too short to make enemies.
TRANSLATION: I'll do anything necessary to put it to you; my life is too short to *worry* about making enemies.

OPPONENT:	My reputation is beyond reproach; you can check me out with my bank.
TRANSLATION:	I've managed to accumulate a lot of money in the bank by screwing guys like you who were stupid enough to think that all they needed to do was check me out with my bank.

Not every guy you face will be speaking old Sanskrit Financialese, but, just to be safe, why not translate his words into it anyway. If it turns out that he was using another version, let it be a pleasant surprise. But if Sanskrit Financialese is his native tongue, at least you won't be standing there in your underwear, scratching your head and trying to figure out what happened to your clothes.

TO BE INTIMIDATED, OR NOT TO BE INTIMIDATED: THAT IS STILL THE QUESTION.

Intimidation is a tool that's used throughout the business world—to one extent or another—by all players. It was discussed thoroughly in covering the People Hurdle, so just assume that everything that was said there goes double regarding financial matters. There will, of course, always be a horde of halo-wearers on the playing field—those self-righteous individuals who claim they've never touched the stuff. But, as always, their denials are irrelevant. Whether or not someone admits he employs intimidation as a tool, or really believes he doesn't, won't change the damaging effects it can have on you. It may only be a now-and-then thing, but, take my word for it, he does use it at times.

In actual fact, my experience has been that, as one can usually expect from a Protesting Lady, the guy who is most horrified by the suggestion that everyone uses intimidation is the very person who's most adept at applying it—and who applies it most frequently. That means he's a Type Two or Three, so look out!

All that need be emphasized here is that there are hundreds of ways in which intimidation can be used against you by business competitors. It takes skill to spot intimidation and it takes determination to refuse to be cast in the role of the intimidatee. Remember, experts don't have all the answers; a big bank balance is not synonymous with integrity; failure doesn't mean you're a loser—just that you're not afraid to take your licks and haven't quite made it yet.

TO THOSE IN THE KNOW, THE GAME IS CASH FLOW.

So long as paper money remains a somewhat viable means of trade, it's important to keep as much of it as possible on your side of the table. To the biggest players, it's one of the most important tools in the Jungle; it's called the Cash Flow Game. In simple terms, the object is to have the free use of the other guy's money for as long as possible.

Why is cash so important to the players? I can best explain it by the

FINANCIAL GEOMETRIC-GROWTH THEORY

This is a two-sided theory; it can work for or against you, using the same powers of multiplication in either case. On the positive side, it manifests itself as the phenomenon of "money makes money." A person with any degree of creativity does not make money in the proportions which surface factors might indicate. Money tends to grow exponentially in the right hands. Consider the following examples of what you've got going for you when you're cash-rich:

1) The cash can be put to work in the best combination of low-risk/high-yield investments possible, thus earning still more cash.

2) Because it creates a good image, it draws the best available people and deals to you.

3) It gives you staying power, which can sometimes be the difference between making or breaking an opportunity for a big killing.

4) You're more likely to make rational, sound decisions as opposed to scared-money decisions.

5) It can be leveraged—sometimes without putting up a dime. Just the use of a cash-rich balance sheet can be worth a fortune.

In other words, you can't really measure how much money can be made from a given amount of cash. The only limitation is the individual's creative use of his cash position.

Unfortunately it works the other way around, too. When you're in a cash squeeze, everything tends to go to hell. The negative momentum looks something like this:

1) When word is out that you're down on your luck, the good deals don't find their way to your desk anymore; the legitimate players avoid you.

2) Because you don't have staying power, you're always dealing from a position of weakness.

3) You're likely to make scared-money decisions—an example of short-term patching—instead of sound, long-term-solution decisions.

4) You have no leverage and nobody wants to loan you money.

5) To make matters worse, you have to spend a lot of time putting out fires, while the fellow with the cash is concentrating on how to make his pile still larger.

Comparing the two possible directions in which geometric growth can travel, it's not hard to understand why the biggies place such an emphasis on cash. No matter how hard you try, I doubt you'd be able to think of a unique cash-flow scheme. It seems that the big corporations have already come up with every conceivable ploy for using the other guy's dough interest free.

The "security deposit" on rental property is an old favorite. The non-interest-bearing checking account (where, in fact, banks usually make you pay a "service charge" for allowing them to have the free use of your money) is always a great laugher—for the banks. Basic monthly charges, unbeknownst to most people, are billed in advance by many utility and telephone companies—before the customer has had the use of the service for the period being billed. One way or another, everybody's doing it. If you're not, then you're at a decided disadvantage.

The big corporations, of course, are the best players of the Cash Flow Game, which is one of the reasons they were able to get so big in the first place—and remain big. They're also the most adept at camouflaging how they pull it off. The idea is to use just a few dollars from thousands, or preferably millions, of customers. This is not too noticeable to the individual, particularly when disguised as something like a "deposit," but to the giant corporation it can mean the interest-free use of millions of dollars—setting in motion the positive aspects of the Financial Geometric-Growth Theory.

The American Express Company is one of the few that talks about it openly, but that's because it's virtually their whole business. They bluntly refer to it as "the float." Here's how it works: American Express sells travelers checks to you, knowing that an average of sixty-five days will elapse between the time you give them your money and the time you cash the travelers checks. During that 65-day period, a large percentage of the cash is invested in, among other things, tax-exempt municipal bonds.

The obvious question is, why does a giant corporation, run by sophisticated money experts, invest in an entity which they certainly realize is bankrupt? (Local "governments" are merely extensions—subsidiaries, if you will—of the federal-government sham.) The answer, as Lysander Spooner detailed more than a hundred years ago, is fairly obvious. If you're a major government creditor, you *own* the government. Unfortunately, since the government has no means of paying back its creditors on its own, it must extort money from its "citizens"—through taxation, inflation, Social Security, tariffs, and any other scheme necessary. As Spooner also pointed out, money buys guns and manpower, which gives government the wherewithal to continue to get its hands on your assets without fear of physical resistance on your part. In short, money begets guns and guns beget more money.

Obviously you don't have the power to pull off the cash-flow schemes of giant corporations or the government, but you still can use the principle to your advantage on a smaller scale. Your circumstances are unique from those of all others, so you should lay out your own game plan regarding this matter. Just proceed from the basic axiom that every day during which someone else's dollar is in your pocket is like borrowing money interest free. On the other side of the coin, every day in which your dollar is in someone else's pocket, you're losing the use of that dollar and all the advantages it can give you through the Financial Geometric-Growth Theory. Put up a fight, whenever and wherever possible, before relinquishing money for security deposits, advance payments and other Cash-Flow-Game ploys. You don't always have alternatives, but there are many cases in which you do. Be alert for such opportunities and attempt to hang onto as many chips as possible for as long as you can. The chips are the material necessary to implement the Financial Geometric-Growth Theory on your behalf.

Legalman: The Croupier of The Game

Legalman is one of the players who shouldn't have been in The Game in the first place, but it's too late; he's already there. Worse yet, he's been endowed with incredible gall. He not only got into the park by sneaking under the fence, but once inside he took it upon himself to assume the role of head skimmer. Like a croupier at a crap table, while the suckers roll the dice, Legalman keeps raking in his take right off the top. He technically refers to this take as "legal fees." In theory, he doesn't actually skim. What he really does is charge you money in return for creating problems for you.

But the result is the same. Over the long haul, all the legitimate players (professionally referred to by Legalman as "clients") lose. The name of the game from Legalman's standpoint is to keep the hostilities flying back and forth, dragging each mess out as long as possible, and preferably making it messier. Time is always on Legalman's side. As the fighting continues, he just keeps raking in those chips with his awesome croupier stick.

Carl Sandburg seemed bewildered by the relentless raking prowess of Legalman:

> *When the lawyers are through*
> *What is there left . . . ?*
> *Can a mouse nibble at it*
> *And find enough to fasten a tooth in?* [7]

As previously emphasized, Legalman is the classic expert—the guy who can tell you all the reasons why you can't do something. In his case, it's not a matter of trying to convince you that you're incapable; rather, he either implies that there's a mysterious legal reason why something you want to do isn't possible or suggests that it would be a bad business move on your part. (How Legalman also managed to get into the picture as a business expert, in addition to being head croupier and interpreter of the law, is still one of the great snow jobs ever pulled off by any master intimidator.)

GREAT LEGALMAN MYTHS

Legalman is able to get by with this incredible hoodwinking because he has succeeded, mostly through government help, in enshrouding himself in a cloud of mystery. It's the old government protection racket again

"Don't be shy, boys. Step right up and keep the hostilities going."

—only those with government-approved "licenses" can practice. The easily intimidated mistakenly take this to mean that the law is beyond their comprehension—that only Legalman has a thorough understanding of it.

That, of course, is nonsense. First of all, the government has made just about everything illegal (and is working on outlawing whatever has not yet been covered), and that's easy enough for anyone to comprehend. Whether it involves sex, eating, drinking, owning a gun, or just about anything else you can think of regarding your private life and natural rights, the government either has already outlawed it or will do so as soon as it's called to its attention.

Even so, millions of naive people still believe that the services Legalman performs are sacred—that his government-approved certificate gives him some mystical powers of understanding. The truth, of course, is that you can obtain a divorce, form a corporation, and even die without the aid of Legalman. (On second thought, you can probably die more quickly—if not more easily—*with* the help of Legalman.)

Then there's Legalman's innate superior intelligence. It's assumed he's just plain smarter than the other players. But if this were true, there wouldn't be so many attorneys stupid enough to get caught breaking the law; they've been going to jail in record numbers the past few years.

THE ADVENTURES OF LEGALBOY

As to IQ-deficient attorneys, I specifically recall an experience I had with one who really wasn't Legalman, but Legal*boy*. He was one of those cubbies who just recently had sneaked in under the fence, fresh out of his final course in law school—Circumcision 401—and brimming over with Perry Mason fantasies. He was extremely anxious to begin wielding the spanking-new, pink croupier stick he had received as a graduation gift. In the Jungle, they call this being "wet behind the ears." The more sophisticated players just ignore Legalboy—as he runs around in his $85 permanent press suit and vest, shouting incoherent legal phrases at anyone who will listen —assuming he's just a member of the Diaper Corps who's gone straight and taken a job as a bank teller.

But if he's persistent, eventually a few brainwashed old-timers will begin to listen and he'll be able to start building up a "clientele." One of those unfortunate old-timers happened to be a creditor of mine from my Beverly Hills leprosy days. He had obtained a default judgment against me in the amount of approximately $24,000, only because, at the time he sued, I was in such a state of chaos I didn't even take the trouble to file a defense. I only owed him $8,000, but a government "law" allows a plaintiff to file for treble damages if he so desires; if you can't afford to defend yourself, the penalty for being poor is that you are deemed to owe three times the actual amount of the debt (just another example of government logic).

My creditor had stumbled upon Legalboy—unfortunately for him—at about the time I was starting to make it back up the financial ladder. He explained to the cubby that he had already obtained a judgment but hadn't been able to collect on it as yet. That's all Legalboy needed to hear. He went into his "go-get-'em" routine, calling me every five minutes, threatening, harassing, talking rapidly and incoherently—the normal approach for an overzealous cubby. It was an amateurish and phony tough-guy approach which—to my amusement— seemed to have his client completely mesmerized. Legalboy was on stage and loving every minute of it as he pressed forward with his "just-watch-me-nail-this-tortoise" routine.

The complete version of the story is fraught with typical Legalboy muffs, but the end result is all I'll trouble you with here. Cubby knew where my office was, and I knew that my bank account was right next door—with about $100,000 in it. All he needed to do was walk into the bank

with our old friend, the sheriff, and in five minutes they would have handed him $24,000 in cash. I've always reckoned that, at the outside, in about half a day—and for no more than a hundred bucks—I could find out in what bank or banks any guy in my home town had an account. But you don't learn important details like that in school. The moneymaking education comes in the Jungle—chiefly through experiencing adversity.

Having a lack of both Jungle experience and cerebral material, Legalboy didn't know how to go about this routine procedure. Luckily for me, he didn't even have the sense to take a logical, educated guess and at least check out the bank right next door! Instead, he was totally wrapped up in his "hard-nosed negotiations" act, which ended up costing his client dearly.

I had figured that if I got off for $13,000—considering the delicacy of the situation—it would be a bargain, so naturally my initial offer to settle was $3,000. The final settlement? When it was all over, Legalboy, who had put on a great show for his entranced client, "nailed" The Tortoise for $10,000—not in cash, but in monthly installments (an example of the Cash Flow Game) over a period of one year. Legalboy bristled with pride until I feared the cheap plastic buttons on his vest would pop off and ruin his whole image. His client was in complete awe. "How in the world do these legal brains do it? They're simply amazing," he must have been thinking to himself. Of course, what he would never know was that Legalboy had just lost him $14,000 by not being smart enough to walk next door to my bank and get more than twice the amount of the settlement—in cash—without having to go through his ferocious-cubby routine.

It's a nice story, because everyone got what he wanted. Legalboy had raked in a fee, solidified his relationship with a new client and, most important, had his ego massaged. The client believed he had succeeded in collecting on a debt owed to him—managing to forget that he had ended up with only about 40% of the face amount, less croupier's fees—and would go on to help perpetuate many of the great Legalman (and boy) myths. And The Tortoise was happiest of all—he had saved $14,000 and would gain the use of varying amounts of the $10,000 settlement money, interest free, over a period of one year.

DEFENDING AGAINST THE CROUPIER STICK

If you're one of the legitimate players, obviously you'd like to minimize the effects of Legalman as much as possible. To do so, you must first wake up to the reality that Legalman is just an average Joe—with a croupier's license—who happens to have discovered the secret of perpetuating myths and mysteries about himself and his "services." Apparently there is a trend toward this awakening, because a recent Harris Poll showed that less than one-fourth of the American public could find anything favorable to say about attorneys. But that's encouraging only if you're among the three-fourths who couldn't find anything nice to say.

Also, get it out of your head that everything is a "legal problem." Over the years, I came to realize that most of my legal problems weren't legal problems at all. They were just problems, problems I could resolve much better myself—and at no cost. I observed that, more often than not, once Legalman entered the picture, legal problems did suddenly begin to occur. The original problem usually gets relegated to a minor status with the advent of the new problems Legalman manages to inject into the situation. There are times when you may actually need Legalman, but exhaust all other possibilities first. He should be a last resort, and when you do have to call him, be prepared for a long, drawn-out struggle. Also, check your bank balance: you're going to need plenty of bread.

Unfortunately, your refusal to use Legalman is only half the battle; he also can be dragged into the deal by someone else. If you sell real estate or insurance, for example, you know what the appearance of Legalman all too often means: the loss of your deal. In businesses like these, where it's hard to keep Legalman on the sidelines, your best bet is to try to out-finesse him.

In the old days, when I had to go up against him regularly, I became adept at anticipating his "problems" in advance. I always tried to stay one step ahead of Legalman, solving the problems before he even brought them up. After a while, you get to know what his standard deal-killing favorites are, so you try to cut them off at the pass. And, of course, I never talked in terms of problems; everything he thought of as hindrances to the deal became "items to be taken care of" when expressed by me. To the degree I was then able to follow through and actually take care of them, I was usually successful.

The ideal, naturally, is to be in an occupation which affords the luxury of not having to deal with people who think it's illegal to consummate a transaction unless Legalman is on hand. The biggest deals of my life were made without Legalman's representing either the other party or me. That has to be more than mere coincidence. The fact is that in every one of those cases, the other party not only was sophisticated, but wanted to conclude the deal as much as I did. Those were the big differences—sophistication and the common desire to work the situation out.

All this firsthand experience with Legalman has led me to the

LEGALMAN PROPER-USE THEORY

From the stories I've related, this one should be obvious to you. Legalman definitely has his place; it's just not on the playing field, getting in the way of the real players. There is, however, a proper time for Legalman's services. I'll state the case simply:

When to use Legalman: If you desire to back out of a deal but are embarrassed to do so on your own.

When to lock Legalman in his cage: When you're serious about closing a deal.

That rests my case for and against Legalman.

The Only Player Who Plays with Guns

Schmexperts are harmless if you know how to handle them. Competitors vary in ability, and you generally can avoid those with whom you do not wish to play. Legalman is a serious obstacle, yet with enough effort you often can succeed in keeping him off the field. With the government, however, you have a problem of a completely different dimension. While Legalman sneaks in under the fence and only uses a croupier stick, the government uses gunpower to enter the stadium and continues using it down on the playing field. This puts all the other players at a decided disadvantage, because it's hard to maneuver around a bullet.

Of course, the average Magoo or Ostrich doesn't see, or refuses to see, the reality that the government makes all its moves under the threat of force, which helps its cause enormously. There are many reasons for this behavior on the part of Magoos and Ostriches. To begin with, such people are intimidated through custom and tradition into blind cooperation with the government's wishes. They are further intimidated into peaceful cooperation through the government's use of slogans—usually "patriotic" in nature. Finally, the government is so big that few people give any thought to challenging it. This allows it to maintain control through the unspoken threat of violence, without its actually having to use its gunpower.

It's no wonder there's an "anything-goes" attitude in business when you consider that one of the players "legally" uses guns to steal from the other players. Seen in this light, the Financial Hurdle becomes a game played by you and every other citizen, using your wits and skills to collect your share of the available chips, but at the same time trying to protect your assets from a giant robber baron who intends to grab as many chips as possible. Worst of all, this robber baron has the free use of guns to make sure no one interferes with its theft.

Never deceive yourself by refusing to face the reality that the government is your chief adversary when it comes to making money. All your competitors combined are not a force formidable enough to compare to the government, if for no other reason than because the government won't allow them to use guns. The plain truth is that Big Government is the most ominous obstacle in the path of the person seeking to look out for Number One.

GOVERNMENT MYTHOLOGY: A STUDY IN WORD USAGE

Compared to the mystique behind which the government has managed to hide, Legalman's myths are elementary. It's amazing what can be done by spending a few billion dollars on propaganda and by allowing a sufficient number of years to pass to give the propaganda time to become second nature to people. Enslavement, for example, can be made to seem both acceptable and respectable merely by rephrasing it as "military duty."

Another clever use of words is demonstrated by the fact that the government itself is thought of as a living entity to the average unthinking individual. This is a premeditated illusion. The government doesn't have wants, needs, desires and emotions of its own. The word *government* is a label given to a group of individuals who draw government paychecks, but, in its most practical sense, it refers to the individuals in that group who possess the most power.

One of the reasons the government acts in a conglomeration of contradictory ways, and why virtually everything it attempts ends in colossal failure, is the very fact that it is not a living entity. As a result, the most powerful government individuals, acting in their own best interests, are constantly struggling against one another—vying for more power and trying to bring about "legislation" which

"Mind if Big Brother plays, too, fellas?"

they desire. The natural result is the slapstick comedy you've been witnessing in Washington for years.

To think of the government as some sort of sacred entity, then, is to believe that the human beings who actually comprise it are sacred. Many people cherish the government because they see it as a means to an end for them. But the government is not a means to an end for the individual who is looking out for Number One and not trying to interfere forcibly with others. The government *is* the end—for every person who draws a government paycheck, particularly those at the top of the ladder.

The question is, if what the government has to offer is so great for the individual—if everyone really wants it—why must the Washington Gang use force? The obvious answer to that question is that what the government offers is not great; it is restraint of freedom. The practical consequences of government are that it uses the threat of violence either to

1) Force you to stop doing something you want to do,

2) Force you to do something you don't want to do, or

3) Force you to give up something that's rightfully yours.

Who needs the government for this? You can walk through Central Park at night and accomplish the same things.

Setting the Example for the "Anything-Goes" Philosophy

Then there's the mythology of "law." Aside from the government's use of force inviting an "anything-goes" atmosphere, government laws set an open example for everyone. It's monkey see, monkey do. If Big Brother can "legally" confiscate the assets of individuals, force them into "kill-or-be-killed" situations (patriotically referred to as "war"), interfere with their sexual freedoms, and perpetrate thousands of other violations of natural human rights, then you can't blame the poor guy who's just trying to make ends meet for having an anything-goes attitude, too.

You don't have to have a very high level of awareness to realize that one doesn't prove that a law is right or moral merely by stating that it *is* a law. The only relevant consideration with regard to government laws is whether or not they are in violation of natural laws and natural rights. Academicians have used various terms to define natural law and natural rights, but I think they can be summed up rather simply: Every man has the natural right to pursue his own happiness in any way he chooses and to retain ownership over all the fruits of his labor, so long as he does not forcibly interfere with the same rights of others.

To say that laws are necessary to protect individuals sounds all right until you realize that most laws interfere with the freedom of individuals—particularly the endless number of absurd victimless-crime laws on the books. How can any group of people—whether it calls itself a government or any other name—know what's good for you when you have desires, ambitions, needs, beliefs and standards different from anyone else's? How can they act in your best interest when they don't even know you? Only you can decide what's best for you; anyone who tries to do it for you, through force, is an aggressor and is in violation of natural law.

No matter what kind of fancy words one uses to decorate the facts, the truth always remains: government restrains you, and restraint violates natural law. In the case of money matters, that restraint manifests itself as a barrier which keeps you from transacting business freely in the marketplace, thus presenting the biggest obstacle to your clearing the Financial Hurdle.

HOW FORMIDABLE IS THE GOVERNMENT AS AN OPPONENT?

All the government really does is: steal a large portion of your personal income; close the doors to your business if you don't fork over a specified percentage of your profits; make the money you do retain worth less every day by illegally printing new currency that has no value behind it; charge you for the privilege of living in your own home ("property taxes"); tell you what minimums you have to pay your employees and whom you must hire; dictate what you can charge for your products or services (through price controls handed down by the FTC); pass judgment on what products you can sell (through the FDA); and—the real coup de grace—make it illegal for you to compete against its own poorly run monopolies (such as the Postal Service).

My God, even a walk through Central Park can't accomplish all that!

Defending Against the Monster

In this day and age, the government's mystique and sanctity are slowly disappearing. The true facts are becoming too noticeable in your pocketbook, in your home and in most aspects of your life. But that doesn't do you much good if there's no way to stop the illegal aggression it carries out against you.

Is there any way to stop it? In all honesty, you can't expect to put a complete stop to the interference, but you certainly can do a number of things to hinder the government's efforts to hinder your efforts to succeed. Just start with the assumption that if you can think of a way to make a profit by creating a beneficial product or service for which people are willing to pay you, sooner or later the government will get wind of it and try to make it illegal. If ever there were a situation in which the Theory of Sustenance of a Positive Attitude through the Assumption of a Negative Result could save you from utter frustration, it's on the playing field vis-à-vis the government.

This attitude is very important where the government is concerned, because it has the power to make sure (through laws and regulations) that circumstances will constantly change. And as we've discussed before, you're in a much better position to move in another direction if you're prepared for changing circumstances in advance. The major-league entrepreneurs like Hughes and Kennedy always seemed to have a knack for moving quickly from one business to another—just in time to escape a new law or take advantage of an old one in another field.

With the "Sustenance" attitude as a foundation, your best bet from a business standpoint is to try to avoid as much contact with the government as possible. It drives the power-holders crazy when they don't have a means of keeping tabs on your day-to-day activities, but even with their millions of employees, they can't watch over everyone around the clock. In order to compensate for this deficiency in the system, they've set up a network of "regulatory agencies" and "commissions," the number and scope of which are staggering. These bodies—the SEC, FTC, FCC, ICC, FDA, CAB, and hundreds like them—are all totally illegal, of course, in every respect. But that's also irrelevant from your standpoint, since the reality is that they do exist and will continue to exist.

All of the agencies are headed by nonelected officials who have virtual carte blanche to make or break any individual or company. More often than not, their arbitrary regulations see to it that competition is eliminated, which protects giant corporations and, as always, guarantees that you, the consumer, will pay higher prices for less service and worse products than you would in a free market.

If you're in business for yourself, my best advice regarding government is to try to pick an industry or occupation that's regulated less than most of the others. For example, promoters who still try to play the acquisition/merger public-company game are just asking to be shot down. The SEC is the most gestapo-like of all the agencies and has gone so far beyond even its original illegal purpose that it's virtually impossible not to be in violation of some SEC regulation if you're in any way involved in a public company. The SEC has not only single-handedly destroyed the entire stock market in this country, but continues to leap into areas far removed from "policing" the securities industry.

If you're already in a heavily regulated business and don't think it's practical to get out (which may be a bad long-term judgment), then all you can hope to do is keep a low profile and abide by the particular regulatory agency's unreasonable demands with as little fuss as possible. Never take regulatory agencies on head-to-head. You'll only be wasting valuable time, energy and money. The deck is stacked from the beginning so that even if you win in court, they'll see to it that you lose down the road.

If you do manage to stay out of an industry or occupation not currently burdened with a strong-arm government agency, make the safe assumption that such will not always be the case. Remember the Changing Circumstances Theory and be prepared to make your move when the player with the gunpower changes the rules.

Government Securities: An Investment in Toilet Paper

Another thing you can do to protect yourself from your foremost adversary is not risk any of your dollars investing in it or taking its guarantees seriously. Since the government is bankrupt, its "securities" are necessarily worthless, too. Its ability to repay bonds and notes depends solely on its continued success in confiscating an ever-increasing percentage of your income, and at some time there could very well be an all-out tax strike by the masses. (By some estimates, the number of persons now refusing to file tax returns is nearing five million.) When the percentage of income which people take home is no longer enough to meet even ordinary expenses, rebellion may be their only alternative. Should an all-out tax revolt ensue, the government will be without means to make good on its obligations to you or any other citizen who has invested in it. If the government defaults with giant corporations, or a select number of families in the financial-empire class, these biggies will merely clamp down on the government leaders a little harder and dictate to them even more than in the past. On the other hand, a default on any securities you hold will mean only one thing: you're out of luck.

The same goes for government "guarantees." Since there's nothing behind them, they're a complete joke. For goodness' sake, don't have everything you own tied up in a bank or savings and loan, feeling secure because you're told that your funds are guaranteed by the Federal Deposit Insurance Corporation. In a crash, there won't be enough of a reserve even to cover administration expenses of the inevitable mess, let alone pay off a dime to anyone. Like the Social Security scheme, the FDIC is a cruel hoax on millions of innocent people who have been lulled into a false sense of security.

Since the government is so slogan-oriented, try this catchy one on for size: *Don't invest in the government!*

Hitting You Where It Really Hurts

Finally, there's the heart of the whole matter: the outright theft of your income. If you've been a victim of intimidation through custom and tradition, intimidation through slogan, or any other form of government intimidation intended to enlist your cooperation in the government's taking of your chips, catch hold of yourself and think rationally. Put an end to the nonsensical perversion that surrounds evasion or avoidance of income tax. A man isn't cheating a thief when he attempts to prevent the thief from robbing him. He's merely defending his natural rights in trying to protect his assets from intruders. A "loophole" isn't something naughty; it's a "legal" way of combating an illegal law until such time as the government passes still another law to make that method illegal, too; it's a currently "legal" way to keep someone from taking what's rightfully yours.

You have a moral obligation to yourself to defend your

possessions against a robber—no matter what mask the thief hides behind. The only valid consideration is the risk involved. I would never suggest that you haphazardly break tax laws—or any law—though they may be immoral. What I am suggesting is that you realize that just because something is a law, that doesn't mean it's right, moral or legal (by the standards of natural law). You owe it to Number One to do everything possible—within the limits of common sense and good business prudence—to protect your assets from the government. The wise man, however, will carefully weigh the risk—the odds of getting caught and the potential downside penalty—against the money to be held back from the robber, then act accordingly.

You can also go to extremes. I've known many people who have set up complex tax structures to protect themselves, forming foreign corporations and using various tax shelters, but I sometimes wonder if the time and money spent putting it all together is worth the amount of money that is actually protected in the end. Again, your individual circumstances will dictate what's best for you, but don't overcomplicate your situation unless it's the most practical type of defense—meaning that the net dollars saved justify it.

In my case, because I publicly state the kinds of things I'm writing here, the cheapest way for me to deal with the gun-wielding player is to keep my structure simple and fork over the loot demanded of me with as little fuss as possible. Because many people are willing to pay for my ideas, that more than offsets the disadvantage of having to make my financial life an open book to the government's henchmen. I lay my possessions right on the table and allow them to frisk me without resistance. But if I were in a different type of business, I would undoubtedly be seeking every way possible to keep the theft down to a minimum, always weighing the risks against the potential savings before deciding on a game plan.

One last thing about the government and its relationship to you as a player: it's up to you to decide how many chips it's going to take to buy the freedom necessary for you to be happy. But do consider the realities of the situation—that the government does steal from you and continues to pass new laws which make it increasingly difficult for you to realize your financial objectives. Incentive, as it was once known in this country, is pretty much dead, because virtually every method for making big dollars is illegal. In view of this reality, if your financial goals are great, you should be fair with yourself and honestly weigh the odds against your achieving such aspirations under the ever-worsening tide of government interference. Then ask yourself if the risk (the years and energy you'll have to expend, not to mention potential run-ins with the government) is worth it. The pragmatic question becomes: Are the odds against me too great to warrant my paying an inordinately high price for something that may be impossible to accomplish in this day and age?

It's just something to think about. On reflection, you may decide to lower your ambition a few rungs, carve out your little niche, avoid the player with the guns as much as possible and concentrate a little more on enjoying life. If that's the way you can gain the greatest amount of pleasure during your lifetime, isn't that really what looking out for Number One is all about?

The Invisible Player: Murphy's Ghost

The ghost of old man Murphy has played a major role throughout this book, so there's little I can say about him that you don't already know. I must list him as a player, even though he's not a living entity, because he is a major factor in The Game. Murphy has a special attachment to the Financial Hurdle. Love, friendship and other aspects of life are fun to mess up, but making people trip over the Financial Hurdle gives Murphy his greatest delight.

The amazing thing is that he doesn't have to use guns or a legal license to accomplish it. As you'd expect of any ghost, he's just out there somewhere, creating problems to thwart your every financial move. What to do about him? Well, you can't fight something you can't see, so you're about as helpless against him as you are against government guns. The only answer is not to let him throw you, which is achieved by being prepared for his ever-recurring appearances.

One of the best methods of preparation, as you know, is to keep the "Sustenance" Theory in mind. Hope for the best, but assume the worst; if you're prepared, you'll be able to handle the worst when it occurs—which is often. All Murphy really wants is a little respect. It's when you start getting cocky and assume you have everything under control—when you can't see how anything can possibly go wrong—that you raise his ire and are in danger of his really putting it to you. He's relatively happy so long as you heed his bylaws. They're worth repeating:

> *Nothing is as easy as it looks.*
> *Everything takes longer than you expect.*
> *And if anything can go wrong—it will*
> *At the worst possible moment!*

And if Murphy has tripped you up to the point that you haven't been able to make it out of the starting gate, don't despair. He's just testing your guts. A wise old man once told me, after I had long tried in vain to get to the first step on the Financial Ladder, that once you got the hang of it—once you started making money—it would come in such abundance and so quickly that you'd wonder why you had so much trouble making it in the first place. I found that hard to believe at the time, but he was right. Having made the trip more than once, I can tell you that his description was completely accurate. But Aristotle was also correct: it's that first step that's such a bitch.

WHAT TO DO WITH IT ONCE YOU'VE GOT IT

Let's assume that you've come through The Game successfully. You've ignored the schmexperts, outplayed your competitors, out-finessed Legalman, dodged government bullets, and shrugged off Murphy's best attempts to confound your efforts. You've now cleared the Financial Hurdle. You've attained the monetary success necessary to give you the freedom to concentrate properly on looking out for Number One. Is it time to lie back and wait to be awarded your freedom trophy?

It doesn't quite work that way. First of all, it's important to your long-term happiness to concentrate on not changing who and what you really are; don't try to be something you're not. Your financial condition may have improved, but you still are you. If you start deluding yourself, you may lackadaisically fall into the Tend-To trap and end up right back at the starting gate again. Don't overfeed your ego; it should require less intake than it did before you achieved your financial aims. Continue being honest with yourself and keep advertising the real you to the world. Don't suddenly start expecting things of people; go right on taking matters into your own hands.

Unfortunately, even if you're able to handle your success, you can't expect everyone around you to accept it without a few neurotic pangs. Though you may not change in the slightest, it's inevitable that some people will alter their attitudes toward you. It's part of the price you pay for success—something you have to learn to accept and deal with.

Sometimes this will manifest itself as slander, which, as we discussed, stems from jealousy and self-contempt. Don't be naive enough to expect everyone to stand by, without envy, and allow you to enjoy your triumph. The smaller the person's mind, the more he wishes you to be unhappy. It aggravates him to see others succeed. His irrational ego is fed by the smashing of yours.

There's nothing you can do to change a person's attitude toward you—but you *can* ignore him.

Money can't buy happiness, but it can get you all the guilt you want.

It's perverted nonsense to believe that your success causes others to suffer (unless they're neurotic, which is something you can't control). Be proud of your achievements, not ashamed. If you're lucky enough to obtain material wealth, don't allow anyone to cheat you out of enjoying it.

It's irrational to think you should repent because there are people who live in poverty. Unless someone is poor because you robbed him, no downtrodden individual is your responsibility and shouldn't be a mental blockade to your happiness. On the contrary, you're not being a burden to the rest of the world if *you* aren't living in poverty.

The worst cases of wealth-guilt complexes are generally seen among people who have inherited, rather than earned, their fortunes. They often feel they don't really deserve their money. If one has this neurosis, the rational thing for him to do is use his assets as a base for accomplishing productive feats of his own, rather than sit around and pout about not being worthy of his station in life.

I recently read an alarming article about a group of guilt-ridden heirs. All were from wealthy families, and, in an effort to rid themselves of self-imposed guilt, they had formed an organization for the purpose of figuring out "socially useful" ways of giving away some of the chips they had inherited.

How sad that they felt compelled to waste potentially productive and creative energy, as well as capital, just because they had allowed certain members of society to saddle them with guilt feelings for something they not only weren't responsible for, but which wasn't hurting anyone else.

Who shall be the ruler, you or your money?

If you don't allow people to get to you via jealousy or guilt ploys, the only thing that can stop you from enjoying your financial success is you. Your attitude toward money is critical. Either you control your money or it will control you. There are two opposite ways in which your chips can gain the upper hand.

The first is if you let them burn a hole in your pocket. If you've never had big bucks before, it's easier than you might think to get carried away by the great feeling that comes with financial strength. If it's been a long, hard struggle to get over the Financial Hurdle, it's natural to want to enjoy so much of it so fast that you wake up some morning only to find yourself back in the starting blocks. There is a far more rational approach you can take.

TOUCHIES AND NO-TOUCHIES THEORY

The idea for this one comes from an old friend of mine who is affectionately referred to in the Jungle as Black Bart—a down-home, shoe-shufflin' boy from Kansas. Black Bart's simplistic approach to business always amazes me. In just five years he went from working as a salesman of inexpensive tract-homes to a guy with a net worth in the neighborhood of $15 million, so when he talks, I listen.

Black Bart reckons that once a guy has made it, the wise thing to do is have two piles of chips—one labeled "Touchies" and the other "No-Touchies." The Touchies are the chips you use to buy houses, cars and other goodies and also for risk investments. The No-Touchies are the ones you don't use for luxuries and with which you don't take chances. The objective revolves around an "if." If you happen to screw up and have your Touchies wiped out, you don't have to start all over again; you still have your No-Touchies to fall back on. (The last time I saw Black Bart, his knack for playing The Game was causing his Touchies pile to become so large, I doubt that he'll ever have to worry about the "if" factor in this theory.)

The other way that money can control you? Put it like this: there's only one thing worse than living beyond your means, and that's living beneath your means. In that case, money becomes an end in itself. Money can buy objects and labor which not only make your life more comfortable, but which can directly or indirectly give you the freedom which is the real reward for crossing over the Financial Hurdle in the first place.

What good is money if you still perform tasks you dislike—tasks which you easily could afford to pay others to do? If you're so afraid of losing your money that it's a traumatic experience to cough up a dollar for something you truly desire, you haven't gained freedom—you've imprisoned yourself. Or, put another way, if you allow money to rule you rather than the other way around, you're out of control, which means you aren't in a position to make rational decisions, which in turn means you aren't looking out for Number One.

The truest words ever spoken: Fame is fleeting.

Oh, how it burns your tailbone to make that long slide back down the hill. It's so sweet at the top—the luxuries, the applause, the attention. However, as I've so unhappily discovered in the past, it's at the precise moment when you're enjoying it most that you're in the greatest danger of losing it all so fast you'll think you were dreaming.

If you're fortunate enough to make it to the top, never forget how quickly it can all turn into a nightmare. Be comfortable and enjoy life, but if you're going to do a proper job of looking out for Number One, keep a close eye on reality. Competitors are plotting; Murphy's ghost is out there; the government plays with guns and constantly changes the rules; schmexperts will forever give you bad advice if you get lax. Circumstances absolutely will continue to change. If you're not ready for the changes —if you're up in the clouds somewhere, off on a Tend-To tangent—look out! Remember that reality has no regard whatsoever for your faulty perception.

In reminding myself of how quickly fame can slip away, I think of David Seabury's likening life to a game of chess, warning that "Fate sits on the other side of the table watching your moves. . . . Make your moves according to the shifts of fortune, play by play. . . ."[8]

I'm on my third time around now. Because of future circumstances which may be beyond my complete control —mostly due to Murphy and his hidden land mines—I never discount the possibility of being knocked from my perch. If it happens, it happens. But being knocked from the top is one thing; diving is quite another. The two times I made the trip downhill, nobody laid a hand on me. I managed it all by myself.

How? By being lackadaisical and failing to abide by the very rules which had lifted me to the top in the first place. The principles in this chapter have always worked for me; it's only when I become lax and fail to remember and apply them that I begin doing belly-smackers. And if I carelessly wander from these principles again, I have little doubt that I will most certainly—and deservedly— bite the dust once more.

But frankly I'm getting tired of the climb back to the top. While it's a reality that many factors are beyond my control, I'd like to think that at least I won't ever again be foolish enough not to follow my own philosophy.

I guess only time will tell . . .

7

The Friendship Hurdle

AFTER THE VICTORY, THEN WHAT?

It was a long and treacherous climb from the Ryder truck to the top of Fat Cat Hill. I'll never forget the day when the conclusion of a certain financial transaction lifted me over the top. I finally was free to concentrate on happiness.

I worked the same number of hours that day and went about my usual routine as though nothing had changed. But a strange atmosphere pervaded my office. There was a certain solitude—a lack of elation—which I couldn't quite put my finger on. After all that struggling, shouldn't I have been more excited?

When my staff left the office at the end of the day, I lingered behind. I sat down at the head of my conference table and began to reflect. There was total silence in the office as I sat pondering the distance I had traveled in those last few years. It exhausted me even to think about

253

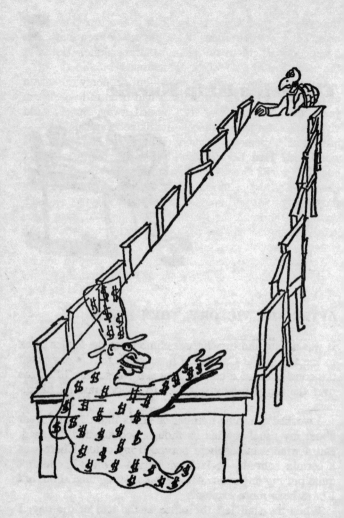

"Well, junior, how does it feel?"

the arduous road I had taken back to the top. Somehow, none of it seemed right. I should have been out celebrating, I thought to myself, not sitting alone, staring at the other end of an 18-foot conference table.

It was strange—really strange—but suddenly the vision of Harold Hart came to mind. It had been at least fifteen years since the old guy had passed away, but I could vividly see him sitting there—in silk robe and pajamas— in his Park Avenue apartment. Where was Harold now, I wondered? Had he discovered that life really wasn't a hoax, after all? Or was he now nothing but dust?

As my thoughts flowed, I pretended I could see him sitting at the far end of the table. He was saying, with an eerie kind of smirk on his face, "Well, junior, how does it feel? You've paid the price—you've gone through the struggles—and you're finally on top. Now what?"

The smirk I imagined was his (or my) way of letting me know that, after all those years, I had *become* Harold Hart. But I couldn't accept that; I had invested too much of my life to believe that it might all be a hoax. There had to be more to life than just struggling to make it financially, then finding nothingness once you got there.

But something definitely was missing. After pondering for more than an hour, it finally came to me. It was the empty table. Victory celebrations for a party of one aren't much fun; they tend to be on the quiet side. I was bucking another law of Nature—attempting something that was virtually impossible—by trying to be all things to myself.

What a paradox: to maximize my possibilities for a joyous life, I needed people—the same species which had caused all the complications and roadblocks in my attempts to look out for Number One. The pieces finally were beginning to fit into place. One requires people in his life because one has needs, and it simply isn't possible for an individual to fill all his own needs. The number of friends required to do the job depends on how many of one's needs can best be filled by others rather than himself. That was quite a revelation. With all his negative characteristics, man was still a necessity in the happiness formula. There were some damn great human beings out there; I knew there were, because I'd had occasion to meet them in the Jungle. There were individuals in the People Store who were considerate, who had self-esteem, who didn't expect something for nothing, and from whom one could derive great enjoyment.

I scanned the gigantic empty table once more. There was no question about it: the missing element in the victory celebration was people. Then and there I faced the reality that life can be a very lonely experience without them. It had seemed that men ought to be able to find fulfillment without being involved with others. But I had long since dispensed with "ought to's." The "is" of the situation had clearly identified itself. It was now my job to act on it.

THE BIG L

Many surveys over the years have pinpointed loneliness as one of the biggest problems most people face, if not the biggest. Before you can cultivate friends, you have to conquer loneliness. So let's get it under control once and for all—lay it right out on the table and give it a thorough once-over. I'll begin with a very basic reality, one which puts loneliness in its truest perspective.

ONE-TO-A-BOX THEORY

No matter who you are, no matter what you've accomplished in your lifetime, no matter how many friends you have, and no matter how close you may be to one or more persons, the reality is that when you go down for the final count, you'll be in that wooden box all by yourself. I've yet to attend a funeral which featured two people in one coffin as the main attraction. You came into this world alone and, whether you like it or not, you'll be going out the same way. Once you face the reality of man's ultimate aloneness, you have the foundation for understanding and conquering loneliness.

I've seen people do some mighty self-destructive things out of the fear of being alone. How can one overcome such a fear? There's only one way to cope with the trauma of loneliness and that's to come to grips with the realities regarding it, which in turn means coming to grips with yourself.

To do this, you must understand that no matter how close you are to one or more other persons, you will always be an entity unto yourself. No one else can ever know all there is to know about you—how you think, how you feel, what your secret desires are—no matter how close they are to you. In that respect, you're alone all your life. You're a unique entity and no one can crawl inside your brain and bring about a psychological merger of two separate beings. A part of your life, yes—but not a part of *you*. Once you understand that, you'll be able to put loneliness in proper perspective.

Since you entered the world alone, will be alone all your life (in the context just discussed), and will go out alone, it would be wise to examine yourself thoroughly. If you're going to be spending so much time with Number One, doesn't it make sense to get to know him a little better? This is what coming to grips with yourself means. If you can reach the stage where you're able to appreciate the great things you have to offer Number One, you'll clearly understand what it means to be "never less alone than when alone."

You can't fully appreciate the company of others if the fear of loneliness is always in the back of your mind. You can't enjoy people if you can't enjoy yourself. Those who can't seem to grasp this principle often go to embarrassing and frustrating lengths to conquer loneliness through overkill—by surrounding themselves with too many people too much of the time.

A female singer-friend of mine, who had been involved in a three-year love affair with a famous male vocalist, described the effects of this irrational approach to the loneliness problem. She explained that after his performance each night, her lover would invite a mob of people up to his hotel suite, talking and drinking until five or six o'clock in the morning. He would do just about anything to keep the last guest from leaving. She described him as being virtually terrified of being alone. Regardless of all the glamour, adulation and publicity, he apparently never had taken the trouble to know and/or learn to like himself.

But such action is self-deceiving. The solution to loneliness isn't to flood your environment with every make and model in the People Store. Some of the loneliest moments in my life have been spent in large crowds. Being "popular"—if that's what you're after—has nothing to do with how many people you know. It's having relationships which are held together by mutual admiration and respect. If you have just one solid friendship of that kind, you're probably more "popular" than most. In simple terms, it's a matter of quality over quantity. You can have many acquaintances and still be very lonely, indeed.

People will compromise their integrity in many ways in an effort to avoid loneliness. Some, for example, seek to attract "hangers-on." One doesn't need to be a celebrity to have them; they're readily accessible to all of us. Men and women also get trapped into conforming to the ways of others—against their own principles—in an effort to gain the acceptance of the greatest number of people. Sadly, such a blanket approach usually backfires because one actually decreases the chances of his finding that handful of meaningful relationships which really *could* add to his happiness.

Don't panic and try to use the quantity approach; you're being unfair to yourself. If you feel the necessity to be "one of the boys" (or girls), then you should re-enroll in high school; you have no business running around loose in the adult world.

A Need for Segregation

The healthiest orientation is to see your life as divided into two distinct halves: a social life and a solitary life. There's not only room for both, but both are necessary. If you can learn to enjoy both of these areas to the fullest, loneliness will cease to be a problem.

The whole point is that being alone doesn't have to be, and shouldn't be, a lonely experience; it can be very enriching—if you have admiration and respect for Number One and are able to develop a good friendship with him. Appreciate solitude for what it can be—an opportunity to do a multitude of things which cannot be done as well when others are around. "I never found the companion," said Thoreau, "that was so companionable as solitude." [1]

Reading is one of the most delightful of all experiences —one you should explore if its treasures have escaped you. It's also something that's far more enjoyable when there's no one around to distract you. Along with the pleasure it brings, it also broadens your horizons, giving you more to offer people when you're living the social side of your life.

Meditation—understood and practiced correctly—is definitely more rewarding when experienced alone. It relaxes you and, in the case of Factual Meditation, helps bring forth solutions to many problems which you aren't able to think through properly when others are around. The bonus is that, by improving your own state of mind, you increase your value to others.

Aloneness should not be synonymous with loneliness. Both it and your social life have their places. Come to grips with yourself and you will have come to grips with loneliness. If you can keep aloneness in its proper perspective—see it as an opportunity to experience some of life's greatest joys—you can eliminate the word *loneliness* from your vocabulary.

If you can't enjoy your own company, you certainly

can't expect others to. When you use your moments of solitude intelligently, rather than allow them to produce unfounded fears of loneliness, you'll find yourself enjoying much more those hours you do spend with other human beings.

The Social Side

If you're successful in developing an appreciation for the private, solitary side of your life, the friendship area becomes much easier. But let's not talk about friendship until we've defined exactly what it is we're after. What is a friend, anyway?

The dictionary, in its usual vague approach to definitions, says, among other things, that a friend is "one attached to another by affection." As you've already seen, I'm not particularly big on dictionary definitions, but this one aids me in making a key point. Friendship, like happiness, is not an either/or situation. Someone cannot be classified merely as "a friend" or "not a friend." It's a matter of degree. You can be "attached by affection" to a hundred different people, but it won't be the same degree of attachment or affection in any two cases. You have casual friends, good friends, best friends, and perhaps one person you consider your very best friend.

You also have different friends for different reasons. One person fills one need, someone else another. A certain friend may represent apples to you, another may provide the oranges in your life. If you happen to like apples much better than oranges, then you'll have a desire to see your apples friend more often. He might be a once-a-weeker, while the oranges friend is a once-a-monther. Others might fit in nicely if you see them only once every few months. At the extreme, you might even have friends who fill needs on a once-a-year basis. If you can't take someone's company at least once a year, I think it's safe to assume that you're not attached to him by affection or anything else.

260

Regardless of the degree or variety, what it all boils down to is that a friend is a person who fills a need for you. And from his standpoint, your function is to fill a need for him. It's losing sight of the latter that causes so many friendship problems. When both sides understand the entire equation and perform accordingly, the basis for a solid, value-for-value relationship exists—the only kind of relationship which can be both honest and lasting.

WHAT A FRIEND ISN'T.

Since people often have perverted ideas about friendship, perhaps the best way to define a friend is to explain what he *isn't*. A friend

Isn't someone who loans you money whenever you need it, regardless of the amount or circumstances involved;

Isn't someone whose responsibility it is to be available to serve your needs twenty-four hours a day;

Isn't someone upon whom you should feel free to impose;

Isn't someone with whom you can be as presumptuous as you desire;

Isn't someone ordained to spend the rest of his life "sacrificing" for you;

Isn't a robot who's been created to act in your best interest without any regard to his own.

"What are friends for?" has been a legendary intimidation line for as long as anyone can remember. If anyone ever tries to cheapen a friendship with you by the use of such an intimidation ploy, answer by telling him what friends *aren't* for.

Money is a particularly touchy subject when it comes to friendships. When I was at The Bottom, I asked Black Bart to loan me $10,000—a seemingly paltry sum in relation to his ever-growing pile of Touchies. But he turned me down flat. In his usual detailed, analytical manner, he explained why such a move would be unwise on his part. Though I was in dire straits, I realized that his reasoning was rational.

Unfortunately, I had more luck with a mutual friend of ours. After much pleading on my part, this particular fellow finally loaned me $5,000. The result? He ended up harboring bad feelings toward me because I wasn't able to pay him back on time. (Having been pressed to the wall, I had made an irrational promise regarding the scheduled repayment of the money, a typical result of the Scared Money Theory.) It was my loss, because I really valued his friendship. I just plain blew it. I imposed on our relationship, the result being that I not only had to pay him back, but had to reimburse Nature, as well.

Black Bart? As always, he ended up with four aces in his hand. He came blowing through town not too long ago—on his way to inspect a ranch he owned up in northern California—and stopped in to see me. I actually thanked him for having had the good sense not to loan me the ten grand I had begged for years earlier. I complimented him for having done the right thing instead of having been intimidated into doing the instinctive thing. His refusal had been a very valuable lesson to me, and I felt he deserved to know it. I was lucky; he saved our friendship.

THE BUILDING BLOCKS OF ALL FRIENDSHIP FOUNDATIONS

There are two essential elements in the foundation of any worthwhile friendship. The first is the admiration/respect factor. If someone doesn't admire and respect you, how can you possibly fill any of his needs, assuming he's rational and bases his actions on long-term consequences? Likewise, if you don't admire and respect the other fellow, what does he have to trade with you?

On the basis of short-term patching, I guess it's possible to develop a foundationless relationship with someone you don't respect and try to masquerade it as a friendship.

Although such a relationship may bring you or him something you desire today (such as companionship), it probably will result in frustration and bad feelings for both parties. If admiration and respect aren't there from the outset, then it's not a friendship; it's an unhealthy relationship.

The other building block of a successful friendship is rational selfishness, which provides the basis for the essential component of value for value. Those who have difficulty making friends are usually afflicted with the negative results of the World-Owes-Me-a-Living Theory. No one owes you, or anyone else, anything—certainly not friendship, love or respect. Don't seek an unearned friendship. Deal with people on an honest, value-for-value basis and you'll be amazed at how willingly they in turn will fill your needs (assuming they, too, are value-for-value oriented).

The modern context in which *friend* is usually used has no doubt been partly responsible for the failure of many people to understand that friendship is something which must be earned. To many, the word somehow implies an individual who will do anything for you, regardless of the circumstances—who can be counted on when a favor, as it were, is needed. And *favor* has likewise evolved—to imply one's receiving something for nothing. The whole syndrome is dangerous. In truth, a friend should be someone you admire and respect and to whom you are attached by affection; a favor should be something you do for a friend because your Weight-and-Balance Happiness Scale tells you that it's in your best interest to do so, long-term.

Therefore, when you "sacrifice" for a friend, it is, hopefully, a conscious, rationally selfish action on your part. It's a goodwill gesture toward another person whose friendship gives you pleasure. It's not a complicated proposition at all, except that you do have to be careful that you're feeding your Scale correct information.

Because a friend is someone who brings you pleasure,

it's essential that you understand that he, too, has a Weight-and-Balance Happiness Scale. When you realize that, you're in the correct mental frame of mind to appeal to him intelligently through acts which make him feel good. Because of custom and tradition, many people have trouble accepting the reality that the most meaningful relationships are based on selfishness. But when both of you are operating in this honest and realistic manner, you have a solid foundation for a beautiful, long-lasting, value-for-value relationship.

That's not to say that both parties must derive the same kinds of pleasure from a friendship. One person could be gaining good advice and intellectual stimulation from it, while the other enjoys the interesting conversations and companionship.

Is there such a thing as a "true" friend?

The dictionary: *true* (in the friendship sense) refers to one who is "loyal, faithful, sincere, etc." If one accepts this definition, then certainly there is such a thing as a true friend. There are people who will be loyal, faithful and sincere to you, and I'll tell you exactly who they are. They're individuals who have analyzed—either consciously or subconsciously, through personal experience with you—that what they get in return is worth their efforts to be loyal, faithful and sincere.

Again, it's a matter of degree. Based on his stake in the relationship, one rational person will be more faithful and loyal than another. Remember our discussion about risking one's life for another person? Your willingness to put your life on the line for someone depends on the degree of your loyalty, which in turn is based on the value you place on the relationship—the amount of pleasure you derive from it.

Furthermore, the total picture must be considered when making decisions regarding "favors" for "true" friends—particularly if they're decisions which are critical in nature. Money is always a good example—and always a problem. You would have to place an inordinately high value on a friendship to put yourself in a serious financial bind in order to help bail someone out of his money problems. But no two situations are exactly the same; you play each according to the factors involved. It behooves you to have some general guidelines on how you intend to act when emergency situations arise so you're not caught off balance. If you haven't given it some rational thought ahead of time, you're likely to make irrational decisions in such cases, which usually means doing the instinctive thing instead of the right thing.

One factor which should always be considered is what the long-term consequences might be (don't forget my friend who loaned me the $5,000). In money matters with friends, it sometimes takes a lot of strength, as well as rational thinking, to do the right thing. More often than not, a person who loans money to a friend is someone who ends up a victim of the You-Won't-Get-Credit-For-It Theory. It never seems to fail that the friend can't repay the money at the promised time, if ever. (This is usually because an unrealistic date was promised when his emotions, rather than his intellect, were in control.) If you happen to be the lender, you may end up losing both a friend and your money. By saying no in the first place, the most you can lose is one; and if your friend is rational, you might not lose either.

When someone tries to coerce or intimidate you into loaning him money by appealing to terms like *true friend*, it's a good sign that *he* may not be a true friend. If he continues to chastise you for "letting him down," etc., I suggest you turn the whole thing around and put it in proper perspective. The fallacy in his conclusion that you're not a true friend just because you won't loan him money is this: if the money he's asking for is necessary to hold the friendship together, then it couldn't have been much of a friendship to begin with. Black Bart didn't loan me the money I asked for, but that didn't sever our friendship. That's because he offered many other qualities which were important to me.

To hell with money as a barometer. I'll tell you one which I believe *is* a good indicator of friendship: how friends react when anything unfavorable or slanderous in nature is said about you. The people who are most important to you shouldn't be affected by negatives volunteered by others. It's another process of self-elimination. Anyone who knows you well enough to call you a friend, yet takes into consideration the negative remarks of others, is telling you something about his character or his inability to think rationally. If secondhand remarks override his firsthand experience with you, he's doing you a favor by eliminating himself from your life. Had he not shown his colors in this manner, his lack of character or inability to think rationally might have surfaced at a far more critical moment—at a time when it could have had devastating effects on you.

I not only completely disregard unfavorable remarks about friends, but discount anything unpleasant said about *anyone*. Again, I do this for rationally selfish reasons. All too often I end up admiring a person someone else has put down.

Can friends be bought?

Can you buy friendship? You not only can, you must. It's the *only* way to obtain friends. Everyone buys all his friends—in the Free-Enterprise Friendship Market. The prices vary in size and form, but there is always a payment involved. Same rule: everything worthwhile has a price. The payment might require your investing a given number of hours per week in conversation, it might mean that you're counted on for inspiration, or that you have to forego some facet of your life which you presently enjoy.

Every person in the Free-Enterprise Friendship Market has needs. When you fill one or more of those needs, you're paying for someone's friendship. It's when you aren't willing to pay for a friendship—when you aren't prepared to fill some need of his on a value-for-value basis—that you begin having problems with the Friendship Hurdle. We all have the something-for-nothing urge within us, so don't feel guilty about it; just concentrate on suppressing it, because it produces bad long-term consequences. To the degree you're successful in keeping it under control, your chances of making and keeping friends are greatly increased.

Whenever I become acquainted with someone I think I might enjoy as a friend, I try to determine two things. One is what the price for his friendship is likely to be; the other is whether I'm willing and able to pay it. For example, an interesting conversationalist may require more of my time than I'm willing to give in exchange for such conversation. Don't delude yourself about the total, long-term price.

CAN A TORTOISE FIND HAPPINESS OUT OF HIS SHELL?

Perhaps we should back up a step. You can't decide you'd like to be someone's friend until you've met him. And you won't meet him if you aren't willing to expend the effort to do so. It's a form of the Waiting-to-Be-Discovered syndrome. Friends won't discover you any more than will people in the business world. You have to open the door in order to see who's out there. You should employ the Sure Theory—take matters into your own hands. If you want friends, go get them.

That doesn't mean you should wander the streets grinning at everyone like a person who's just completed a personality-improvement course. But it does mean you should wander. Get out, go places, try doing things you've never done before. Unfortunately, that automatically means you'll have to experience a certain amount of pain and embarrassment, but by now you certainly know the reason why: it's part of the price which must be paid for a better life. Another theory applies here: One in the Sack Is Worth a Hundred in the Face. If you haven't experienced failure in seeking friends, you probably haven't tried very hard.

While it's true that grinning for no apparent reason might make people think you're a lunatic, it's perfectly natural—and doesn't cost a thing—to be humane, friendly and generally cheerful toward others. Concentrate on what they're saying; try to feel their emotions. It's when you appeal to a person's natural selfishness that he becomes more interested in you. That opens the door for you to get to know him better, which is the only way you can find out if he does have qualities you admire and respect. If you do decide that you have admiration for an individual, keep right on appealing to his selfishness. Then, after a while, invite him into your world so he can begin to understand your needs. From that point on, you'll both be deciding, at least subconsciously, if you have the ability and desire to fill the other person's basket.

Above all, *always advertise your true self; never try to be something you're not.* If you don't adhere to this basic principle, those people in whom you're most interested—individuals with values similar to yours—will not recognize you when you make your appearance. Worse yet, those whom you would prefer not to have in your private world will probably be the very ones most attracted to the disguise. That's the beginning of a dishonest relationship, and the Pinspotter will treat you quite shabbily when it slams you into place.

Advertising my true self at all times is so important to me that I'm always checking my actions. If I find that I'm talking, gesturing or generally acting like those in my presence, I call a mental time-out, pull off my mask and start over again. You shouldn't become a new person each time you're in the presence of new people. The only way to survive socially, on a long-term basis, is to be the same individual—the real you—at all times, no matter what the atmosphere. If you don't adhere to this honest approach, you're again out of control—being what you think others want you to be rather than what you really are. Don't try to be all things to all people. It won't work. There's only one you; show yourself off as you really are if you wish to attract those people who can add the greatest amount of pleasure to your life.

As Usual, No Guarantees

There is at least one factor beyond your control in every prospective friendship situation, and it would be unrealistic not to acknowledge it. The other person simply may not want you as a friend. Ouch! Well, who ever said life was supposed to be easy? You have to accept the fact that the old ego is going to take a good blow now and then. But it cuts both ways. Just because someone wants your friendship doesn't mean you want his, either—or that you're obligated to accept it if it's offered.

If you want value for value, you both have to feel you're going to get as much out of the relationship as you put into it. The other person's reasons for feeling he won't receive satisfactory rewards from the friendship can be very personal and private in nature. It's not always something over which you have control. Therefore, it's in your best interest to take the rational, wise approach; as always, think in terms of the "Sustenance" Theory. If an individual with whom you'd like to be friends doesn't reciprocate, don't take it as a personal insult. It's just one of those things. He may have any number of reasons for feeling the way he does, but when you have self-esteem—when you know where you're at and where you're going in life—philosophically you can look at it as his loss, not yours.

A GUIDE TO SCREWING UP EXISTING FRIENDSHIPS

The simplest way to destroy a good friendship is to

forget that friends are people and that people aren't perfect. They possess, to one degree or another, every negative trait we discussed in "The People Hurdle," and more. They'll disappoint you; they'll hurt you; they'll let you down. Depending on the degree and frequency, this doesn't necessarily mean that a person isn't a good friend; it just reaffirms what you already know about human beings: they have faults. If the friendship is worthwhile from your standpoint, then the key to surviving such actions on his part is forgiveness. The poor guy didn't ask to be born a Homo sapiens; it just happened. Forgive him for his human weaknesses.

Keep in mind, too, that something which disappoints and hurts you might look very different through his eyes. Like all human beings, he, too, plays the Definition and Line-Drawing Games. With a friend, what it sometimes amounts to is a nicer version of the Screwor-Screwee Theory. No matter how positive you are that you're in the right, your friend's lines may vary from yours at times and he may occasionally define things in a different way. If this happens too often, of course, you should question whether your values are similar enough to sustain a healthy friendship.

I seldom have flare-ups with friends anymore, because I make it a point to give them the benefit of the doubt. Whenever I'm aggravated by something a friend does to me, I try to remember that people have been mad at me at times for reasons I felt were unjustified. Therefore, I automatically assume that whatever he might have done, it wasn't meant in a detrimental way.

There may be all kinds of extenuating circumstances which could cause a friend to act in a manner that displeases you. He could be having financial pressures, or he may not be getting along with his wife, or it's possible that *you* may have done something which he misunderstood. Give him the benefit of the doubt. My reason for being forgiving is pragmatic in nature: it's simply not in my best interest to harbor grudges, particularly toward those from whom I derive pleasure. Forgiving is a rationally selfish action on my part.

For the same selfish reasons, I go one step further. I've discovered that the foolproof way to shield oneself from the disappointment and hurt brought about by the actions of friends is not to expect anything of anyone. It's easy to be forgiving if you assume nothing to begin with. From the day I established this attitude, making and keeping friends became an amazingly easy proposition. A friend might surprise me—on rare occasions even disappoint me—but almost never can he "hurt" me. And anything one does to keep hurt out of his life is a contribution to looking out for Number One. Any conscious, rational effort to avoid pain has to be a move in the right direction.

Does this mean you should put up with any amount of irritation a friend throws your way? Of course not. You put up with it in relation to the value you place on the friendship. So long as what you derive from the relationship is worth it, you forgive; when it's not worth it, it's time to get out. Just don't depart in a moment of anger—when you're reacting emotionally to something you may see differently once you've had time to think it through. One moment of anger can produce a lifetime of regret, particularly where friends are concerned.

This brings ego back into the picture. We talked about the fact that when one "stands on principle," often it's his ego that's doing the "standing." As a result, the friendship may fall. Watch out for your ego; when that dinosaur gets up to step on your house, make sure none of your friendships are inside. If you can't afford to feed an overstuffed ego, you can be certain your friends don't want the obligation of supporting it, either. Just as the cost of an insatiable ego can be financial failure, it can also be the loss of friends.

Get it out of your head that you're Elasticman. You can't stretch in every direction at once. The result of trying to spread yourself too thin among friends is, quite naturally, a reduction in the quality of your friendships. The easiest thing in the world is to make commitments; the hardest is to keep them. Don't leave the word *yes* lying around on the tip of your tongue; put it away somewhere for safekeeping, to be used for special occasions. You're far better off, in the long run, if you learn to say no politely and pleasantly, but immediately and firmly.

That doesn't mean you should say no to everything a friend asks of you; just be sure you don't make a habit of making promises you can't keep. It's short-term patching versus long-term solutions again: the friend may love you for promising to do something, but he may end up disliking you intensely for not actually following through when the time comes. Conversely, he may have a degree of negative feelings toward you for refusing him at the outset, but later on down the road he may forget it or even respect you for having had the strength not to make a commitment you weren't prepared to keep (particularly if you honestly and rationally state your reasons for the refusal at the time of the request).

The problem becomes more delicate in nature when you've made a commitment, then realize you either can't keep it or don't wish to (say, for reasons of integrity). As a generality, I believe that one should try to keep his commitments. But if it becomes apparent that you've made a serious mistake, you're under no moral obligation to follow through—particularly if you feel it might be detrimental to Number One—just because you said yes before carefully analyzing the consequences.

Like your friends, you, too, are entitled to make mistakes. Abide by the principle of precipitating crises sooner rather than later. The ideal time to precipitate a "crisis," of course, is at the outset, by saying no without hemming and hawing. But the "sooner-than-later" rule applies even if you've botched your first opportunity to say no. If you agree to do something and later realize you've made a mistake, explain your position simply and honestly, in a pleasant manner, but leave no doubt in the other person's mind that your decision to back out is final. If you wait until tomorrow to confront your friend, it will be that much harder, and the day after that will be even worse.

A farfetched example to make my point: Suppose, in a moment of anger, you agree to help a friend carry out a vendetta against someone both of you dislike. When you come to your senses and realize that such an action is immoral by your standards, you certainly have the right to change your mind. In this illustration, *not* backing out of your commitment would be immoral.

Save everyone problems by learning to catch yourself *before* you make a rash commitment. There are all kinds of things you may wish to do for your friends, but the reality is that you simply can't do all of them. In view of that, it makes sense to choose those things which you're best equipped to handle, under present circumstances, for those friends who are most important to you. Don't try to be all things to all people; do what *you* think is right under the given circumstances. You'll never please everyone, so you'll only succeed in frustrating yourself if you try. Repeat: *don't spread yourself too thin.*

The Impossible Stretch

Overvolunteering is even worse than overcommitting oneself. In a desire to make or keep friends, many people develop the dangerous habit of trying to solve everyone's problems. If you make this mistake, all too often the result is that you somehow end up being the bad guy, while those who didn't offer to lift a finger get off scot-free. Back to the You-Won't-Get-Credit-For-It Theory: if you go overboard trying to be a good guy (by becoming too involved in others' problems), you run a high risk of being tagged a bad guy in the end. It can be a very frustrating experience, to say the least.

The self-sacrifice sham, of course, doesn't work. You can't win or keep friends by drowning them in your "unselfishness." You'll only be hiding your true self, and that might be the very person they would admire and respect if they just could see him. Consciously or unconsciously, friends won't respect you for trying to be unselfish. Ironically, however, once you've established such a pattern, they may dislike you later on for not delivering still more—at a time when your help may really be needed, but when you, for one reason or another, are unable to give it.

Miscellaneous Ways to Lose Friends in Case All Else Fails

One good way to drive people out of your life is to be the ever-present bearer of bad tidings. There's nothing wrong with discussing problems with good friends; just don't bury them with your troubles. People don't like problems; they have enough of their own. It's natural for human beings to seek pleasant surroundings.

Another excellent way to reduce the quality and quantity of your friendships is to stand naked before the world. It's nice to have intimates in whom you can confide, but that doesn't mean you should expose your every thought. The reality is that when there's no more to learn about you, you lose some of your luster.

That's not to say you can't tell select friends certain personal things about yourself, but in each case the closeness of your relationship should have a direct bearing on the intimacy of the information you're revealing. As I stated in the One-to-a-Box Theory, no one can climb inside your body and literally be a part of you. No matter how close the friend, you're still an individual entity, so don't feel an obligation to make certain that no facet of your life remains unknown to a close friend. There are some thoughts which should remain the private property of Number One.

When I was much younger, I had a tendency to get carried away with telling on myself; I was my own stool pigeon. All too often, at some later date, the volunteered information would come back to haunt me. Nature has a nasty habit of converting friends into nonfriends—or sometimes even enemies—and when that happens, it's nice if they're not carrying around a mental diary of your private life.

As always, I had to learn this the hard way. During one such blabber-mouthing incident many years ago, one of four people with whom I was spending an evening remarked, "That's quite an admission; you've just undressed yourself in front of everybody." That really bothered me; I realized I had said something so personal that the people I was with were surprised anyone would reveal such a thing about himself. Then and there, I made a mental commitment to Number One. I still repeat that commitment out loud whenever the urge to strip arises: *Never undress yourself in public!*

THE RESPECT VIRUS

Respect is contagious. If you have self-respect, it's likely that you'll maintain the respect of others, too. But if you lack it, certainly no one will be able to contract it from you. All you have to do to create a lack of respect for yourself is engage in an activity which is against your moral standards—usually in an unthinking moment when you're trying to please others, or possibly as a result of attempting to take a shortcut instead of paying the full price for something.

Self-respect—the result of faithful adherence to one's standards—is a rare treasure. As should be the case, the price to maintain it is enormous—usually in the form of self-discipline, which may sometimes make you unpopular in the short term. But in the long run, even those who may have chastised you for not going along with something which you believed would be a compromise of your integrity will end up respecting you (though not necessarily liking you) for your stance.

An important reiteration: Never compromise your integrity; always respect yourself.

ARE YOU OPERATING IN THE RED?

But the easiest way of all to destroy a friendship is to wake up one morning and realize that your accounts payable to someone have far outgrown your receivables. If a person is a good friend, it's easy to be presumptuous and take liberties you wouldn't think of attempting with your worst enemy. Does it make any sense to treat friends worse than enemies? Remember that your friends have Weight-and-Balance Happiness Scales, too. They can't afford to carry overdue receivables on their books forever, any more than you can. When you allow a friendship to become too one-sided, your friend being the creditor and you the debtor, it moves out of the realm of friendship and becomes an obligatory relationship. Your friendship debts become so great that you lose the freedom necessary to look out for Number One.

I've only mentioned a few ways in which you can bust up friendships. But if all these fail, I'm certain you can think of a number of other methods without taxing your creative powers too much.

WHERE ARE THE VALUE-FOR-VALUE RELATIONSHIPS?

What if you can't find value-for-value friendships? I have empathy for that dilemma, because there was a time when I couldn't find them, either. Until I started looking for them. And when I did, I realized it was I, not the other guy, who hadn't been willing to give equal value for that which I hoped to receive. The Weight-and-Balance Happiness Scales of others were telling them to stay away.

You *can* find value-for-value relationships. It has amazed and excited me to discover how many beautiful, value-for-value people there are out there. In percentages, the figure is small; but in actual numbers, they're all over the place, hiding among the millions of hardcore something-for-nothing adherents. What makes it nice is that you're only looking for a handful of friends, not thousands. Your odds of finding just a few are very good if you're willing to put forth sufficient effort to locate them—willing to pay the price.

Cherish each rose you do manage to find. Nurture every value-for-value friendship which comes into your life. If you haven't been able to find and/or keep such relationships, are you sure it's not because you haven't been willing to pay the price? Be honest with yourself; it's your life and happiness that are on the line.

What to Do About a Lousy Personality

People have sometimes confided to me that they have trouble making friends because they have "bad personalities." I always respond that, in all honesty, I'm not sure exactly what a bad personality is. Even Genghis Khan and Mussolini had friends. It's another category which isn't black or white. Personality traits not only come in degrees, but, as a total package, each individual is unique from all others. People don't have "bad personalities." They just act in ways which lead others to believe they have nothing to trade in the Free-Enterprise Friendship Market.

If you think your personality has been a roadblock to finding and holding meaningful friendships, then it's up to you to pay the price to do something about it. Take the trouble to honestly analyze what it is you're doing (or not doing), then correct it. More often than not, when one takes the trouble to factually meditate about this predicament in an honest and rational manner, he finds the real problem is that he's been hiding his true personality. We're all so defensive and so afraid of getting hurt that we often go to great lengths to create an artificial personality with which to protect ourselves. God forbid we should invite a person to go somewhere only to find that he's already made other plans; our sensitive egos simply can't bear the pain.

Get out of your shell and allow others to see the real you. Don't worry about being a rejectee; either the rejector has a valid reason for the rejection or, if not, you should have enough self-esteem to see it as his loss. Forget it and keep right on looking around the People Store; finding the good ones takes time and effort. The question, then, is not, "What can I do about a lousy personality?" but, "Am I willing to pay the price necessary to figure out what I'm doing wrong, correct it, ignore rejection, and continue searching for value-for-value people who can appreciate what I have to offer?"

HOW TO GET OUT OF A CRUMMY "FRIENDSHIP"

If you've accumulated a lot of excess baggage in the way of "friends" who contribute more discomfort than pleasure to your life, by now you should be convinced that you can't afford the extra weight—not if you're going to succeed in looking out for Number One. We spoke earlier of the wisdom of precipitating a crisis sooner rather than later. I'd like to reemphasize that point with the

CRUMMY-FRIENDSHIP THEORY

A crummy friendship is one in which you consistently give more than you receive. It's okay now and then, but after a while it gets to be a drag. If you've made the mistake of getting into a friendship which you now realize is going in the wrong direction, cut it off before it gets out of hand. Just because you made an initial error doesn't mean you have an obligation to perpetuate the relationship and endure further suffering.

Remember, it's unwise to attempt to smooth over irritating situations; they'll only get worse. The other person misinterprets your nonresistance as encouragement, and the end result is one big mess. If you're thinking long-term, you should have the foresight to see what a situation can become.

Have a little self-esteem. You're a completely unique person—one of a kind—whether or not you've realized it in the past. Don't yield to everyone who has a desire to come into your private world. If, through a lax attitude on your part, someone does manage to slip in who doesn't belong, take control once you realize what's happened. You do the deciding as to which people you want in your life, then go after them. Don't leave the matter of your friendships up to the whims of others.

And don't procrastinate. Take matters into your own hands starting today. Anyone who causes irritation in your life—whether he's a "friend," relative or uninvited guest —is an aggressor. He's aggressing against your right to a happy life—your right to look out for Number One. It's neither cruel, heartless, nor cold to get out of a relationship which is causing you discomfort. On the contrary, it's wise; long-term, it's good for both you and the other guy. The result of failing to take action will be unnecessary bitterness and displeasure, which could cause those people who can add happiness to your life to shy away.

THE EFFECTS OF THIS CHAPTER ON THE LIFE OF THE TORTOISE

How do the things I've said in this chapter affect my friendships? Is it wise to let my friendship philosophy be made public? Yes, that's the whole point. I want my friends—and everyone else who might cross my path—to understand exactly what my thoughts are regarding this important subject. By being honest—by advertising the real me—I increase the chances of drawing to myself those people with whom I have the most in common. It also brings me closer to existing friends who see friendship in the same value-for-value light that I do.

On the other side of the coin, it operates as a self-policing device. It eliminates from my life those people who don't understand the necessity of paying for friends. Rather, it would be more correct to say that they eliminate themselves. This in turn spares me the unpleasant ramifications of becoming involved with the wrong kind of people, as well as the discomfort of having to break off any existing friendships which are, or could later become, unhealthy.

If the Friendship Hurdle has seemed a bit easy to you, it's because it really is, especially in comparison to the one which lies ahead. Well, you knew it was coming; we're almost at the end of the book. We can't avoid it any longer, so let's get on with that last, gigantic obstacle —the Love Hurdle—the one we'd all like to clear in perfect form.

The Love Hurdle

If friends are one of the great joys in life, then lovers are probably the greatest. Lovers, like friends, are people to whom you're attached by affection, but there's an added element of coziness to it. It's a different kind of attachment. You may love a friend, but not in the same way that you love a parent. Nor is your love for a friend the same love you feel for a lover.

The dictionary partially defines love as "a feeling of warm personal attachment or deep affection; a strong or passionate affection for a person of the opposite sex." That the sex should be "opposite" is a little presumptuous, perhaps, but to keep things simple, I'll take the liberty here of dealing only in terms of the opposite sex. That, however, does not mean that I'm judging your sexual preferences. Those are entirely your business.

I believe this feeling of passionate affection to be, in its purest form, an inexplicable physical attraction—an indefinable chemistry, as it were—which, while it does not equate to sex, does find its ultimate celebration in sexual expression. The physical-attraction aspect is important, because without it I don't think you can have real romantic love. You may love many things in a person, but if the romantic affinity isn't there, all you really have is a good friend. I label this physical-chemical phenomenon "The Other Element." It's the ingredient which distinguishes between lovers and friends.

The Other Element relies on beauty only insofar as one acknowledges that beauty is not an absolute; it's a matter of personal taste. What you see when you look at the woman you love can be quite different from what others see. In actuality, the deep affection you feel for someone is based on a total package—a combination of physical and intellectual qualities, as well as other personal characteristics. It's this total package to which you are physically attracted.

Like friendship, love is not an either/or proposition. There's no rational reason why you can't have a deep passionate feeling for more than one member of the opposite sex; lacking control over such feelings, however, can lead to irrational behavior which may not be in your best interest. Like all emotions, love is measured in degrees. The extent of your love for one person will exceed the love you hold for another. And, of course, the added complication of variety is there—the *kind* of love you feel for one individual is different from that which you feel for another, because each person has unique characteristics.

HOW MANY LOVERS?

From the standpoint of an uncomplicated life, one lover is probably the ideal number, depending on the needs of the individual and whether one's lover has the ability and desire to satisfy those needs.

This brings us to that fine line separating lovers and "luvers." A *luver* is a person positioned somewhere in that vast area between a lover and an overnight fling. He or she doesn't quite make it as a lover, but there's a little more to the relationship than just pure sex. Some people tend to accumulate luvers to see them through the lean times when their search for a lover isn't going too well.

The biggest danger I can see in the volume approach is the problem of spreading yourself too thin—physically and mentally. It not only takes more time than a normal person can afford, but requires too many promises—which inevitably leads to some of them not being kept. That in turn breeds bad feelings on many fronts, not to mention the danger of the thin-spreader ending up with gouge marks on his face.

THE BIGGER L

The loneliness one feels for the love of a lover is different than the loneliness one feels for friendship. It's an empty feeling which can't really be described. You've been there; we all have. Since love-loneliness is more painful than friendship-loneliness, understanding the reality of the One-to-a-Box Theory becomes even more imperative.

There are two dangers in not being able to cope with love-loneliness. First of all, as with friends, you won't be able to enjoy a love relationship fully if you equate aloneness with loneliness. Since we've already covered coming to grips with yourself by learning to appreciate what you have to offer, I won't go into that. But it is important that you put your lover (or potential lover) into proper perspective.

No matter how close your relationship with a lover, you are, and will remain, an entity unto yourself. You and your lover aren't a package deal; you're two separate people who happen to feel deeply for one another. But your every desire is not identical; your every thought is not parallel; your every need is not the same. A lover can be a part of your life, but not a literal part of *you*.

283

Another danger in letting the Bigger L get out of control is that you become vulnerable to making "scared-money" decisions. A famous comedian once made the profound, not-so-funny statement that we all spend our lives in misery out of the fear of dying alone. There was a ton of perceptivity in that little observation and I've often fetched it from my memory tank when my self-discipline needed a booster shot.

Although one can never be certain about what goes on behind closed doors, it doesn't take a very observant individual to make an educated guess that a majority of unhappy marriage partners are in their present unfortunate circumstances out of the fear of dying alone. They may not admit it to themselves, or even think about it consciously, but the price they're paying for not being alone at the time of death is a lifetime of joyless co-existence.

What a sad hoax these people play on themselves. They haven't taken the time to factually meditate—to think it through rationally; if they did, they'd realize that they'll be alone at the time of death anyway. Don't victimize Number One. Don't get into a bad relationship—or stay in one which is making you miserable—out of the fear of loneliness. I seldom make promises, but I'll stick my neck out on this one because there's no risk involved: The Tortoise personally guarantees that you will die alone. Accept it; put it away in your reality chamber; then forget it. That done, you can get on with the more important subject of living.

Can the volume approach cure loneliness?

If you enjoy quantity when it comes to love, that's your business. But if you try to use it as a solution for loneliness, I doubt it will bring you the desired result. To me, building up a backlog of luvers (or lovers, if that's possible) creates the same lonely feeling one experiences when trying to escape loneliness by being in a large crowd. Some of the loneliest-looking people I've seen have been so-called ladies' men. After coming to grips with yourself as an individual—learning to enjoy those wonderful periods of solitude—the chances of finding the kind of love gratification you seek are much better if you have the self-discipline and patience to concentrate on finding one great human being rather than trying to use lovers and luvers for the purpose of drowning loneliness.

The Slow, Fast Way to the Rescue Again

There's no other facet of life in which patience and self-discipline have the potential to pay greater dividends than in love. Unfortunately, in no other area of life are these more difficult to exercise. That's not surprising, since the price/reward ratio never fails to assert itself.

Loneliness for love is a potential panic situation. But panic is something you must avoid at all costs if you wish to retain the hope of finding that someone special. There no doubt are times when the odds against your finding that person seem so overwhelming that it's hard to keep the faith. During one period several years ago I came up with a complicated formula for calculating the number of women in greater Los Angeles (an area containing about eight million people) who were "eligible" by my standards. I took into account such factors as age, physical appearance, intelligence, availability and, most important, my own individual quirks. You know the figure I came up with? Eighteen! Eighteen eligible women in a city of eight million people. My God, I thought to myself, how do I begin to search for eighteen human beings scattered among eight million people? And when I finally find one—if ever—how do I know the situation will be right? Maybe it will be at a party when she's with Warren Beatty and I'm walking around with mustard on my tie. Just like that, the list goes down to seventeen.

No sooner had I begun considering the priesthood as an alternative than an amazing thing happened: I hit a hot streak. In the next six months I stumbled upon a whopping total of four of those eighteen women, each under the right circumstances—a reaffirmation of the feast-or-famine syndrome when it comes to love. The famines are murder, but oh, those feasts. It's what is commonly referred to as a Good Problem—being in the rare position of having to make a choice between two or more delightful alternatives. The only danger is the greed factor. When greed is allowed to take control of a Good Problem, the tortoise who hesitates loses everything. Then it's back to famine, with only the good memories left to tide you over until the next opportunity presents itself.

Obviously there was something wrong in my complex formula for calculating the number of available prospective lovers in the area. Now I'm no longer sure what the real odds are, but I do feel certain that they're not as overwhelming as most people tend to imagine when they're enduring a bad streak of loneliness. Seen from the proper perspective, the odds aren't nearly as bad as you might think, provided you're willing to pay the price of exercising patience and self-discipline. And the proper perspective from which to view the odds is that you only need to find one person—not eighteen or thirty-six or a hundred. Think of it: only one love victory in your whole lifetime is all that's needed—if it's the right one.

THE SEARCH

You can't expect to find the right person if you don't know what you're looking for. And to know that, you first have to know a great deal about yourself. This is a crucial area of your life, so tenaciously adhere to the rule of being totally honest with yourself about who and what you really are and what you want out of life. This self-examination has to be done at a time when your intellect is in control. If you allow your emotions to guide such an analysis, you may as well forget it. Factual Meditation, when practiced under the influence of panic, can produce dangerous illusions. Think. Have the courage to acknowledge reality. After that, it's a matter of exercising self-discipline—sticking to your rational conclusions at future times when you're under the influence of your emotions.

Rational Thoughts for a Rational Search

In matters of love, there are a multitude of factors beyond your control, so never allow yourself to get into a mental state where the failure to make it with any specific lover—or potential lover—can be your undoing. Your life is too important to be shattered by outside circumstances—including the quirks of another person.

Just as you don't need any one client, customer or job, neither do you need any one mate. You may need a lover, but not any specific lover. While it's true that you only need to find one person, that doesn't mean there's only one person available. There's no such thing as looking for the right man or woman. Anyone old enough to have graduated from the Diaper Corps knows all about the number of fish in the sea. Since no two are exactly alike, you're absolutely right if you think you'll never find another love like the last one. You won't, but what you will find is a different love, one which can bring you happiness in many new ways. The old and the new can't be compared, so don't try; it's the apples-and-oranges fallacy again. The plain truth is that there are many people with whom you can fall genuinely in love.

When people blow love situations out of proportion, they create unnecessary emotional problems for themselves. If you insist on believing there's only one individual who is just right for you, you're certainly going out of your way to create false pressure for yourself. When an individual gets emotionally sucked into believing that the deal he happens to be working on is the only one in the world, the tendency is to press, and the harder one presses, the worse his chances for success. If a situation doesn't work out, it's in your best interest to forget it and get on with your search for the Real Thing. Knowing the coy ways in which Nature operates, she undoubtedly had good reasons for calling in Murphy to gum it up.

How the "Sustenance" approach aids your health.

The "Sustenance" Theory not only gives you the proper frame of mind to sustain a prolonged search for the right person, but can also save you from a potential letdown once you've found her. It's best explained by a derivative of this theory, which I call the

BOYFRIEND THEORY

Whenever you run across a woman who intrigues you so much that you light the wrong end of your pipe, try to keep calm. Don't get too carried away until you've had an opportunity to assemble some background information. Experience has taught me that you're far better off—particularly physically—if you assume the following two probabilities:
1) She already has a boyfriend (or fiancé or husband).
2) He's big, hairy and mean.
Adherence to this theory substantially increases your chances for a longer and healthier life. To ignore it can cause considerable complications, particularly if you're troubled by the sight of your own blood.

WHAT A LOVER ISN'T.

A female lover
Isn't a maid who should be expected to be constantly busy at her chores;
Isn't a cook whose job it is to have your dinner on the table at a specified time;
Isn't a governess whose duty it is to shield you from the unpleasantries children can cause;

"Hi, honey, don't I know you from somewhere?"

"I don't know—why don't you ask my fiancé? Just call him 'Gorilla' for short."

Isn't someone whose only male friend is you.

A male lover
Isn't a painter, carpenter or general handyman;
Isn't a printing press whose sole function is to keep rolling off bills in order to support you in a style he can't afford;
Isn't a Ken doll to be propped up at social gatherings he'd rather not attend;
Isn't someone whose only female friend is you.

At various times, to one degree or another, a lover might be any or all of these things, but not at all times and under all circumstances. When any of these items becomes the sole function of a lover, there's no longer a basis for a meaningful love relationship. The building blocks of a rational relationship between lovers are, as you'd expect, the same as those in a sound friendship: admiration, respect, and rational selfishness. It's not possible to have a value-for-value love relationship with someone you don't admire and respect. What can such a person possibly have to trade with you?

SELFISHNESS—THE ROOT OF ALL GOOD

It's necessary to understand the beauty of rational selfishness if you're to free yourself from intimidating "unselfishness" myths which can rob you of your chance for a happy life. Since rational selfishness is one of the primary elements in looking out for Number One (the conscious, rational effort to seek pleasure), and since love is probably the most pleasurable of all experiences, it's critical that you understand the role it plays in love relationships.

If you fail to seek value for value in love relationships, you're coming out of the starting gate with a load of problems under your arm—a load that certainly will slow you down in your search for a better life. Extra weight is

290

something we've already decided you need to get rid of to succeed in looking out for Number One.

It goes without saying that you can't afford to forget your lover's Weight-and-Balance Happiness Scale, either. Your lover doesn't owe you a thing—especially not love. This definitely is the wrong area for you to become an unthinking victim of the World-Owes-Me-a-Living Theory. I'll tell you exactly how much love you *can* expect to get from a lover: the exact amount you *earn*. You can never be free to enjoy the goodies in life unless you seek to earn everything you wish to receive. That goes for money; it goes for friendship; it goes for self-respect; it goes for love.

As with friendship, the parties in a love relationship do not derive the exact same benefits from it. The issue isn't to fill the same needs in one another, but to give your lover those things which *she* needs. All other things being equal, to the degree your lover fills your needs, she makes you happy; to the degree she makes you happy, you love her; to the degree you love her, you're anxious to fill her needs. Simple . . . now if we could all just learn to do it, we'd cut the divorce rate to shreds. Value for value translates into balanced love equations.

Love for Sale

Can you buy love? You know the answer by now: you must buy it—in the Free-Enterprise Love Market.

How do you pay for a lover? Well, mink coats have always been a big favorite; unfortunately, however, they won't get you the Real Thing. Material luxuries are nice additions to the various types of negotiable love currencies (consideration, kindness, warmth, and a whole array of abstract satisfiers), but that's all they are—additions.

What I like best about the Free-Enterprise Love Market is that it works so smoothly. There are no government controls, the result being that each individual is free to go after whatever he likes; by the same token, no one is forced to do business with him. And since there's no other you in the whole world, you have no real competition. Through the natural processes of the Free-Enterprise Love Market, competition is actually reduced to the benefit of everyone.

If you're rational enough to be able to decide what it is you want—not allowing yourself to be influenced by the opinions of others—then all you need to do is be loyal to your own standards. By doing so, you'll run across fewer "competitors"—fewer men and women who are searching for the same thing you are. Values which are important to you aren't significant to them, and vice versa. The result is that you're not in competition with one another.

HOW, WHEN AND WHERE TO GO "FISHING"

If friends won't discover you, you can be sure that lovers won't. You have to get off your behind and see what's out there. Your life isn't all that long; you don't have time to sit around and mope about how lonely you are. The "when" to go fishing is now.

Where? Everywhere. Try new places, new experiences, new people. If you haven't previously put forth much effort, you'll be amazed at the variety of activities that await you—activities you may not have known about or things which you never seriously considered doing. There's a hell of a lot more to life than eating, sleeping, working, going out to dinner once a week, or taking in an occasional movie. The "where" of the problem is easy as long as you're willing to try new experiences.

The "how" is the tough one. Anybody who's ever been fishing knows all too well what a tricky proposition it is. You have to use the right pole, the proper bait, cast your line just so; it's a delicate sport. To talk about it is easy, to actually do it can be very painful. Unfortunately, that's part of the price you must expect to pay for finding the right person. If you're not willing to pay the price, I can tell you this: there are millions—or certainly thousands—who are. They're the ones who will reap the rewards of finding the Real Thing—and deservedly so. Those who are willing to shell out the necessary payment in the Free-Enterprise Love Market are entitled to go home with the goodies. Those who aren't willing to pay should be prepared either to live without love or, worse yet, to live with someone under a false pretense of love, which certainly is more painful in the long run.

I have a friend who specializes in fishing. While our values are very different when it comes to women—and though I have neither the desire nor the capacity to emulate his style—you and I can both learn a lot from his basic philosophy. His strength lies in his unique application of the realities of the "Sustenance" Theory and the "One-in-the-Sack" Theory. He uses these two effectively in one of his fishing methods, which he refers to as the Police Approach.

It works like this (although I doubt that you're going to believe it): When things are on the slow side, he cruises the streets in shopping areas, looking for attractive women. When he spots one, he jumps out of his car (double-parking, if necessary), walks alongside her and tries to strike up a conversation. I've asked him what he says to these strangers, and he's explained that the "secret" is not to plan anything special. He blurts out whatever happens to come to mind, which he believes alleviates any unnecessary "pre-game pressures." Usually it's something to the effect of, "I was just driving down the street and there you were; it suddenly occurred to me that I'd never see you again unless I jumped out of the car and introduced myself."

The result? He admits matter-of-factly that these women usually just ignore him. What does he do? He persists. And what do they do when he persists? They usually tell him to get lost. When the confrontation reaches that point, his final ploy is to jump in front of the woman's path, spread his arms like a traffic cop, look her in the eye (with a smile he assures me is irresistible) and give her a speech like, "Look, I'll make you a deal. I'll leave you alone if you'll give me your name and phone number. All I want to do is take you out."

His percentages are lousy. But he's trained his mind to ignore the misses. He's only interested in the times he lucks out. And believe it or not, he's actually turned up some very interesting women. Why? Who knows? Maybe the girl had a fight with her boyfriend, maybe she was in a whimsical mood that day, or perhaps his approach was so ridiculous it struck her as "cute." The law of averages is a strange phenomenon—strange because it always works. It works to the extent that *sooner or later* it works.

While I could never pull off his Police Approach, I must admit that his basic idea—practiced on a sane and reasonable level—is sound. He tries and tries again. That's his secret. It's the key lesson to be learned from the Police Approach. The next time you're feeling sorry for yourself because you can't find a lover, think about this acquaintance of mine, because the chances are very good that at the same time you're despairing, he's out there trying. If there's a guy running around loose on the streets pulling off a caper like this, surely you can think of a sane, subtle, workable approach that's easy by comparison. The only requirement is that you be willing to put forth the effort.

And don't forget the part his "Sustenance" attitude plays in his success. I once asked him how he could withstand so much rejection. His explanation was that he realized it wasn't him, per se, the women were rejecting, but someone they didn't know. Therefore, he refused to take it personally. In fact, he admits that if he were in their position, he would be as adamant as most of the women who reject him.

Forget his values; forget the insanity of his Police Approach; forget everything about this story except one point: the man has learned to handle the fear of rejection.

One of the major barriers which keeps males and females from getting together is the fear of rejection—both pre- and post-relationship. Our egos again—if only we could get rid of them. They just can't survive a turndown. But as my Police-Approach pal pointed out, in most cases the other person really isn't rejecting *you*, but a stranger.

Pre-relationship fears of rejection can close the door on a new experience before it's begun. One especially self-protective device is the standoffish approach to a first meeting—a refusal to indicate an interest in someone you've just met out of the fear that your interest may not be reciprocated. Unfortunately, this tends to backfire. No one can read your mind, so if you fail to demonstrate any interest, it will undoubtedly be assumed that you have none.

For my part, I don't respect a woman any less for being friendly, open and relaxed when I first meet her. In fact, all other things being equal, I respect her more. By not being defensive and uptight, she's telling me a good deal about herself: that she probably has fewer hangups than most; that she has high self-esteem, which makes her less afraid of rejection than the majority of people; that she isn't a prisoner of custom and tradition; that she has a mind of her own. So right off, I like what I see and hear; I admire individuality. I respect people who are relaxed and able to display their true selves to the world.

Pre-relationship fears are often directly related to a post-relationship feeling of rejection. Once you've been burned, it's hard to turn around and subject yourself to the possibility of being hurt again. If you're not able to handle your emotions and think rationally, this fear will increase with each love relationship that goes sour. Unfortunately, the result is that most people become hardened with age—more defensive, more cautious, less open, less relaxed, and less themselves when meeting members of the opposite sex. Pain is bad stuff. Who needs it? Looking out for Number One is an effort to avoid pain, not endure it.

In that respect, it's a kind of paradox. To find pleasure and eliminate pain, part of the price one has to pay is undertaking the risk of the pain of rejection. If you don't like that fact, I certainly can't blame you; I'm not wild about it, either. But I must ask you once again: Who ever said life was supposed to be easy?

Love, being one of the greatest of all joys, carries an enormous price tag. The inherent risks are incredible. How can Nature possibly ask us to go through all the rejection, the pain, the tremendous effort, and not even guarantee us that we'll succeed in finding, winning, or keeping what we're after? I can't answer that; I only understand the reality that it's the way Nature has decided she wants the game to be played. And since it is a reality, you'd better get your "Sustenance" and "One-in-the-Sack" attitudes down pat. Without them, I don't see how you can muster the strength necessary to pay the price.

False advertising begets false love.

If you understand the importance of assuming the worst and hoping for the best, coupled with the reality of the law of averages, you've got a good start on learning how to go fishing. Unfortunately, though, even if you master those two crucial items, there's still a lot more to it. Making the effort and having rejection under control are only the beginning. The other person still has to recognize you when you cross her path.

You've been told to advertise your true self so many times in this book that it should practically be imprinted on your subconscious by now. For your sake, I hope it is. If you don't adhere to it, I'd hate to quote odds on your finding the Real Thing. When you're out there trying all those new activities you've never experienced before, always remember there are members of the opposite sex who will like you for what you really are. If the real you isn't a guy who feels comfortable using something as ludicrous as the Police Approach, don't fake it just because

296

it happens to obtain results for someone else. You're *not* someone else, so you don't want to end up attracting the same kind of women my "traffic cop" friend is looking for. To misrepresent yourself is a waste of time, because any relationship evolving from such a meeting will be in big trouble when the real you is discovered.

On the other hand, by advertising your true self, you sometimes can compensate for the other party in the event that he or she isn't fortunate enough to have grasped the soundness of this policy. Suppose you're a gal who likes the quiet type, who enjoys intellectual stimulation and good one-on-one conversation. You've somehow ended up at a party where the atmosphere is zany and everyone is acting pretty raunchy. Included among those at the party, however, is a man who is quiet, intellectual, and who enjoys good one-on-one conversation. The only problem is that you can't find him because, though he doesn't enjoy the swinging life, he's playing the "swinger" role in the mistaken belief that it's in his best interest to conform to the surrounding atmosphere.

But because *you* understand the practicality of advertising the real Number One, you're easily recognizable to everyone. The result? It's highly possible that the quiet intellectual in swinger disguise will find you. If this should happen and you end up floating off into the sunset together, you can credit it to the fact that your persistence in advertising your true self compensated for his false advertising. By placing an honest ad, you controlled your own destiny.

The ultimate in the false advertising game is the so-called singles bar. It's really just an indoor, nighttime version of the Thousanduplets. When it comes to finding the Real Thing, the atmosphere is wrong from the outset. Everyone is there for pretty much the same reasons— usually to find a luver or lover—but the problem is that they all are working too hard to act like everybody else.

I suppose the singles-bar scene is all right, but I certainly wouldn't hold out too much hope of finding the Real

Thing there. Though being in a bar doesn't make a person better or worse than anyone else, it's a matter of correct application of the law of averages. Some people argue that the odds are good in a bar because of the sheer volume of the inventory. But, again, that's a matter of the Definition Game. If one's objective is to see how many men or women one can seduce, I can't argue with the numbers. But if to you the Numbers Game means finding *one* for Number One—the Real Thing—then it's my opinion that the odds are very bad.

OBSTACLES ALONG THE WAY

The path leading up to the Love Hurdle is so bumpy, it's no wonder that very few people manage to clear it successfully. In addition to the roughness of the course itself, Murphy has placed several obstacles in strategic spots along the route, snickering at the thought that you and I will trip over them every time we take our eyes off the Hurdle.

The "What-Others-Think" Obstacle

Should you care what others think of your lover? With all the problems involved in finding the Real Thing, you don't need the opinions of others to add to the confusion. Naturally, it makes you feel good to know that other people have admiration and respect for your lover, but if their opinions become your primary emphasis, you've become a victim of intimidation through conformity.

In the event you solicit the advice of friends regarding matters of love, you'd better be very sure who your friends are. You and I know all too well the reality that misery loves company. Insecure, unfulfilled people feel just a trifle better if you're unhappy, too. It's what I refer to as the old "roommate syndrome." Two friends live together, one has something going and one doesn't. If you happen to be the "have" in such a setup, be careful. You can throw away a lifetime of happiness by listening to the opinions of a have-not "friend" regarding someone you love.

The question is, if a friend advises you to give up someone you love, can he or she furnish you with someone better? Or if a friend encourages you to become more deeply involved with a person about whom you have doubts, is he or she prepared to step in and take your place five years from now if it turns out to be a mistake? Since you're the one who will have to endure the pain of a wrong decision, don't you think it would be a good idea to maintain control of the situation, taking third-party opinions with a grain of salt, if at all?

The idea of trying to please or impress others is always dangerous business. Back in my Diaper Corps days, I had a friend who pulled off a real coup. He managed to win over the most sought-after young lady at a certain university. She was absolutely perfect—just what every *other* man wanted. After the wedding, my friend put his "trophy" on the mantel, sat back in his chair and waited for . . . well, I guess he wasn't exactly sure what he was waiting for. What he got, however, was just about everything he never wanted.

Men and women aren't trophies to be won. They're people. They have needs to be filled and represent potential values to you to the extent that they can fill your needs. Violate this law of Nature and you can expect to pay according to the degree of your crime. Going after the woman everyone else thinks is the "sharpest" gal around is an unconscious (usually), irrational (always) effort and can bring you a potful of pain you never realized you were bargaining for.

The corollary to this syndrome is to pursue a woman for the main reason that her looks are stunning. The pursuit of beauty for beauty's sake is always trophy-winning in concept. The pursuer runs the danger of winning a trophy whose more important qualities are the kind he would normally go out of his way to avoid.

Another problem with the beauty-for-beauty's-sake approach is that good looks have a way of staying behind as age moves on. The trophy disappears and all that's left is a human being. At that point, you've got a real problem—unless you just lucked out and later found, to your surprise, that the trophy had wonderful built-in qualities you hadn't even known about.

If you're shooting for the Real Thing, don't dwell on beauty alone. Above all, don't worry about what others think is beautiful. Have enough self-esteem to go after what you really want—what *you* value.

Should you care what others think of your lover? Yes, if you're trying to decide who to ask to the Senior Prom. But if you're too old to go to the Prom, I wouldn't give a great deal of thought to the opinions of others, including friends. Trophies are nice to flaunt at proms, but in the home they just sit on the mantel and rot.

The Boy-Girl Obstacle

The Boy-Girl Theory applies to all facets of life, but derives its name from the fact that its workings are most visible in matters of love.

BOY-GIRL THEORY

There's a basic human weakness inherent in all people which tempts them to want what they can't have and not want what is readily available to them. It's a dangerous instinct, often amounting to a gigantic illusion which can have devastating effects on an individual's life. It tries to shove aside our rationally selfish wishes and replace them with unfounded desires for "forbidden fruit."

I've often thought of renaming it the Sucker Syndrome, because it not only trips everyone up at one time or another, but also makes us feel like suckers when we come out of the ether. You've stumbled over the Boy-Girl obstacle when your mind plays tricks on you and makes you think you're in love with someone just because he or she is giving you a hard time. You also display Boy-Girl tendencies when you toss aside a wonderful person—who perhaps represents many of your highest values—just because he or she is readily available to you.

The Boy-Girl Theory is another phenomenon that's real big at the Senior Prom. It has no place, however, in the adult world. The reality, unfortunately, is that it's a major motivator in the adult world.

Realistically, it's probably not possible to conquer it completely, but you can certainly bring it under control. For many years I've worked very hard at keeping the Boy-Girl instinct in a state of animated suspension. Since I first became aware of its existence and the mirages it creates to my detriment, I've made a conscious, rational effort to quash it from my life. Realizing it's a theory for suckers, and understanding the dangers it holds, I feel it's imperative to be on guard against its effects at all times. It takes intense concentration and rational thinking to be honest with yourself in analyzing whether you want someone because he's "playing hard to get" or because he really represents values which you admire and respect.

Don't let the Boy-Girl obstacle ruin your life. Don't allow your emotions to pull you into its illusory trap. It's strictly for people who have a low reading on the Awareness Meter, not for those looking out for Number One.

Then there's the other side of the Boy-Girl coin: when you take the easy way out and marry someone out of habit—the habit of having been with him or her over a long period of time. The word *love* is thrown in now and then merely as a convenience factor. In a case like this, the love partners are so accustomed to one another that they just sort of relax into staying together. What motivates an individual to take the so-called easy way out is that he knows all too well how tough and cold it is on the outside.

The chronic nothingness that usually results from such a lackadaisical attitude toward love is well deserved. Whether you've been going with someone for a long time, have recently met a person who represents the potential to end a long string of loneliness, or have been married for many years, the only valid reason for getting together and/or staying together on a permanent basis is love, not availability. Factual Meditation will serve you well in this area. If you don't feel the excitement that's an integral part of the emotion of love, you should be asking yourself if you really are in love with the other person. And be very honest in your answers. If the reason you're together is not that you admire and respect your lover or prospective lover, or that he or she satisfies or has the potential to satisfy your highest values and needs, you're in the wrong place. Love is not a subject one can afford to take lightly—or lazily.

The Better-Dealers Obstacle

Each of us probably has the Better-Deal instinct in us to one degree or another. But it's not as prevalent in most people as is the Boy-Girl instinct. The Better Dealers are those persons in whom the Better-Deal inclination is totally out of control; they've gone over the top, usually past the point of no return.

BETTER DEAL THEORY

It's human nature, once you have a "deal" sewn up, to wonder about the possibility of there being a better deal down the road. And theoretically there probably is—simply because the People Store is so big. But the question is, how far down the road is it practical to travel before reaping the rewards of a meaningful love relationship, and how much of your life are you prepared to spend on such traveling?

An even bigger question is: after you find your mythical "better deal," how can you be sure that down the road a piece there isn't one still better? The answer is that you can't. One would have to be omniscient to know such a thing, so it's not a human possibility. The seriously afflicted Better Dealer is an individual hopelessly chasing his tail, cheating himself of happiness within his reach by conducting a life-long impossible search for the ever better deal.

You have the tendency—every human being does—but as with the Boy-Girl instinct, work hard at keeping it as dormant as possible. Better Dealing is even less rational than Boy-Girling. With the latter, there's an illusion that the grass is greener on the other side of the fence, but at least the illusion involves real people. When you're Better Dealing it, however, you're flying blind. You're just assuming that there are greener pastures that can satisfy you, and you'll probably continue to assume it all your life, no matter how many green pastures you find.

The Emotion Obstacle

Emotions have a way of clouding reality and shattering logic. When that happens, a best friend, marriage counselor or psychiatrist can't wave a wand and bring your emotions under control. You have to deal with your emotions head-on in order to dominate them on a permanent basis. It's a matter of your rational thought processes winning out over actions derived through emotion. If your emotions rule too often, the impression others get is that you're a self-destructive individual.

The Boy-Girl Theory is a good example of one's emotions controlling his actions. When you desire forbidden fruit, giving no thought to whether the object of your desire represents values you hold in high esteem, your emotions are very much in control.

Sex is another culprit which can produce the illusion of love. Though you've been through it before, it's always a threat to entrap you. It oftens takes too long to realize that it's sex alone which attracts you to another person and that there's no real love involved.

Another old emotion-trap favorite is one that's man-made. Allow me to introduce you to the chemical phenomenon which can instantly inject the emotion of love into a seemingly innocent relationship: two martinis. That, fortunately, can be conquered easily. If you can't drink, don't!

Then there's infatuation. This is a common illusion which takes place most frequently between the ages of thirteen and thirty. Unfortunately, many people carry infatuation symptoms well into their fifties or sixties. That can sometimes be embarrassing, because a fifty-year-old man doesn't wear it as well as a high-school kid.

When I was a young tortoise, I had more trouble with the infatuation obstacle than all of the others combined. Infatuation is hard to pin down. It's part chemical attraction, part physical attraction; it's kind of Boy-Girlish, kind of crazy, kind of fun—and very immature. It can also be extremely dangerous at times.

The West Side Story Caper

In the days when I was roaming the streets of New York looking for wealthy old guys who would listen to my LSD Deals, I occasionally found time for a little entertainment. At my young age, I still was able to burn the candle at both ends without sacrificing too much in the quality of my work.

Through a little luck—and an ever-watchful eye—I had the good fortune to meet an absolutely gorgeous Puerto Rican girl who had infatuation written right across her forehead. Unfortunately, it was written in Spanish, a language I couldn't read. As a result, I thought it said *love*. I had recently seen *West Side Story*, so I was ripe for infatuation—particularly in this kind of situation. I was like Clark Kent going into a phone booth and coming out as Superman; I'd go in to visit Harold Hart, and when I departed I suddenly was Tony—straight out of the movie. Considering her beauty, transforming the girl into Maria was a very easy task.

When your emotions are in control, you're in danger of doing things you wouldn't even consider under normal circumstances. In my case, after several romantic lunches at the local automat, I managed one evening to end up on the fourth floor of an old tenement house on the Lower East Side. There I was—in bed—in a room with no lights. If that weren't bad enough, there also was no fire escape and no elevator. And there was only one exit from Maria's apartment. I tell you, tortoises were never meant to be in such situations.

Then of course it came: the knock on the door at 4:00 A.M. The knock soon turned into a ferocious banging, interspersed with Spanish words I didn't understand, but there was no doubt in my mind that the person at the door wasn't serenading us with "Guantanamera." Very calmly I asked Maria, "Wh—who is th—th—that?" Very calmly she answered, "My husband." Oh, no problem, I thought to myself. I'll just hold my breath till I die—that way I'll never have to know what he did to my body.

I frantically searched for clothes in the dark—any clothes—hers, mine, his—it didn't make any difference. After partially covering my body with a variety of garments which made me look like a candidate for first prize at a Halloween party, she opened the door and let him in. The moment of truth—what do I do? Tortoises aren't fast; I had no weapons; I'm not adept at fisticuffs, particularly on the fourth floor of a tenement house at four in the morning. While Maria began explaining that I was a priest from Jersey City, I began edging casually toward the door. As their conversation continued, I kept edging . . . and edging . . . and edging.

In the end, I set two tortoise records which still stand today. One is the time for descending four flights of tenement-house stairs (conditions: after midnight, with no wind at the runner's back)—3.5 seconds. The other

"Thees ees Father Goldstein from Jersey City."

record I set was for covering the distance from Avenue B to First Avenue in the shortest time any tortoise had ever done in the snow—7 seconds. And mind you, all this was accomplished while wearing only one shoe. Finally, a little good luck. A cab was zipping by at that ungodly hour. I flagged it down, jumped in, and thus ended the saga of Tony the Tortoise.

Watch out for infatuation. It can lead you to dangers you haven't even dreamed of, but which can become permanent nightmares.

The "Falling-in-Love-with-Love" Obstacle

Love—even when it's real—is always illusory to some extent. Love mirages abound because our thirst for love is insatiable. This often leads people to fall in love with the emotion itself.

If you find yourself falling in love as often as you fall in and out of bed, the chances are excellent that you're in the habit of falling in love with love. And that doesn't work out too well. Love itself does not make a good lover. It can't go to a movie with you; it can't converse with you; the two of you can't have a good laugh together; it can't even mix you a drink. Real people make much better lovers. As long as you have a pulse rate, love will always be a little illusory in nature, but don't allow yourself to become so addicted to its wonderful feeling that you imagine you're in love with everything that wears a skirt.

The Transformation Obstacle

Nothing is more frustrating than being in love with (or thinking you're in love with) someone who isn't exactly what you'd like him to be. The failure to face the reality of what your lover (or prospective lover) really is can lead to one of two irrational procedures on your part, both unhealthy. The first is to try to imagine him to be something other than what he really is. The second is to try to *mold* him into what you want him to be. In either case, you violate the laws of Nature. The first is a matter of lying (to yourself), the second a matter of tampering with the impossible. And the latter is based on the rather arrogant assumption that you have some sort of right to "improve" someone.

I once went with a woman who rated "A's" in about eight categories on my "ten-highest-values" chart. Unfortunately, she could do no better than "F's" in the other two. But because she was so outstanding in eight of the areas, I tried to sweep the two "failures" under the rug—imagine they weren't there. Then I went from bad to worse: when my refusal to acknowledge reality didn't work, I attempted to help her "correct" the two "problem" areas. I'm sure you can guess the result. When you start "helping" a person change, what begins as a passively unhappy situation suddenly becomes an emotional holocaust.

If a person has many qualities you admire and respect, that doesn't erase qualities which are displeasing to you. Nor does it mean you can change those qualities—or that you have the right to. Forget about your lover's basic traits changing; they won't. You must weigh the *existing* pluses and minuses against each other, then allow your Scale to provide you with the verdict.

The Opposites-Attract Obstacle

There's probably a great deal of truth to the old adage that "opposites attract." But the more important reality is that they don't stay together too long, and when they do, it's not on a very happy basis. Finding the Real Thing is tough enough as it is. Common sense tells you that if two people don't enjoy most of the same things in life, the chances of long-term success are considerably reduced.

Three possibilities lend themselves to a relationship based on the opposites-attract illusion. One is an eventual parting of the ways, all too often after many valuable years have been wasted. A second is the irrational non-action of staying together and being at each other's throats over an entire lifetime. But the third is worst of all: The Compromise.

Compromising as a way of life (as opposed to the occasional giving in on a rational, value-for-value basis) means that both parties eventually deteriorate to the point where instead of concentrating on pleasurable activities, they're usually choosing between the lesser of two painful ones. As we discussed, a compromise isn't really a compromise at all; it's sacrifice. And a sacrifice isn't really a sacrifice; it's an irrational selfish action. Looking out for Number One requires *rational* selfish action.

Intimidation through custom and tradition tells you that people must "give their marriage a chance," that they should "try to work things out." What this traditional myth doesn't tell you, however, is how many years of your life you're supposed to risk trying to "work it out" with someone who doesn't share your interests and/or values.

Fortunately, there's a more intelligent solution. Make the conscious, rational effort to find a lover whose main interests coincide with yours. Why start a love relationship with two strikes against it? It's hard enough for two people to live together even when their interests are similar.

It goes without saying that if you're already in an opposites-attract situation which is causing you chronic pain insead of the pleasure you have the right to seek, the only rational solution is to get out of it. Pay your price—in pain—now. Make it a clean, final payment.

The "Jumping-Before-You-Test-the-Water" Obstacle

Over the years, I've done some beautiful swan dives into steaming hot love-jacuzzis, without taking the trouble to stick my toe in the water. All too often I've ended up exiting the pool with third-degree burns. But as I've staggered into the sunset of my life—my once smooth, green skin covered with red blotches—I've become a little cautious. I've learned the wisdom of testing the water before jumping.

Lovers have a natural tendency to be on their best behavior in the early stages of a relationship. That's something you can't control, but you can beware. Before making commitments which can turn your life into an eternal 110-degree jacuzzi, take the trouble to stick your toe in first. Try to experience as many "real-life" situations as possible with a prospective lover.

One such situation—which soothed many of the burns I had accumulated over the years—I affectionately refer to as the Baked Ham Saga. I was dating a beautiful young lady who seemed almost perfect (a danger signal?). I found her intelligent, sensitive and agreeable. But remember this well: a few movies, a half-dozen romantic dinners at elegant restaurants, and a handful of parties are not real life. They would be more appropriately described as the dessert; unfortunately, there's far more to life than just dessert. The fact is you can end up with ptomaine poisoning from the main course before you ever get to the dessert.

With the passing of time, I began to sense a puncture—ever so slight—in her perfection bubble. In a most innocent manner, she began making suggestions regarding my lifestyle—an eccentric one, I admit. I like things to be done in a certain way, at certain times, and by certain people. I'm not very flexible when it comes to my lifestyle, but, then, neither do I try to impose it on anyone else. I never suggest that anyone change her way of living, nor do I expect her to adjust to my eccentricities.

Then came Baked Ham Day. It started innocently enough. I had invited a few friends out to the house for a casual afternoon, figuring we would grill hamburgers and hot dogs later in the day. But this particular young lady didn't quite see it that way. She kept insisting, in a sweet and calm manner, that "you just don't entertain that way." Understanding the Translation Game, I realized that what she was really saying was that *she* didn't entertain that way. I knew for a fact that I entertained that way, because I had done it many times in the past.

She apparently knew well the art of winning bees with honey, because she was all sweetness in her relentless effort to make me see the light. She was so persistent that she finally outlasted even The Tortoise. After hashing over the subject about twenty-five times, I threw in the towel; I was too fatigued to discuss it anymore. I have a quirk about women entering my kitchen, but, in the name of peace, I relented. She gingerly went about her task of preparing a beautiful baked ham dinner with all the trimmings. And here were the results:

1) Everyone enjoyed the meal immensely; it not only looked scrumptious, but was absolutely delicious.

2) Because of the baked ham—entertaining the "correct way"—my guests may have enjoyed themselves 1% more or 1% less than had we just grilled hamburgers and hot dogs.

3) My unhappiness with the situation caused me to be a bad tortoise and do a number of things which turned this sweet young lady into a very mad cook.

4) After her inevitable indignant departure, The Tortoise found himself muttering swear words and crying in soapsuds—at midnight.

5) Another nightmare was added to the guys in the turbans and the race from Avenue B to First Avenue. I still wake up in a cold sweat on occasion, dreaming that I'm trapped in a kitchen with no doors or windows, adrift in a sea of soapsuds.

The young lady was, and is, a very fine person. She only was trying to do what she thought was right—meaning what *she* wanted to do. Which was fine—for her. But having had substantial experience in jumping without testing, I had enough sense to know that what I was seeing that day was only the tip of the baked ham. It's the part I hadn't yet seen that scared me.

You're under no obligation to allow another person to impose his or her lifestyle or standards on you, no matter how abnormal they may think yours are. Allow them to do so only when your Weight-and-Balance Happiness Scale tells you that what you get in return is worth it. Then you're not compromising or "sacrificing"—you're price paying.

Always test the water first! If you don't, at least make certain that your prospective lover is going to stay around long enough to help with the dishes.

WHAT IF YOU CAN'T FIND VALUE-FOR-VALUE LOVE RELATIONSHIPS?

If you've really had a tough time with the Love Game, the first place to look, as always, is in the mirror. If you're faring badly, are you sure it's not because you haven't been willing to pay the price of making the effort to get out and look, the price of enduring the pain that comes with rejection, the price of contributing sufficient value to another's Weight-and-Balance Happiness Scale? Don't kid yourself in this self-examination; it's too critical in your effort to look out for Number One.

Love is not a favor to be automatically bestowed. If you haven't had enough of it in your life, it's very likely that you haven't earned it. Of course, you can't begin to earn love from someone else until you've earned it from yourself. The Real Thing requires self-esteem. True love is an expression of one's admiration of qualities in another individual—qualities which often reflect the traits one most admires in himself.

I once dated a woman I thought was the greatest thing since bubble-gum trading cards. But she didn't see herself that way at all. She had a complete lack of self-respect and no self-confidence whatsoever. I kept trying to convince her that she was outstanding, but she kept insisting she wasn't. The result was that she finally convinced *me*.

Remember, the respect virus is contagious. The only way anyone else will catch it from you is if you have it yourself. You develop self-respect by determining exactly what your values are, then having the self-discipline to stick by them at all times. When you refuse to compromise your integrity with a prospective lover who has similar values, that trait alone should gain his or her immediate admiration and respect.

If you haven't been able to find love, look harder. There are plenty of roses among the weeds out there, but they won't discover you; you'll have to take matters into your own hands and do the discovering yourself.

CAN A LOUSY PERSONALITY OR LACK OF AESTHETICS CHEAT YOU OF LOVE?

Trying to pin down what makes for a lousy personality or what is or isn't aesthetically pleasing is the ultimate in the Definition Game. I've seen some of the world's handsomest men escorting women whose looks were "average," and I've seen the loveliest of ladies on the arms of very plain-looking men. But those assessments were made through *my* eyes; what you see may be quite different. That's one of the things which makes the Free-Enterprise Love Market so great; we're not all competing for the same people. Not only do our values differ, but we see two different images when we look at the same person. That's good for you and good for me.

The lousy-personality problem we've already covered. It, too, is something that's indefinable. If, however, you feel your personality is causing you problems in the Love Game, it's up to you to pay the price necessary to find your weak spots and correct them. Start by making absolutely certain that you're not concealing the real you, which is by far the most common error. A second area to examine is whether you have the fear of rejection under control. You don't need to become a Police-Approach advocate, but don't put on a false front or act defensively out of the fear of being spurned. Assume the worst and hope for the best. When the worst does happen, pick up your self-esteem and go on to the next shelf in the People Store.

A GUIDE TO SCREWING UP EXISTING LOVE RELATIONSHIPS

The easiest way to ruin the Real Thing, once you've got it, is to forget that the other person is a human being. Let's go back to the drawing board: people will hurt you, disappoint you and let you down. Your lover is a person, so if you expect her never to do these things, you're expecting the impossible and are likely to get the probable: trouble. Her views will sometimes vary from yours as she unconsciously engages in those two human sports, the Definition and Line-Drawing Games.

The rationally selfish, pragmatic approach to a lover's mistake is to give her the benefit of the doubt. Avoid flare-ups; they not only don't solve anything, but often do irrevocable damage. Once the words fly out, you can be sorry all you want, but you can't "un-say" them. Angry words which enter her ears become her property for life.

As usual, I'm writing from firsthand experience. I once had what I thought was a wonderful love relationship blown to pieces for no other reason than the fact that I'm nearsighted. The woman in my life had a number of fantastic qualities, but they didn't include the capacity to forgive. The detonation came one afternoon when I happened to be in a parking lot having a strictly platonic conversation with another female. As typical tortoise luck would have it, my girl was walking down the same street, saw us, and began waving. But, alas, my eyesight failed me.

I will say, however, that she handled it very calmly—

sort of like a blitzing all-Pro linebacker stalking a quarterback. Once the charge was lit, I was less worried about the survival of our relationship than I was about coming through the incident without the need for plastic surgery. It was a case of the woman's not giving me the benefit of the doubt, although her firsthand experience definitely gave her no reason to assume I was doing anything wrong.

Give your lover the benefit of the doubt—particularly if he's nearsighted. Forgive until the frequency of such occurrences causes your Scale to begin tipping in the wrong direction. At that point, of course, you have a whole different ball game to consider.

Standing on principle—mostly an ego problem—goes hand in hand with the failure to forgive. That's because once you fly off the handle, you imagine that backing down is a difficult course of action. But that's all in your mind. Backing down actually is easy—particularly if you love someone. All you have to do is do it. I can't think of a more meaningless way to waste a love relationship than by standing on principle.

Being Guilty of Love-Homicide

Sadly, so many people are fortunate enough to find love, then turn around and kill it. In such cases, love doesn't grow stale or fade away; it's annihilated. It's done through jealousy; it's accomplished by interfering with the growth of a mate; it's brought about through possessiveness. You and your lover equal two people, not one. You can't think as a single entity, agree on all issues, or have interests which coincide 100% of the time. In fact, if these things were possible, it would be a dull and unhealthy relationship. People who strive for such oneness reflect a basic insecurity in themselves, and the Pinspotter will soon be along to jostle them into their proper slots.

David Seabury said it all: "Love is not so simple and malleable as many suppose. Put it in prison and it dies. Restrict it and it turns into hate. Force it and it disappears. You cannot will love, nor even control it. You can only guide its expression. It comes or it goes according to those qualities in life that invite it or deny its presence." [1]

Amen.

Seabury was right: love isn't a simple proposition. There are many ways to destroy it. Taking your lover for granted, for example, can wreak destruction before you even realize what you've done (or haven't done). If your lover represents values which are important to you and does her part in keeping your Scale well-balanced, be careful about getting lax. Don't unthinkingly toss aside her great qualities and the joy you experience through her very existence just because you've become used to her. If you've got a good thing going, be conscious of it; avoid losing it through a low rating on the Awareness Meter.

Like friends, lovers are people with whom you should be able to share bad news as well as good. But, being human, your mate doesn't particularly relish problems (unless she's neurotic). Don't bury her with bad news on a daily basis. Tell her about the half of your cup that's full; after a while she tires of hearing only about the empty half.

If you're making it worthwhile for your lover, she'll want to share your troubles with you, but don't relegate her to a dumping ground for the crummy stuff. It's also not her duty to be your echo; in fact, it would be an injustice to you. If all you want is a person who will agree with everything you say, go out and hire someone to come in and regurgitate positive responses to all your remarks. But if you want the Real Thing, you'll encourage her to be honest with you.

Finally, there are the Scales again—both yours and hers. Don't let either of them tip too far in one direction. If you try to be self-sacrificial, you'll upset the laws of Nature and assure the loss of her respect. By the same token, if you operate in the red—accumulate a big credit balance—you'll never feel free to enjoy the love relationship. Fill her needs and make sure yours are taken care of, too; think value for value and you can't go wrong.

SIGNALS THAT TELL YOU YOU'RE IN THE WRONG PLACE

As the experiences have rolled by with the years, I've found myself becoming less and less willing to get close to any situation that has the potential for the one thing which is intolerable to me: hassling.

If you're already in a shaky relationship, hassling can't be avoided very easily. If your lover is hassle oriented, it can't be avoided at all. I like the way a friend of mine puts it. He believes that everyone has a little Happiness Plug at the back of his head. Should a person's Plug be pulled, he's doomed to a frantic life of hassling, problems and general unhappiness.

Men and women are equally susceptible to losing this vital plug. In my friend's case, he became convinced, after many years of marriage, that his wife had lost her Happiness Plug. He swore there was an empty hole where the Plug should have been and that all her happiness fluid had drained out. He'd tried everything to make her feel good, but to no avail. If he had won a million dollars in a sweepstakes, she would have been depressed about the taxes they'd have to pay.

How can you tell if someone has lost her Happiness Plug? If you're sufficiently attracted to a woman to spend a lot of time with her, be alert to how often you get boxed into "can't-win" situations. If the Plug is either gone or deteriorating, you'll often find yourself in positions where you're "damned if you do and damned if you don't."

Such situations are unhealthy; they hold the dangers inherent in being in close proximity to a neurotic person over a long period of time. Under such circumstances, it's easy to become a victim of the I'm Crazy/You're Sane Theory. And since you're more closely involved in a love relationship, you're not only a convenient target, but your ability to think rationally can be impaired by emotion.

I, too, had the experience of living with a woman who had her Happiness Plug pulled. People made her self-conscious; a lack of them made her feel lonely. Poverty depressed her; money made her resentful because she didn't "deserve" it. She hated the routine of working; not working made her feel worthless. Everything about this woman was fabulous—except for the fact that she couldn't be happy.

It was hassle, hassle, hassle—around the clock—week after week, month after month. I kept thinking modern medicine would come up with a technique for transplanting Happiness Plugs, but in the meantime my life was wasting away. One of our typical can't-win, I'm-crazy/you're-sane conversations sounded something like this:

TORTOISE: Look at that rain; it's the worst storm I've seen in years.

LOVER: It's not raining; the sun is shining.

TORTOISE: *(recovering quickly, as the rain begins coming down even harder)* Hmm, you're right; the sun is shining.

LOVER: I think you're trying to humor me. You know damn well it's raining.

TORTOISE: *(nervously thinking through all possibilities as he realizes he's getting boxed into another can't-win corner)* You're right. It is raining. *However,* it's possible that the sun may eventually come out or, on the other hand, it may continue to rain.

LOVER: I know what you're doing; you're trying to prove you can outwit me. Well, it won't work. You can go straight to hell.

TORTOISE: Sorry.

If you're lucky enough to be living with someone who *doesn't* have her Happiness Plug pulled, you'll easily recognize it. She'll be going out of her way to seek pleasure rather than conflict. When the Plug is missing, your lover will display a perverted delight in finding, if not synthetically creating, can't-win situations for you.

318

"Hmm, you're right; the sun is shining."

If the latter sounds familiar, you're probably involved—or have been in the past—in a can't-win situation. If you're still in such a relationship, get out—now! Don't beg, don't argue, don't reason; it won't work. The hassle-oriented person has the deck stacked before you even open your mouth. You must avoid can't-win situations—and rid yourself of existing ones—if you're to be successful in looking out for Number One.

The Compromise Signal

We've already talked about compromising. A compromise is either a rational or an irrational selfish act. You "give in" to your lover when your Scale tells you it's worth it—that what you get in return justifies your actions. When you "compromise" in this manner, you're being rationally selfish. But if you give in too often, and don't feel good about it, you're probably being irrationally selfish. Giving in too often is the result of cheating—feeding your Scale incorrect information.

If a love relationship requires too much compromise on both sides, it's probably an opposites-attract situation. That's not good for either party. Both you and your mate should be spending the majority of your time doing those things which bring you pleasure. If you're not—if your prime interests vary too much—what better signal do you need to tell you that you've made a mistake? The solution isn't to continue compromising, but to find someone whose interests are similar to yours. It's better to lose love now—temporarily—than to wake up years from now and realize that you never had the Real Thing to begin with.

If a lover wants to play by a set of rules that you either don't approve of or don't understand, that doesn't make him a bad person. It just makes him different. What's exciting is that there *is* someone out there—there are many, in fact—who already see life much the same as you. It may not be the same kind of love you have right now, but, in its own way, it can be just as good or better.

Listen to the compromise signal if it's trying to get your attention, then do the right thing instead of the instinctive thing. Don't yield to the tormenting myths of custom and tradition which intimidate you into believing that for some unknown reason you should spend still more of your limited supply of time trying to work out an unworkable situation.

The Looking Signal

If you're looking, something's wrong. I can hear the howls already. Sorry, but after years of observation and hundreds of conversations, that's my honest opinion. By looking, I'm not just referring to an occasional stare at a beautiful woman or a handsome man. I'm talking about looking for someone to *touch*. Being human, I suppose we're all entitled to a slip now and then when it comes to "cheating." It's not advisable, but it's understandable to some degree; forgiveness is certainly justifiable under the right circumstances.

What bowls me over, though, is the man or woman who cheats regularly on his or her spouse, yet claims to have a good, or even great, marriage. You'll never sell me on it. Perhaps I'm old-fashioned—maybe I'm missing some key point—but if the person you're living with is so great, why the necessity to look elsewhere? Sex? Bull! That's only a cheap escape from frustration, usually a result of some deep-seated problem; most likely it stems from an insecurity one doesn't have the courage to face on a conscious level.

I emphasized at the outset that I feel physical attraction is an irreplaceable element in meaningful relationships. I also believe this inexplicable chemical affinity is enhanced over the years as respect and admiration between two lovers grow. If such a feeling slips away, it's an indication that admiration and respect have slipped away. If you're looking elsewhere, it may be a sign that something's missing at home. Don't hide from it; shielding oneself from reality never brings good results. Two people who are honestly and selfishly in love—who derive pleasure from one another's existence on a value-for-value basis—don't lose the feeling of physical attraction with age. If they're meeting each other's needs and growing in the same direction, the physical attraction will increase.

It amazes me how many people delude themselves on this point. They'll argue irrationally for hours on end, trying to explain why fooling around on the side has nothing to do with their feelings toward their spouses. I have one acquaintance who put more effort into cheating on his wife than he did his occupation. His office was in the city, his home in the suburbs (sound familiar?). This was convenient for him, since he had something lined up in the city four or five nights a week. The man was an absolute genius at devising sophisticated schemes to assure that his rendezvouses remained unknown to his wife.

He used to "work late" virtually every night, so it was understandable that he seemed tired on those rare occasions when he was home; his wife, of course, assumed his exhaustion was the result of long, hard hours at the office (which to some degree was true, since he did a lot of "work" on his office couch). He pulled off his all-timer the day he purposely rode to work with someone else, asking his wife to pick him up at the office around 11:00 P.M.

When she picked him up that night, he insisted on doing the driving (mind you, this was all premeditated—down to the last detail). As he drove home, he periodically pretended to doze off. At one point, he deliberately ran off the road (he had picked, days in advance, what he considered to be the perfect spot for a groggy swerve). His wife screamed and he "awoke" in a startled manner—a performance which should have won him an Oscar. But i paid off. You know the first thing she said to him? She told my carousing acquaintance that she would never again let him risk driving home late at night after putting in a grueling fifteen-hour day at the office. She insisted that h

322

stay in the city overnight when he had to work late (i.e., four or five nights a week).

The topper? The next day she went out and bought him a suitcase to make sure he'd keep his promise to stay overnight when he was too tired to drive home. By the way, they're no longer married—which I'm sure is no great shock to you. The amazing thing to me is that his wife never found out he'd been cheating all those years.

Remember: looking out for Number One requires the ability to recognize and the courage to acknowledge even the most painful and unpleasant realities. If you're looking, it's a warning signal that something's wrong in the relationship. Whether it's you or your lover who's doing the looking, the signal is there. In either case, don't delude yourself. Have the courage to acknowledge reality; analyze what's wrong and do something about it.

More often than not, The Other Element has evaporated—which means it's no longer a love relationship. That chemical affinity may have died without your being consciously aware of it, but it's unlikely that the factors which contributed to its death over a long period of time can now be corrected.

If your tendency to "look" stems from a basic insecurity within you, then you must make a conscious, rational effort to resolve that problem. If that isn't the case, the rational solution, although most people dread facing it, is to sever the relationship and look for a partner who satisfies your needs to the extent that you won't have the urge to look.

The "Everything's Fine" Signal

Another acquaintance has openly stated on many occasions that he has absolutely no affection for his wife. When I asked him the usual absurd question—why he didn't get a divorce—he didn't try to rationalize. According to him, his sole reason for staying with his wife was that he loved his small son too much to leave.

While I had empathy for his attachment to his son, I persisted in wanting to know how he could stand to live under such circumstances. He replied that it wasn't that bad. "She really doesn't get in the way and hardly bothers me at all." Statements like that cause me to blink and scratch my head a lot. All I can say is that if the function of a husband or wife is not to get in the way and not to bother his or her mate, it's no wonder that marriages are crashing to the rocks in record numbers and that adultery has become a way of life.

The Perfect-Marriage Signal

So as not to paint a false picture that would indicate it's always the men who wear the black hats and the women who specialize in naiveté, I'll throw in one last story. I have a very close friend who seemed to have the perfect marriage—twenty-five years with the same woman. On the surface, they appeared to have a great deal in common, were sincere and affectionate toward one another, and generally very happy. I often remarked to him that they had the kind of love relationship everyone dreams about. He would respond with a warm smile, "I guess I just lucked out."

One day, however, a not-so-funny thing happened on the way to the office: his wife, then in her early forties, ran off with a twenty-nine-year-old chap. Some time later after the shock had worn off and we had a chance to discuss it, I told him that the whole thing had taken me by complete surprise, that I'd always believed they had the perfect marriage. His reply was one that I won't forget—ever. Staring blankly and forlornly at the floor, he responded: "So did I."

HOW TO GET OUT OF A CRUMMY LOVE RELATIONSHIP

The burden of excess baggage on your journey throug

life is, as we discussed, costly; being saddled with a bad love relationship is totally debilitating.

CRUMMY LOVE-RELATIONSHIP THEORY

A crummy love relationship is one in which you consistently give more than you receive. If you're in that predicament now, cut it off before it goes any further. Just because you've invested a number of valuable years in a relationship which has caused you more pain than pleasure, that doesn't mean you should throw away additional years enduring more of the same. Don't try to hide it or smooth over it; ignoring the realities will only cause it to get worse. Don't leave the determination of your happiness (or unhappiness) in the hands of another person; you should be in control of your own destiny. Don't put it off. Do it now; you're running out of time as each second goes by.

No reason is sound enough to keep a crummy relationship together. The worst excuse of all is children. If kids are involved, give them a break. Get out of your mate's life so your children can enjoy both of you at your best— in happier states than they now see you. If you stay together under miserable circumstances, not only do you and your spouse suffer, but the children, who had nothing to do with creating the mess in the first place, are forced to endure the pain of watching you quarrel or be exposed to a bad advertisement for marriage.

Guilty? Come on, now, we've already thoroughly covered intimidation through guilt. Both of you are adults; each had the right to say no to the relationship before becoming too deeply involved. The only reason for feeling guilty is if you desperately and irrationally try to hold together the pieces of a crumbling relationship. You have no right to make your mate suffer any longer, even if he or she erroneously believes that it's best to stay together. Usually such a thought on the part of your lover is inspired by irrational selfishness, which in turn has been brought on by the emotion of fear. Change is a scary thing, and it grows scarier as you get used to a set way of life.

The only reality is the present. What a person is today and what you feel for him today are realities. The past is over; it's something that no longer exists. The future is a possibility or, at best, a probability, but not a reality. Only that which you are now experiencing with your lover is reality.

If you were an honest, faithful husband for ten years, it might be reasonable to expect your wife to forgive you for cheating once. But if it becomes an addiction at age forty, a rational woman will realize that what you did yesterday was what you *were* yesterday. What you're doing today is what you are today. If she had rational reasons for loving you yesterday, those reasons are no longer valid if you're no longer the same person. Sure, you accumulate a certain number of credits over the years for good deeds, but never do you build up a backlog great enough to give you the right to mistreat your mate consistently.

People change as the years go by. When two lovers grow in different directions, they end up looking at strangers across the breakfast table. The divergent growth normally takes place over a period of many years, being unnoticeable on a day-to-day basis. As a result, it's impractical—if not impossible—to retrace your steps and teach one another everything you've learned over a long period of time. You may have started out as two individuals with similar interests, but evolved into a classic opposites-attract couple.

There's only one relevant factor to consider when determining whether you're in a crummy love relationship: does your Weight-and-Balance Happiness Scale tell you that what you're getting out of the relationship is worth what you're putting into it? No matter how good the good, if the bad outweighs it, it's a crummy relationship. Staying in it can only be a fatal blow to looking out for Number One.

Looking Back

If you've decided that your love relationship no longer meets the requirements necessary to your living a happy life, and if you've rationally made the decision to split, let me suggest you do one thing with regard to looking back: *don't!* There is almost always a temptation to go back and give it another try. I suppose it's possible—anything's possible—but it seldom works out.

Subconsciously, at least, one of the biggest influences in tempting a person to go back is to recall all the pain he or she endured while searching for the right lover. This is enough to discourage anyone. Having been away from the seeking-and-rejection pattern for years, the prospect of having to go through it all over again can be quite frightening. In fact, there's only one thing I can think of that could be worse: a continued lifetime of dull, nagging nothingness. Better to be alive and hurting; where there's life, at least there's hope. And the chances of that hope transforming itself into reality increase dramatically with your increased efforts, determination, self-discipline and patience.

Are you willing—at age thirty or forty or fifty—to pay the price for a better life? It always seems to get back to the bottom line, doesn't it?

The Great Reward

Whether you've never been in love or are now in a bad relationship and desirous of finding the Real Thing, it's out there for you; I guarantee it. And when you finally discover love, don't fail to nurture and cherish it. Don't let anyone stand in the way of the Real Thing once you've found it—not a father or mother, son or daughter, husband or wife.

The husband or wife, of course, should not be a factor when the time comes; if the relationship wasn't right, it would have been severed by that time, freeing both to search for the Real Thing. Be a big boy and make the move *before* you find what you're looking for. You not only increase your chances of finding it, but ease the pain for everyone else involved. The well-known syndrome of waiting until the kids are grown and the woman is past her prime is the most irrationally selfish action a husband can take. Such a man wastes the best years of his life, as well as his spouse's, and unfairly subjects innocent children to a daily lie. In such a situation, it's not surprising that children grow up thinking that love isn't a necessary ingredient in marriage.

Be rationally selfish and have the courage to start paying the necessary price right now. And when you're lucky enough to find the Real Thing, don't be afraid of it. I've heard people comment—when finding love—that they're "so happy it scares them." Don't be afraid of love. Tomorrow will come soon enough and bring with it its share of unpleasant circumstances. More important to consider is that tomorrow may not come at all. Only today is reality, and if you're happy today—if you're feelin' good—you've got it.

Let yourself go when you find the Real Thing. Become totally involved with the pleasures of the present. Don't just go through the motions; live each moment to the fullest. Don't cloud your mind with the nonexistent past or a future that may never arrive. Love and be loved and don't look for problems. Fill each other's needs and keep your Scales balanced. It all adds up to pleasure, the end result of looking out for Number One.

THE EFFECTS OF THIS CHAPTER ON THE LIFE OF THE TORTOISE

How might my philosophy on love relationships affec my love life? The same as with friends. It saves me wor by encouraging all prospects who don't understand th beauty of value-for-value love relationships to eliminat themselves. That's good for me; I'll accept any help I ca get in the elimination process. It increases the chances of those roses out there perking up and making themselves seen.

I guess you might say "The Love Hurdle" has been a want ad. Summarized, it reads something like this:

Woman with following qualifications send picture and resume to:

The Tortoise
Los Angeles, California

No history of disease (e.g., World Owes Me a Living, Waiting to Be Discovered, Tend-To, etc.); Boy-Girl instinct under control; no experience as Better Dealer; large quantities self-esteem and self-respect; thorough understanding of beauty of rationally selfish, value-for-value relationships; intelligent, mature, courteous, friendly; likes racquetball.

The Starting Line

You know something? Now that I'm through, I'm glad life isn't as Madison Avenue portrays it. Because writing this book, instead of vacationing in Rio, has reminded me how exciting and beautiful real life can be.

And that, above all else, is what I hope has come through to you: that by clearing the hurdles we've discussed, your life can be a joyful experience, a journey where the pleasures far exceed the moments of unpleasantness. What greater epitaph than to be able to say that when you passed this way, you were feelin' good and didn't interfere with anyone else?

If we're on the same wavelength, you know that won't happen by accident. To clear those hurdles, you've got a lot of work to do. Work is the price; happiness is the reward. It takes effort on your part to be aware and to make conscious, rational decisions; it takes effort not to delude yourself into feeding your Weight-and-Balance Happiness Scale incorrect information; it takes effort to concentrate on the "is's" of life, ignoring the "ought to's" which constantly tempt you to go off course.

In addition to effort, it takes courage—the courage to change an established way of life and move on to a better one. You begin summoning the necessary courage when you place your problems in proper perspective. They aren't insurmountable. Remember, there's always a way out—a method for getting from where you are now to where you want to be. It's not impossible to make changes; it's only hard. Compromising won't do it; sweeping irritations under the rug won't do it; continuing to load yourself down with excess baggage won't do it.

What will do it is price paying. Pay the price of uncomplicating your life. Pay the price of trying unique experiences, some of which will cause you pain; others, however, will lead to pleasures beyond anything you may have dreamed. Pay the price of looking around the People Store—and shop carefully. Buy as many of the good ones as you can afford; they'll add untold happiness to your life if you're willing to deal with them on a value-for-value basis.

And the others? Leave them in the Store. Those who would intimidate you—through credentials, custom and tradition, conformity, guilt, or any other ploy—have no place in your plans for looking out for Number One. In some cases, people who cause you problems will try to invite themselves into your life anyway. They will only bother you, however, until you learn not to let them.

Starting today, take control of Number One. And when you're ready to start clearing those hurdles, don't let anyone hold you back. Before you get into the starting blocks, however, one caution: don't cheat. When I say *starting blocks,* I'm talking about the starting blocks on a track which leads to long-term solutions. After you begin, no short-term patching is allowed. Make patience and self-discipline—adherence to your game plan—your trademarks once you spring forward toward the first hurdle. Do it the long-term-solution way: pay the full

331

price for love, friendship, and material gain. That way your life won't be a perpetual rerun at the hurdles that stand between you and the freedom which comes from looking out for Number One.

Oops—I almost forgot Murphy. Do remember that he's out there and that he'll get you as often as he can. But at heart, he's only a playful old trickster. I sometimes suspect that he secretly enjoys seeing you thwart his little pranks; I think he actually admires your rational use of the "Sustenance" Theory. Murphy or Nature, or both, will continue to see to it that circumstances change, but once you get the hang of it, you'll start handling that phenomenon as though it were an everyday occurrence—which is exactly what it is.

Okay, if you're ready, get down in the starting blocks. Remember, the clock doesn't start when you take off; it's *already* running. If you have the ability to make conscious, rational decisions that will lead to pleasure, the only question which remains is: do you have the courage?

Personally, I think you deserve the joy of looking out for Number One. How can I make such a statement if I don't even know you? Because I believe that every individual has the right to seek a happy life so long as he doesn't forcibly interfere with others. Begin today to do good deeds for someone you've probably neglected far too long: Number One. The world may not owe you a living, but you owe yourself the world.

Good luck and watch out for your toes as you go over each hurdle. If you happen to trip over one, Murphy's just testing you. Be aggravatingly persistent and I think he'll respect you; pick yourself up and try again until you clear it.

And when you've cleared all the hurdles and broken that tape, it's not the finish line you will have reached; it's the *Starting Line*. It's the beginning of a life where rational dreams have a way of coming true.

Acknowledgements

Whenever the subject of writing comes up in discussions with non-authors, I'm reminded of how little is generally known about the complexity and wide range of specialized effort that goes into the making of a book. I'm not referring here to "group effort," but rather to the principle of specialization—each individual lending his particular talents on a value-for-value basis, the synchronization of these talents being the responsibility of the author.

In this regard, I wish to pay specific tribute to my research editor, Ellen Shahan, who was instrumental in editing the book and overseeing a great number of details which went into its mechanical preparation. Her intelligence, insight, thoroughness, and relentless advocacy of simplicity have been invaluable to me.

Patti Zimmerman, Lynn Michelson and Eldo Callico deserve credit for contributing to the final product—either directly or indirectly—by competently handling an endless number of details which made it possible for me to concentrate on the creative area of putting my ideas in writing. All three are living proof of the soundness of the value-for-value concept between employers and employees.

I'm indebted to many people for contributing to the evolution of my philosophy over the years, notably Ayn Rand and Harry Browne, whose works have been instrumental in this respect. Other writers whose ideas have been particularly helpful to me are Henry Hazlitt, Eric Hoffer, David Seabury, and Lysander Spooner. The principles espoused by the Libertarian Party have been stimulating and have helped to cement many anti-government thoughts of mine which previously were only suspicions. Finally, I deeply appreciate the help Sy Leon has given in crystallizing my answers to a number of philosophical questions regarding government.

Notes

Chapter 1

1. Ayn Rand, *The Virtue of Selfishness* (New York: The New American Library, Inc., Signet Books, 1964), p. 29.
2. Aristotle, *On Man in the Universe*, ed. with introduction by Louise Ropes Loomis (Roslyn, New York: Walter J. Black, Inc., Classics Club, 1971), p. xxviii.
3. Harry Browne, *How I Found Freedom in an Unfree World* (New York: Macmillan Publishing Co., Inc., 1973), p. 51.
4. David Seabury, *The Art of Selfishness* (New York: Julian Messner, Simon & Schuster, Inc., Pocket Books, 1974), p. 236.

Chapter 2

1. Aristotle, *On Man in the Universe*, p. xxviii.
2. Carl Sagan, *Other Worlds* (New York: Bantam Books, Inc., 1975), p. 12.
3. Will Durant, *Our Oriental Heritage* (New York: Simon & Schuster, 1954), p. 69.

Chapter 3

1. Ayn Rand, *The Virtue of Selfishness*, p. 28.
2. David Seabury, *The Art of Selfishness*, p. 119.
3. "The Memphis Smut Raker," *Newsweek* (5 April 1976), p. 62.
4. Dee Brown, *Bury My Heart at Wounded Knee* (New York: Holt, Rinehart & Winston, 1970), p. 8 [*Italics mine*].

Chapter 4

1. Janis Ian, "At Seventeen" (Words and music by Janis Ian, © 1974 by Mine Music Ltd.). Reprinted by permission.
2. Alfred A. Malabre, Jr., "The Future Revised: U.S. Unlikely to Be as Big—or as Rich—as Analysts Thought" (First in a Series), *The Wall Street Journal* (15 March 1976).
3. Eric Hoffer, *The True Believer* (New York: Harper & Row, 1951), p. 14.
4. Henry David Thoreau, *Walden* and *On the Duty of Civil Disobedience* (New York: Harper & Row, A Harper Classic, 1965), p. 255.
5. Aristotle, *On Man in the Universe*, p. xxxii.
6. Robert Froman, *Racism* (New York: Delacorte Press, 1972), p. 46.
7. Ibid., p. 55.
8. Ibid., pp. 53–54.
9. Lewis H. Carlson and George A. Colburn, *In Their Place: White America Defines Her Minorities, 1850–1890* (New York: John Wiley & Sons, Inc., 1972), p. 1.

Chapter 5

1. Eric Hoffer, *The True Believer*, p. 97.
2. Richard K. Rein, "A Princeton Tiger Designs an Atomic Bomb in a Physics Class," *People* (25 October 1976), p. 41.

Chapter 6

1. "Rich–Poor Gap Dominates World Poll," *Los Angeles Times* (21 September 1976), Part I, p. 4.
2. Tynette Hills and Floyd H. Ross, *The Great Religions by Which Men Live* (Greenwich, Connecticut: Fawcett Publications, Inc., A Fawcett Premier Book, 1956), p. 56.
3. "Playboy Interview: Karl Hess," *Playboy* (July 1976), pp. 64 and 70.
4. Ayn Rand, *The Virtue of Selfishness*, p. 52.
5. John Hospers, "The Two Classes: Producers and Parasites," *Reason* (September 1975), p. 15.
6. Ayn Rand, *The Virtue of Selfishness*, p. 55.
7. Carl Sandburg, "The Lawyers Know Too Much," *Smoke and Steel* (New York: Harcourt Brace Jovanovich, Inc., 1920). Reprinted by permission.
8. David Seabury, *The Art of Selfishness*, p. 71.

Chapter 7

1. Henry David Thoreau, *Walden* and *On the Duty of Civil Disobedience*, p. 100.

Chapter 8

1. David Seabury, *The Art of Selfishness*, p. 180.

Glossary

Absolute Moralist: A person who takes it upon himself to decide what is right and wrong for everyone.

Absolute morality: A unilaterally determined moral code which establishes what is right and wrong for everyone.

Anti-Neurotic Theory: Ignore all neurotic remarks and actions of normal people and *all* remarks and actions of neurotic people. In cases where a neurotic person persists, notwithstanding your lack of attention, take swift and positive action to eliminate him from your life altogether.

Awareness Meter: An imaginary mechanism which gauges an individual's level of awareness.

Better Dealer: A person in whom the Better-Deal instinct is totally out of control; *see* Better Deal Theory.

Better Deal Theory: It's human nature, once you have a "deal" sewn up, to wonder about the possibility of there being a better deal down the road.

Billionaire Babies: People who constantly think and talk in terms of billions of dollars (i.e., billionaires, billion-dollar deals, etc.).

Big Picture: The vastness and complexity of the universe, including the wide range of problems and complexities of mankind.

Bottom, The: Financial destitution; the lowest financial point one can experience.

Boyfriend Theory: When you meet a woman who intrigues you, try to keep calm. Don't get too carried away until you've had an opportunity to assemble some background information. You're far better off—particularly physically—if you assume the following two probabilities: 1) she already has a boyfriend (or fiancé or husband); 2) he's big, hairy and mean.

Boy-Girl Theory: There's a basic human weakness inherent in all people which tempts them to want what they can't have and not want what is readily available to them.

Cash Flow Game: A game whose object is to have the free use of the other guy's money for as long as possible.

Changing Circumstances Theory: The one absolutely predictable thing in life is that circumstances will always change. What is not known is *when* they will change.

Confused-Thinking Theory: When a person's philosophy takes a sudden and dramatic shift in an opposite direction, his reasoning is suspect, because: 1) If his previous beliefs were foreign to his present ideas, his thinking must have been confused where his former ideology was concerned; therefore, how can he trust his reasoning power with regard to his new ideology? 2) On the other hand, if his original thinking was sound, his old philosophy should have been correct; therefore, his reasons for joining the new crusade must be incorrect.

Crummy-Friendship Theory: A crummy friendship is one in which you consistently give more than you receive.

Crummy Love-Relationship Theory: A crummy love relationship is one in which you consistently give more than you receive.

Definition-Game Theory: Every word, every act and every situation is defined by each human being subjectively, usually in such a way as to fit in comfortably with his actions and/or the circumstances of the moment.

Diaper Corps: People under twenty-one years of age or people over thirty who still play with rattles; they are responsible for many of the really far-out movements (crusades).

Discouragement Fraternity: Those people in any given industry who will go to great lengths to try to convince you that you can't make it in their field.

Egoruptcy: A form of bankruptcy caused primarily by the investment of too much time and capital in one's ego.

Electronic Thought-Particle Game: A mental game played on an imaginary TV screen, the object of which is to maneuver individual rational thought-particles through a maze of irrational custom-and-tradition particles without a collision.

Expert: A person who is knowledgeable in his field, but not infallible; a guy who can tell you all the reasons why *you* can't do something.

Factual Meditation: A type of meditation which is practiced in a quiet, relaxed atmosphere, and which involves a free-flowing of the facts; as thoughts begin to wander in and out of your consciousness, the idea is to grasp the rational ones and filter out those which aren't rational.

Film Festival Theory: There is a bitter, snobbish element in the film business—people who are so hopelessly out of touch with the desires of the consumer that they try to make themselves believe commercial success in films is irrelevant. If you're interested in financial success, don't put too much emphasis on the critical acclaim of a small, elite group of individuals. That's not where the money lies; it's only where the ego seeks to be fed.

Financial Geometric-Growth Theory: A two-sided theory which, on the positive side, manifests itself as the phenomenon of "money makes money," but which, on the negative side, dictates that when one is in a cash squeeze, everything tends to go to hell.

Forcible-Interference group: A group which tries to bring about change through the threat of force (i.e., pressuring those in power to pass new "laws" to help them attain their objectives).

Free-Enterprise Friendship Market: An absolute market—consisting of all the people in the world—in which one theoretically can "buy" friends on a free-enterprise basis.

Free-Enterprise Love Market: An abstract market—consisting of all the people in the world—in which one theoretically can "buy" lovers on a free-enterprise basis.

Game, The: The game of business.

Grouping and tagging: The application of a label to a group of people, disregarding individual characteristics and abilities.

Happiness Plug: An imaginary plug at the back of each person's head, which, when pulled, dooms him to a frantic life of hassling, problems and general unhappiness.

Human Nature Group: Three realities of human behavior which are grouped together because they are so fundamental and automatic in nature and are present to the same degree in all people (*see* Self-interest, Line-Drawing-Game Theory and Definition-Game Theory).

I'm Crazy/You're Sane Theory: If you attempt to carry on a relationship with an irrational person, given enough time he can make you think that you're the one who's neurotic.

"Is's" versus "Ought To's" Theory: The degree of complications in an individual's life corresponds to his insistence on dwelling on the way he thinks the world *ought to* be rather than the way it actually *is*.

I've-Got-My-Shit-Together Theory: The more someone dwells on a point (particularly if the information is volunteered for no apparent reason), the better your chances of being right if you assume the opposite.

Jungle: The business world.

Leapfrog Theory: In business, you are under no obligation to fight your way up "through the ranks" or let someone else decide when you've "paid your dues." Only you know when you're ready, and when you are, leapfrog to exactly the point on the business ladder where you think you belong.

Legalboy: A cub-attorney, fresh out of law school, still "wet behind the ears," and brimming over with Perry Mason fantasies.

Legalman: The omnipresent defender of the nonexistent problems of people; one of the players in the game of business who got into the park by sneaking under the fence, then took it upon himself to assume the role of head skimmer.

Legalman Proper-Use Theory: The proper time for Legalman's services is when you desire to back out of a deal but are embarrassed to do so on your own; the proper time to lock Legalman in his cage is when you're serious about closing a deal.

Liar: One who correctly perceives a given reality but, for his own reasons, purposely hides the true facts from others.

Life-Complication Theory: People seem to have a tendency to seek ways to complicate their lives.

Line-Drawing-Game Theory: Every person subjectively draws his own lines concerning what is and is not proper action, based either on his own moral standards, the moral standards of others, or what is convenient for him at the time of the action.

LSD Deal: A deal that could only be created by a person under the influence of LSD and which has absolutely no chance of ever coming to pass.

Luver: A person who is positioned somewhere in that vast area between a lover and an overnight fling. He or she doesn't quite make it as a lover, but there's a little more to the relationship than just pure sex.

Mr. Magoo: Someone who does not have the ability to perceive the facts correctly.

Murphy's Law: Nothing is as easy as it looks./Everything takes longer than you expect./And if anything can go wrong—it will/ At the worst possible moment!

One-in-the-Sack-Is-Worth-a-Hundred-in-the-Face Theory: If you aren't willing to make the effort and pay the price—ask for and be prepared to take the inevitable bumps and bruises—you've boxed yourself into a corner where the odds against your succeeding are about 100 to 0. Stated positively, what it really boils down to is the simple law of averages.

One-to-a-Box Theory: No matter who you are, no matter what you've accomplished in your lifetime, no matter how many friends you have, and no matter how close you may be to one or more persons, the reality is that when you go down for the final count, you'll be in that wooden box all by yourself.

Ostrich: The individual who has the ability to perceive reality correctly, but who refuses to do so, preferring instead to live in the fantasyland of "ought to's."

Other Element, The: The physical-chemical attraction one has for a lover; an ingredient which distinguishes between lovers and friends.

Out-of-Step Theory: As a general rule, a person's chances for success will tend to increase the more he's out of step with "society."

Paradigm Restriction: An abstract mental obstacle to an accurate perception of reality which makes it tough to comprehend ideas and circumstances we aren't accustomed to hearing and seeing within the invisible perimeters that surround our lives.

Pinspotter Theory: Life is like a giant pinspotter in a goliath's bowling alley, with billions of humans relegated to the status of bowling pins. In the final analysis, the Pinspotter shakes us down into our proper slots and we end up exactly where we belong.

Plastic Glass Theory: If you base your actions on custom and tradition alone, the likely result is that you will pay for such a lackadaisical mistake in lost pleasure and increased pain.

Police Approach: A bizarre method of trying to meet eligible women which involves, as a last resort, blocking the path of a woman you've spotted on the street, spreading your arms like a traffic cop and then promising to leave her alone if she'll give you her name and phone number.

Pop-Off Mess-Up Man: The imaginary chief aide of Satan, assigned the eternal task of urging incurable pop-offs to let everyone know about their plans prematurely.

Price-Paying Toll Machine: An imaginary toll machine which requires that you pay the necessary price for anything you wish to obtain or accomplish in life.

Protesting Lady: A person who betrays himself by overstating his case or protesting too much; derived from Gertrude's statement in *Hamlet*. "The lady doth protest too much, methinks."

Reality, Theory of: Reality isn't the way you wish things to be, nor the way they appear to be, but the way they actually are. Either you acknowledge reality and use it to your benefit or it will automatically work against you.

Real Thing: A love relationship which is based on the principle of value for value, mutual admiration and respect, and a mutual physical-chemical attraction.

Relativity, Theory of: Few people take the trouble to consider facts in a relative light; until one does so, one cannot intelligently settle on a proper course of action.

Sanskrit Financialese: A translation of business language which assumes the worst.

Scared Money Theory: When you're operating on money you can't afford to lose, or no money at all, it's not only hard to be convincing, it's also difficult to make rational decisions; and it's almost impossible to avoid being intimidated by the player who does have financial strength behind him.

Schmexpert: The nonexpert giver of advice.

Screwor-Screwee Theory: The screwor is always the other guy; the screwee is always you.

Self-Indictment Theory: Don't undress yourself in public and don't wear your problems on your shirtsleeve. Never provide the would-be slanderer with something for nothing.

Self-interest: A concern for one's own well-being.

Selfishness, irrational: Selfishness based on irrational thinking, which manifests itself in behavior which is not in one's best interest, i.e., forcible interference in the lives of others, disregard of the principle of value for value, or any other type of irrational behavior.

Selfishness, rational: Selfishness based on rational thinking, which manifests itself in behavior which is in one's best interest, i.e., noninterference in the lives of others, use of the principle of value for value, or any other type of rational behavior.

Sure Theory: There's only one way to be sure that your objective will be given the best shot possible: *take matters into your own hands and don't expect any help from anyone.*

"Sustenance" Theory (Theory of Sustenance of a Positive Attitude through the Assumption of a Negative Result): Since most things in life don't work out (due to factors beyond your control), it's realistic to assume the worst: the positive result is that you won't be mentally devastated when things go wrong.

Tend-To Theory: Most people have a tendency to believe their own bullshit: when you start believing yours, you're in a state of mind that is dangerous to your well-being.

bullshit; when you start believing yours, you're in a state of mind that is dangerous to your well-being.

Three Type Theory: There are three types of people in the world— a Type Number One, a Type Number Two, and a Type Number Three. A Type Number One understands and openly acknowledges that he always acts in his own self-interest. A Type Number Two understands that he always acts in his own self-interest, but tries to make you believe otherwise. A Type Number Three either doesn't understand or doesn't want to understand that he always acts in his own self-interest. He therefore feels very sincere when he tries to make you believe he's thinking of you first.

Touchies and No-Touchies Theory: Once a guy has made it, the wise thing to do is have two piles of chips—one labeled "Touchies" and the other "No-Touchies." The Touchies are used to buy houses, cars and other goodies and also for risk investments. The No-Touchies are the ones you don't use for luxuries and with which you don't take chances.

Tough Guy: A fellow who suffers either from delusions of physical grandeur or the misguided notion that demonstrations of "toughness" engender respect and admiration.

Translation Game: The conversion of a person's remarks into what he truly means by understanding where he's coming from (i.e., who he is, what his motives are, what his problems are, etc.).

Type Number One, etc.: *See* Three Type Theory.

Volcanic Ash Theory: Happiness is where you find it. Whether it is or is not presently close by, don't be carried away by illusions and make dramatic moves based on emotion. Changes should be made only after careful reasoning convinces you they're warranted.

Waiting-to-Be-Discovered Theory: The majority of people either are too unaware of what's going on around them, or too obsessed with bitterness over some misfortune they've endured, to recognize the opportunities which continually pop up. They fantasize that someone is going to come along and put their names "in lights."

Weight-and-Balance Happiness Scale Theory: Each of us has a marvelous miniature computer—a Weight-and-Balance Happiness Scale—within that larger computer we call the brain. It automatically weighs every known alternative available to you at a given moment and chooses the one it *believes* will bring you the most happiness.

World-Owes-Me-a-Living Theory: A person who has the absurd notion that anyone, particularly "the world," owes him anything is destined not only for a lifetime of failure, but tremendous bitterness and frustration as well. Until a person gets such a presumptuous notion out of his head, he'll never get out of the starting gate, much less succeed.

You-Won't-Get-Credit-For-It Theory: Don't do something for the reason that it's "the right thing to do" if there's no benefit to be derived from it.

Zip the Lip Theory: If you've got something good going, *shut up!*

Bibliography

"American Notes: Looking Ahead." *Time*, 25 October 1976.

Angrist, Stanley W. *Other Worlds, Other Beings*. New York: Thomas Y. Crowell Company, 1973.

Aristotle. *On Man in the Universe*. Edited with Introduction by Louise Ropes Loomis. Roslyn, New York: Walter J. Black, Inc., Classics Club, 1971.

Behrman, S.N., and Logan, Joshua. *Fanny*. A musical play based on the trilogy of Marcel Pagnol. Music and Lyrics by Harold Rome. Copyright © 1954 by S.N. Behrman and Joshua Logan. Copyright © 1955 by S.N. Behrman, Joshua Logan and Harold Rome.

Brown, Dee. *Bury My Heart at Wounded Knee*. New York: Holt, Rinehart & Winston, 1970.

Browne, Harry. *How I Found Freedom in an Unfree World*. New York: Macmillan Publishing Co., Inc., 1973.

Carlson, Lewis H., and Colburn, George A. *In Their Place: White America Defines Her Minorities, 1850–1890*. New York: John Wiley & Sons, Inc., 1972.

Davidson, Jim. "Tired of Being Pushed Around Every April 15? Punch Out the IRS!" *Playboy*, April 1976.

"Double-Talk Outfoxes Educators." *Los Angeles Times*, 8 May 1974.

Durant, Will. *Our Oriental Heritage*. New York: Simon & Schuster, 1954.

Falk, Richard A. *This Endangered Planet; Prospects and Proposals for Human Survival*. New York: Random House, 1971.

Foley, James. "U.S. Develops Secret 'Sleeping' Antisub Torpedo." *Los Angeles Times*, 20 May 1976.

Froman, Robert. *Racism*. New York: Delacorte Press, 1972.

"Galaxy 8 Billion Light Years Away Discovered." *Los Angeles Times*, 1 July 1975.

Greenwood, Leonard. "Amazon Has Enough Iron to Last Centuries." *Los Angeles Times*, 10 August 1975.

Halacy, D. S., Jr. *The Geometry of Hunger*. New York: Harper & Row, 1972.

Hauser, Philip M., ed. *The Population Dilemma*. 2nd ed. Englewood Cliffs, New Jersey: Prentice-Hall, Inc., 1969.

Hazlitt, Henry. *Economics in One Lesson*. New York: Harper & Brothers, 1946.

Hazlitt, Henry. *The Conquest of Poverty*. New Rochelle, New York: Arlington House, 1973.

Hills, Tynette, and Ross, Floyd H. *The Great Religions by Which Men Live*. Greenwich, Connecticut: Fawcett Publications, Inc., A Fawcett Premier Book, 1956.

Hoffer, Eric. *The True Believer*. New York: Harper & Row, 1951.

343

Hospers, John. "The Two Classes: Producers and Parasites." *Reason*, September 1975.

Joseph, Frank S. "How American Express Co. 'Floats' Its Way to Profitability." *The Pittsburgh Press*, 22 June 1975.

Kann, Peter R. "Filth, Poverty, Disease Overwhelm the Citizens of Teeming City in India." *The Wall Street Journal*, 14 June 1971.

Leon, Sy. *None of the Above*. Santa Ana, California: Fabian Publishing Company, 1976.

MacBride, Roger L. *A New Dawn for America: The Libertarian Challenge*. Ottawa, Illinois: Green Hill Publishers, Inc., 1976.

Malabre, Alfred A., Jr. "The Future Revised: U.S. Unlikely to Be as Big—or as Rich—as Analysts Thought." (First in a Series.) *The Wall Street Journal*, 15 March 1976.

Matthews, Linda. "Attorneys and Their Fees: The Pressure Is On." *Los Angeles Times*, 27 September 1974.

"Memphis Smut Raker, The." *Newsweek*, 5 April 1976.

Orwell, George. *1984*. New York: Harcourt Brace Jovanovich, Inc., New American Library, Signet Classics, 1949.

"Playboy Interview: Karl Hess." *Playboy*, July 1976.

Rand, Ayn. *The Virtue of Selfishness*. New York: The New American Library, Inc., Signet Books, 1964.

Rein, Richard K. "A Princeton Tiger Designs an Atomic Bomb in a Physics Class." *People*, 25 October 1976.

"Rich–Poor Gap Dominates World Poll." *Los Angeles Times*, 21 September 1976.

Sagan, Carl. *Other Worlds*. New York: Bantam Books, Inc., 1975.

Sandburg, Carl. *Smoke and Steel*. New York: Harcourt Brace Jovanovich, Inc., 1920.

Seabury, David. *The Art of Selfishness*. New York: Julian Messner, Simon & Schuster, Inc., Pocket Books, 1974.

Shapley, Deborah. "Plutonium: Reactor Proliferation Threatens a Nuclear Black Market." *Science*, 9 April 1971.

Simpson, Janice C. "Rich Young Activists Give to Change U.S.—And to Feel Better." *The Wall Street Journal*, 11 December 1975.

Spooner, Lysander. "Natural Law, Or The Science of Justice." *Libertarian Forum*, September 1974.

Spooner, Lysander. *No Treason: The Constitution of No Authority* and *A Letter to Thomas F. Bayard*. Libertarian Broadsides, no. 5. With Introductions, Annotations and a New Afterword by James J. Martin. Colorado Springs, Colorado: Ralph Myles Publisher, Inc., 1973.

St. Aubyn, Giles. *The Art of Argument*. Buchanan, New York: Emerson Books, Inc., 1962.

Thoreau, Henry David. *Walden* and *On the Duty of Civil Disobedience*. New York: Harper & Row, A Harper Classic, 1965.

von Däniken, Erich. *Gods From Outer Space*. New York: G. P. Putnam's Sons, 1970.

Wickersham, Bill. "One Man's Nucleomitaphobia." *Saturday Review*, 17 April 1976.

Index

350